SICKERT

The Painter and His Circle

SICKERT

The Painter and His Circle

MARJORIE LILLY

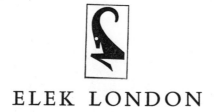

ELEK LONDON

Published in Great Britain by
Elek Books Limited
54–58 Caledonian Rd London N1 9DP

ISBN 0 236 15429 X

Made and printed in England by
The Garden City Press Limited
Letchworth, Hertfordshire
SG6 1JS

The author and publisher gratefully acknowledge their
indebtedness to Miss Lillian Browse for the time and
trouble she has kindly given in helping to locate illustra-
tions for this book, and for her generous loan of photographs of some of the works illustrated in her own book
on Sickert.

Contents

To
Clifford and Julian Hall
without whose encouragement
this book would never have been finished

Illustrations

The best British painting has generally been oblique to the main channels of foreign art. Hogarth lies athwart, not along the line of Northern European genre painting.

Turner arrived at his greatest pictures only after emancipating himself not only from the picturesque but from the continental epic landscape.

Sickert should be appreciated not as a faint parallel to Degas but for a quite distinct view of modern life.

Basil Taylor
Sunday Times, 6 March, 1960

PART ONE

Chapter 1

Meeting : Fitzroy Street

My first encounter with Sickert was in an omnibus.

This happened in the winter of 1911, when I was a student at the Slade School of Art in Central London, during the reign of Professor Tonks the Terrible. He had ordered me to Islington to buy a cast of Julius Caesar from a queer old shop near the Angel. Students liked browsing there among the casts; it was more like a hayloft than a shop, all dust and cobwebs, shades and silence, no one spoke to us or followed us about, we could stay as long as we chose. So I obeyed the Professor's instructions promptly (as who indeed did not?) and returned from Islington one dark winter's afternoon with Caesar under my arm.

Sickert sauntered into the omnibus at the Angel with his usual deliberation, regardless of the impatience of the conductor. His movements were as unhurried as his mind was swift and he chose his seat with care, deprecating the displacement which his large presence was causing among the other passengers. 'I *beg* your pardon! a thousand apologies . . .'

It was a foggy day and progress was slow; I had ample time to study him as he presided over the company. He had chosen to enact the role of dandy and wore a dark overcoat, blue cravat disposed in cunning folds, bowler, gloves and cane. Never did he affect the lovelocks of the poet, but his hair had been allowed to grow a reasonable length and it now waved in thick, crisp undulations above his ears. This was, happily, a close-shaven interlude; long deep lines ran up from the corners of his mouth to his eyes, which were deep-set, light and searching. Where had I seen that head before, I asked myself. Ah, here was Aristotle in modern dress. Remove the bowler and you would have the broad brow, the massive skull and a certain all-over resemblance to the Greek philosopher, except that Sickert's nose was a thought small to conform to classical standards. I fell to wondering how he would be in a toga but no, he was a Northerner after all. In years to come, when I had seen him in every kind of headgear from a cook's cap to a trilby, I sighed for the rightness of that bowler which he had made his own.

After some commotion he was settled to his liking, looking round with his bright, amused gaze to see what entertainment we might provide for him. His eye soon fell on my parcel. The nose of Caesar protruded in tantalizing fashion through his wrappings and, as the horse-drawn, double-decker bus rocked down Pentonville Hill, Sickert craned his neck in a vain effort to identify the cast. At last, feeling that his curiosity should be relieved, I pulled some more of the paper away from Caesar. Sickert met this gesture with a delighted grin and I felt, had circumstances permitted, we should have had a discourse on the antique all the way to Tottenham Court Road.

Some years afterwards, when he saw Caesar hanging in my studio, he remarked that the ears of the cast did not belong to the original head; they had been attached to it at a later period by some inferior hand, a fact which had always worried him.

Our next meeting was some years later, in November 1917.

I had left the Slade School and was now sharing a tiny workshop with a friend from the Slade at Number 15 Fitzroy Street, in central London. Fitzroy Street lies at the heart of a district bounded by Tottenham Court Road to the east, Oxford Street to the south, Marylebone Road to the north and Portland Place to the west. Our cupboard, for it was little more, was the best apology for a studio that we could find in wartime, but as we were both on night duty at the camp in Regent's Park we were too sleepy to do much serious work in the day. Behind us, down a passage, was a huge studio which Sickert had just hired, called the Frith, after the artist who painted 'Derby Day'.

He had moved from Paddington that year to a house in Camden Road. The Frith was most conveniently sited now that he was living in North London; it was opposite the Whistler studio at Number 8 Fitzroy Street, which was occupied by his school, so that he could pop across the road to visit his students whenever it suited him. All his own work was transferred to the Frith and it was here that he and his wife intended to entertain (to avoid confusion, I should state that Sickert's wife was called Christine and that my friend Christina Cutter, who shared my studio and afterwards became my sister-in-law, was always known as Chris). To keep both studios was an extravagant arrangement but all Sickert's arrangements were extravagant. He never worked at home.

At this time, he was in a somewhat peculiar position. Already a legend in Bloomsbury and Chelsea, with a continental reputation as well, the chosen leader of the schools, the painter's painter, his immediate influence was still restricted to a narrow circle. His pictures were bought by a select few, but for years he was not enjoyed by the multitude he so longed to reach, who had woken his deepest sympathies. His radiant humour and zest for life were misleading; strangers saw him as the triumphant artist revelling in popular as well as spiritual success, but he was now nearly sixty and secretly wounded by the indifference of the British public.

To some extent, his own temperament was the cause of this lack of general popularity. He was the proverbial rolling stone, never staying long enough in one place to become fully appreciated. His roots were in London but he drifted to Venice, to Dieppe, back to Venice and back to Dieppe again before he returned to London in 1905, took rooms in Camden Town and made England his headquarters. Perhaps all this wandering about was a preparation for the most important phase of his work, The North London series of music halls and figures in shabby interiors, with some startling portraits too. It was certainly the culmination of his life's work, resulting in a wave of masterpieces which died down in the 1920s; that is to say, with gradually failing health and impaired eyesight, his output became uneven. But impressive as the Camden Town series may be, I do not see how we could do without the Dieppe churches, the Venetian canals or some of the later Bath pictures. If not so intensely personal as his feeling for North London, they reveal his great range and versatility, his abiding interest in architecture.

Had he remained in France there can be little doubt that he would have gained official recognition far sooner, for the sheer vitality and virtuosity of his brush; as Miss Lillian Browse has pointed out, he would probably have been labelled Ecole de Paris, his name today would be of international repute and his prices accordingly elevated. But we must bless the powerful instinct which brought him back to his own country and his own particular brand of realism, to the great storm-dark city which was also the inspiration of two of his idols, Hogarth and Charles Dickens.

Number 15 was razed to the ground by enemy bombs in the Hitler war. It survived the First World War triumphantly and would have stood for many years to come, its solid dingy exterior guarding the secrets of its past from the indifferent passer-by, had it not been demolished in the second. For some years, all that remained of this imposing Georgian façade was a huge gap between its neighbours. I never liked it so well as the house opposite, Number 8, hallowed by memories of Whistler, but it was enough for Sickert that Number 15 had witnessed the birth of 'Derby Day'. He was so proud to be the owner of this very chamber that on taking possession he immediately ordered quantities of writing paper and postcards with 'The Frith' printed on them in the largest, blackest letters he could find. It would be hard to say how much of his enthusiasm was due to his love of Victoriana rather than admiration for the aesthetic qualities of Frith; but there can be no doubt whatever that he really appreciated the robustness, the energy and the rollicking spirits of 'Derby Day'.

Our quiet house was soon all in a bustle. Workmen, all sorts of men, tramped backwards and forwards, the great front door was opening and shutting continuously, heavy weights were dragged over bare passages, snatches of talk and laughter echoed through the November dusk, the light, restless step of the new tenant was everywhere at once, up and down the dark abyss leading to the basement, in and out of the Frith, along the street. No actual noise or clatter; rather a steady ceaseless humming, like a hive of bees.

The basement soon took Sickert's fancy. Huge, eerie, with winding passages and one black dungeon succeeding another like some horror story by Edgar Allen Poe, it was presided over by Mrs Parminter and a mysterious old man whom no one could account for. Even Sickert, whose insatiable curiosity soon ferreted out the secrets of the entire house, had met his Waterloo in Mr X; he was unable to place him. They soon met, of course, and exchanged views but all Sickert could discover was that Mr X had spent years in Jamaica and was an authority on bananas. When Chris objected that bananas were a dull subject of conversation, Sickert reproved her. 'The great thing, my child, is to be interested in *something*.' Mr X was not, certainly, Mr Parminter; Mrs Parminter would have indignantly denied the assumption. She was very strong-minded and must, I think, have been a confirmed feminist. Feminism was all the go in those days and Mrs Parminter, although no doubt unaware of the distinction, was well abreast of fashionable thought. However, in spite of the pallid spectres that haunted the sinister regions below stairs, only to disappear with monotonous regularity as she routed them, one by one, Mr X remained. What is more, he shared her kitchen. But this was nothing to the trial that awaited her on the advent of Sickert. From the first, she was not enthusiastic about the upheaval of our way of life. It was understood all over the house that her basement was sacred territory; only by formal invitation did we drink tea with her and hear the news. This privilege was not extended to those tenants of whom she disapproved, or to recent arrivals who had yet to win her good opinion, so that when she did bestow one of her rare favours we were duly sensible of the honour conferred upon us. (Thus, it will be remembered, did Goldsmith respond to the occasion when he announced proudly to Boswell, who had not yet been distinguished by her attentions, 'I go to tea with Miss Williams.') But it soon became only too clear that Sickert was oblivious to the unwritten code of Number 15; he always did precisely what he liked, no territory was sacred to him, he ascended and descended as the spirit moved him. I fear that, so far as Mrs Parminter was concerned, he never made the grade. She deplored his presence from first to last and he did not take to her; she interfered with his drawings, scattering them far and wide as she cleaned the studio, and he interfered with her basement. I might add that we also were somewhat disturbed by his incursions. It had not struck us that he would be roaming all over the place; if we had considered the matter at all, we should have taken it for granted that he would remain mostly in his own quarters and sally forth at stated intervals from studio to front door. But now we were rendered uneasy because we had carelessly allowed Mrs Parminter to decorate her kitchen with a number of our own canvases, 'throw-outs' which we had intended for the dustbin. Chris had gained applause at the Slade as a draughtsman, but I was mortified to think of my own daubs displayed all over the kitchen and that Mrs Parminter, who admired our efforts very much, would not fail to point out their merits to him at length. When I assured him afterwards that we meant them to be destroyed he made the only answer that I suppose he could have made: 'At any rate, they are sincere.' But this remark held out more consolation than I knew. He hated any tricks in art; tricks of composition, of lighting, of brushwork, the use of any tools save the legitimate tools devised for painting; affectations, falsities, ruses, and gimmicks all were anathema to him.

One morning when I returned, half-asleep, to our studio from the camp in

Regent's Park, Sickert poked his head round the door. He wore working clothes on this occasion, a blue shirt, tweed trousers and the carpet slippers that his wife had embroidered for him, of which he was immensely proud. That afternoon Christina and I went to 'share a crust' with him in the Frith.

We found our host in a huge, bare, carpetless barn engulfed in shadows, thick with dust and the odour of paint and cigars, stacked with canvases and lit by the solitary ray of a bull's-eye lantern. He had achieved a queer sort of comfort, too. A horsehair sofa, draped with his black Venetian cape, stood beside the blazing fire; there were plenty of deep chairs and a kettle singing on the hob. A table stood between the windows, littered with drawings; there was a dresser decorated with china and various ornaments which were constantly being changed. We longed to know what happened to the discarded bric-à-brac but like Dr Johnson and the disposal of his orange peel, the secret was not divulged. The righthand side of the room was furnished with the stove and a huge shelf packed with canvases; by the door stood an iron bedstead covered with a honeycomb quilt and a Victorian bookcase hanging above. He had two fervent crazes at the moment, crime and the princes of the Church; crime personified by Jack the Ripper, the Church by Anthony Trollope. Thus, we had the robber's lair, illumined solely by the bull's-eye lantern; when he was reading Trollope we had the Dean's bedroom, complete with iron bedstead, quilt and bookcase. The ecclesiastical flavour so congenial to him was somewhat marred by the red Bill Sykes handkerchief dangling from the bedpost; but the presence of this incongruous article in the Dean's bedroom was not a passing whim; it was an important factor in the process of creating his picture, a lifeline to guide the train of his thought, as necessary as the napkin which Mozart used to fold into points which met each other when he too was composing. Sickert was working now on one of his Camden Town murders and while he was reliving the scene he would assume the part of a ruffian, knotting the handkerchief loosely round his neck, pulling a cap over his eyes and lighting his lantern. Immobile, sunk deep in his chair, lost in the long shadows of that vast room, he would meditate for hours on his problem. When the handkerchief had served its immediate purpose it was tied to any doorknob or peg that came handy to stimulate his imagination further, to keep the pot boiling. It played a necessary part in the performance of the drawings, spurring him on at crucial moments, becoming so interwoven with the actual working out of his idea that he kept it constantly before his eyes. How it affected his preoccupation with church dignitaries I cannot presume to say but there seemed to be some mysterious connection here too. With gusto, he would refer to his clerical set as he wound the red handkerchief round his neck. 'Do you know my friend, Prebendary Webb Peploe? Such a charming man, we really must ask him to tea.'

His easel, graced by the canvas he was working on at the time, filled the centre of the room; beside it was a small glass-topped table, constructed by himself, which served as a palette; at the side of the easel he had pinned a reproduction of

'Her Mother's Voice' by Frank Dicksee, 'to inspire me', as he gravely explained, tongue in cheek, 'in the more critical stages of my work'. But the scene was dominated by 'Suspense', the big oil of a woman waiting for news of her son or lover. Sickert conceived this picture about 1912 (the actual dates for Suspense are uncertain) in a room on the third floor of Number 8 Fitzroy Street, which Chris and I used afterwards as a studio, since bombed to pieces and restored with the rest of the building. I cannot suppose that Sickert carried out the picture in this third floor back, as it would hardly have been big enough, and he liked plenty of room to move about when he was painting; probably it was completed in the Whistler. He told me that he did some twenty careful drawings of the subject before he squared it up.

I had seen neither the drawings nor the canvas before that afternoon in Number 15; as I entered the studio, the reflection of 'Suspense' filled the depths of a huge misty glass on the opposite wall and the memory of it haunts me still.

He was in meditative mood during teatime, affable but remote. Gravely he filled the teacups and the large bowl that he reserved for himself, rising at intervals to burrow into his cupboards and find one drawing after another for our inspection. However untidy his room might seem sometimes, he always knew where to put his hand on his things. It was not until Mrs Parminter meddled with her broom that he mislaid them. 'God! woman, you'll ruin me,' he would groan as she waddled about, raising clouds of dust in her wake. But even Mrs Parminter respected the red handkerchief and left it where she found it whenever she invaded the Frith.

Awed by the privilege accorded to us in this private view, we gazed at the drawings in silence. Alas, that I could see again, with the fuller knowledge that I now possess of his work, some of those drawings of long ago, which seem to have disappeared for ever! Their finer points escaped me but one black chalk sketch, stabbed my spirit broad awake. A woman struggling on a bed, a faceless man with folded arms beside her lapped in shadow; a subject that Sickert had treated before and would treat again; but the terror conjured up by a few taut lines, the contrast of dark and light, were unforgettable. This was not a working note, to be squared up and enlarged as a picture afterwards, it was a drawing in its own right, the most dynamic Sickert sketch that I have seen. All the subsequent versions of it such as 'The Crisis' (*circa* 1909) seem clumsy by comparison. I thought of the sketch by David of Marie Antoinette in the tumbril on the way to the guillotine; this drawing had the same stark nightmare quality. It was a relief to turn for comfort to the quiet studio, the firelight and the kettle hissing on the hob, with a placid elderly gentleman making the tea. Impossible to connect him with this savage explosion! The scene before me was almost domestic; Sickert always enjoyed making cosy corners in the vast old Frith.

'I sold another version of that to the French President,' he remarked. 'He took a lot of my things.'

He talked about everything under the sun that afternoon. Preoccupied as he was with criminology, he dwelt at length on some famous murder trials. We were more interested in his dramatic exposition of the subject than the actual crime; he told his story with deadly effect, waving his hands to mark his points by the eerie glow of his lantern. Only unsolved crimes detained him, for the solution of which he had endless plausible theories.

His sense of theatre was as keen as that of his idols, Hogarth, Degas and Dickens; he loved to invent fresh disguises, cropping his head like a convict on Monday or producing a vast square beard on Friday, which seemed to grow as fast as Jack's beanstalk. Fortunately, he soon wearied of these pranks and would reappear suddenly clean-shaven and fastidiously groomed, lordly as a portrait by Van Dyck. His dress varied accordingly; at one moment, the painter in open shirt with carpet slippers, at another the farmer with Norfolk jacket and leggings, again the man about town with morning-coat, striped trousers, gloves and cane. If he was making a public appearance somewhere he always shampooed his hair at the last minute, plunging his head under the tap in a lather of soap and water, rubbing it vigorously and planting his bowler on his wet curls, all at lightning speed. We never knew, when we met him in hall or passage, what fresh quirk had overtaken him, whether we should see the artist, the *homme du monde*, the farmer, the professor, the Tichborne claimant . . .

These kaleidoscopic changes were bewildering, as was his habit of reviewing his friends, like his gods, in strict rotation. They formed a sort of giant circle around which Sickert revolved methodically, adding another figure to the circle from time to time but always returning to it and savouring in turn the personages of whom it was composed. He had his Burns days, his Byron days, his Whistler days, his Degas days, his Napoleon days, his Dr Johnson days and many other days, and when his own good nature had involved him with a bore whose visits, in spite of marked hints, appeared interminable, he would murmur, 'What would *Byron* have said to this infliction? *He* would not have permitted it for a moment.'

Before he had been a week in residence at the Frith, he knew every nook and cranny of his own floor and the rambling basement, the names and occupations of the inhabitants, their appearance and their little ways. I never heard that anyone resented his knowledge of their affairs, indeed they all seemed anxious to gratify his curiosity. Later, when we visited the *quartier* and compared notes with him about our neighbours, we found that he had gleaned more information about everybody in weeks than we had in a year. This interest in people was unfailing; in the mornings, after breakfast, he would collect fresh news, leaning against the railings outside Number 15. He deplored the habit in other painters—'How can Porter get on with his work? He's always on the doorstep, looking up and down the street. Now when I was young, I got on with the job.' But he derived much enjoyment from the practice himself.

Moving in continued indefinitely. Loads of furniture arrived at Number 15 and the passages resounded to the tramp of workmen's feet. One afternoon, to my surprise, I found the house quiet and I supposed that Sickert had now arranged

17

everything to his satisfaction. But not for long. Soon it became apparent that he was still moving. Rumbling sounds came from the Frith, as of massive objects being dragged about, succeeded at length by a loud crash. Alarmed, I ran down the passage, fearing that he was hurt; when I entered his studio I saw an enormous cupboard on the floor with Sickert's carpet slippers waving beneath it. As I hurried forward to render first aid the cupboard rose slowly to an upright position and Sickert, dusty but dignified, emerged from the rear. 'I've had lessons in moving furniture,' he explained. 'You lie on the ground with the thing on your stomach, heave and there you are.'

As I have said, he was still renting the Whistler studio at Number 8, across the street, which he retained chiefly for his pupils. Special ties bound Sickert to the Whistler; he always reverted to it from time to time and it seemed to us the ideal setting for him. I never shared his fancy for the Frith, a more prosaic interior, although it inspired one of his best later paintings, 'The Bar Parlour'. But in 1917 he was chiefly interested in the Frith and would have said of the Whistler, 'that orange is now sucked'. He used it merely to compose exciting arrangements for his pupils. Sickert lavished royal hospitality on his classes at the Whistler. I remember one exquisite colour symphony in bronze, apricot and purple; a Negro posed against the chimney piece in the *contre-jour* lighting that he loved, with his grand piano reflected in the dusty glass. How looking glasses recall Sickert's work; those explosions of colour, liquid shapes floating like water plants in the flux of the tides, fleeting yet vivid, piquant yet ephemeral. Sometimes, when he was contemplating one of these compositions that he had built up for his students, it reminded him of Tam o' Shanter.

> 'Or like the snowfalls in the river
> One moment white, then melt for ever
> Or like the rainbow's lovely form
> Evanishing amid the storm.'

The piano had a history which we were never told. One day when the permanent financial crisis was particularly acute, Christine suggested that he might be persuaded to sell it. But we soon found that whatever sacrifices were necessary, he would never part with the piano. It enshrined some precious memory that he would never disclose. However, it proved most useful for students when they were composing; it supplied an exciting background with its sweeping curves and angles, instead of the 'buff vacancy' which surrounds the object in so many art schools, even to this day.

We soon got used to the transformation scenes in the Frith. After the robber's lair, the Dean's bedroom; then the studio would become a sort of parlour overnight with strange or banal objects conjured up from heaven knows where, which vanished on the morrow as suddenly as they came. How Sickert procured his numerous chattels, what he did with them when he got bored with them or they had served their purpose, will remain one of the world's mysteries. During a prolonged cooking craze, the walls were covered with expensive gadgets and pots and pans, with Sickert himself appropriately arrayed in cook's cap and apron. In this rig, he looked about eight feet high and a friend of mine, a shy little elderly person who knocked on his door by mistake one day when I was out, was so overpowered by the vast white apparition who opened it that she was bereft of words. He was quite concerned about her when he related their encounter to me.

'I explained your absence, I did my best I assure you, my manner was most caressing. But the poor lady was dumb . . .'

The cooking utensils, of course, vanished suddenly, to be followed by a sort of clothier's shop; masses of Sickert's wardrobe adorning the walls, rows of suits neatly suspended from coat hangers on his cupboard doors with stacks of headgear on the pegs above them. His wife was particularly interested in this display and enquired the whereabouts of a dark suit which became him. 'It's there all right,' said Sickert, who always knew where he had put his things. 'Did you think I had pawned it?' She was aghast when she discovered that he had just bought four dozen collars made to his own especial design, but collars he found irresistible. Also collar-studs in trays. 'The play of light and shade on them is so fascinating,' he confided to a bewildered shop assistant who was showing him some at a draper's in Charlotte Street.

But the wardrobe scene too, was rapidly superseded by something else. Next day a profusion of little ornaments might be all the go; old prints, jaded curling yellow photographs of bygone beauties and dusty portraits filled every conceivable space; one portrait remained on view for three whole days while he was declaring it to be a Delacroix, after which first fine careless rapture the inevitable reaction set in and it was unhooked, sadly, from its proud position on the wall.

One foggy January morning in 1918, Sickert said suddenly: 'Let's go to Petticoat Lane.' We were working in the Frith when he dropped this bombshell. I gazed at him, aghast. He had seemed so happy and so busy, resurrecting a battered old Gladstone bag, to which he was greatly attached, from the basement in order to paint his new address on its ancient sides in large white letters, 'The Shrubbery, 81 Camden Road'. We could not imagine how he conjured up a shrubbery from his patch of front garden; all we could remember there was a dismal little row of laurel bushes, craving alms of the sun—but he always enjoyed playing 'let's pretend'. Perhaps he really did see those sickly laurels as a green thought in a green shade.

He pulled a letter from his pocket which he handed to us.

'Look here, I can't go carrying letters from my missus to you all day long. She specially wanted me to deliver this one but it must really be the last.'

This was unfair to Christine, who had not offended in this way before, but the letter was handed over without further comment. Christine begged us to see that he did not wander about in the fog, as he had rather a sore throat; she hoped we would be able to persuade him to remain indoors. She must have had some dark premonition about Petticoat Lane. But she could not have been more taken aback than we were by his decision. Already, we knew only too well the futility of trying to stop him from doing anything that he had a mind to; we feared that writing to us about it was really a waste of time. As for Sickert, he was not interested in the correspondence and did not want to hear what she had written.

'What fun! I've always wanted to see Petticoat Lane.'

The fog was rapidly thickening; soon, we should not be able to see more than a few yards in front of us. However, we were hustled into our coats, and bundled out into the sulphurous, bitter tasting street. I was frankly sulky; the Frith was warm, it seemed unkind to flout Christine's wishes, we had no idea how to find Petticoat Lane and to crown all, when we reached Warren Street station we found that Sickert had no idea either. Why did he want to go there? We suspected that it reminded him of an excursion he had made with George Moore and Wilson Steer to Peckham Rye; he was reliving one of his major reminiscent phases at this time and the subject of it happened to be Moore. Also, he had a fancy to take a ride in the tube. I do not believe that he had ever been in the tube before. He was all at sea, even at the ticket office, murmuring 'tiens!' as we shot down the lift to a crowded platform and embarked on a still more crowded train. Meekly, he embraced his strap, looking larger than ever among all the other travellers as the train swirled along. He was much knocked about and every time someone trampled on his feet he said plaintively, 'I *beg* your pardon! A thousand apologies . . .'

Soon, he attracted notice. He was wearing a dark overcoat and bowler hat, suitable City attire, but one by one the seatholders dubiously lowered their newspapers as he hung patiently to his strap; all eyes were focused on him. He was so evidently unused to London Transport and now that he felt less bewildered in his strange surroundings he began to ask everyone the way to Aldgate.

'Excuse me . . . but we are looking for Aldgate Will someone be so good as to put us on our way to Aldgate?'

Everybody began to tell him all at once; he was more lost than ever but gravely bowed his acknowledgements. Finally, a traveller in the corner addressed himself to Chris.

'I'll tell *you* how to take him to Aldgate. He'll never get there by himself.'

I cannot say how we ever arrived at Petticoat Lane. Sometimes I wonder whether we did eventually find the real thing after all; I saw next to nothing then and I have never returned since. The fog exceeded our worst fears. It was now almost black. Chris was behaving well, entering into the spirit of the thing, but when my total lack of co-operation became too marked to be any longer ignored, Sickert paused to deliver a little homily on adapting oneself to circumstances and taking things as they came, which fell on deaf ears. I have seldom spent a more uncomfortable day but Sickert was enjoying himself tremendously. We had to keep a strict eye on him, as every now and then he darted down a side street when he thought he saw a Rabbi or some other elder, sitting on a doorstep. Mindful of Christine, we plunged after him through the murk and secured him before he disappeared completely.

'Such a beautiful head! What a *beard*. A perfect Rembrandt. . . '

Petticoat Lane, and the district, were in fact growing on him and we began to wonder if we should ever reach port again. Now that he had thought of Rembrandt, he was no doubt fancying himself on the quays of Amsterdam, and he certainly had a throat. He might even take it into his head to find a subject in the general black-out, in which case we should be detained here for an indefinite period. In the end, having chased him up and down endless side streets until we were exhausted, we declared ourselves hungry, which gave Sickert pause immediately. He always deplored our light luncheons, and was convinced that we were underfed and needed constant nourishment to counteract the effect of war starvation. So at last, battered and bedraggled, we groped our way back to the West End. Sickert was not at all weary; the trip had braced him, although he admitted that we had not seen much of Petticoat Lane in spite of tantalizing glimpses through mouthfuls of fog. But he always remembered the trip with complacency; some months afterwards I heard him introducing Chris to a perplexed newcomer with this comment, by way of recommendation:

'This child has been down every drain in London.'

We were dining at Camden Road that evening. Sickert had become extremely hoarse and we wondered what we could say to Christine. To our great relief, he was too cunning to mention the outing. Although we were on dangerous ground when he croaked during dinner:

'Listen, Christine! we have seen such wonderful people today, perfect Rembrandts . . .'

Chapter 2

Books and Persons

Sometimes the Frith would become a library, filled with books of every sort, shape or size, scattered in all directions. After breakfast, lying in his long chair, Sickert would unfold *The Times* and when he had read the news, entertain himself with one of his favourite classical authors before turning to the business of the day. He might however show interest in a recent play or novel, book of memoirs or art criticism that he had heard about when he took his walks abroad. Once he asked me suddenly: 'Have you read *The Visits of Elizabeth*, written, I believe, by a Mrs Glyn?' It seems a pity that we have no cartoon by Max Beerbohm depicting the reactions of Sickert to a Mrs Glyn; I am sure Beerbohm would have interpreted them correctly but although I supplied Sickert with a copy of *Visits of Elizabeth* the silence that ensued was profound. At last curiosity got the better of me and I asked him how he did with Mrs Glyn. For once, he seemed nonplussed. The pause that followed was prolonged. Then he observed, with uncharacteristic vagueness: 'No doubt it is all very true.' Further probing, however, elicited the fact that he had not got beyond the first page.

He seemed equally bemused with a strange phenomenon called Ethel M. Dell; I suppose she is forgotten now but she had a vogue in her day and one of her stories, rather in the vein of Mrs Glyn, was actually dramatized and produced in the West End. One wonders what Sickert was doing there but Thérèse Lessore, who accompanied him, assured me that he really went to the play one evening and what is more, sat out the performance.

He was, I think, far more critical of writers than of painters. Which seems odd, as his standard of painting was even more fastidious than his standard of literature. But painting seemed often to arouse a feeling of pity; I have often heard him say 'Poor X!' while fetching a deep sigh, when confronted with a bad picture. On the other hand his criticisms of writers could be severe to the point of harshness, at any rate in private. When he found us reading Gissing's *Odd Women* he borrowed the book and returned it later with scathing comments scribbled over the margins of its pages in his stubby black pencil. It distressed him to discover that I could enjoy anything that he considered to be so badly written.

'All the characters are *voulu* . . . no knowledge of life; it wouldn't have been like that. This Rhoda. There *is* no such person.'

To reclaim us if possible, and darkly suspecting that some of his other young friends might be equally lacking in taste and discernment, he decided to give us a course of reading at the Frith. We began with Balzac; this, he felt, should kill two birds with one stone; it should lighten our darkness about such important matters as style and construction and it might even mitigate those frightful sounds which had assailed his ears when we were airing our French, if we heard the language properly spoken. Curtains were drawn, lamps lighted, the fire mended; we sat stiffly on our chairs, a row of solemn youngsters encircling the Master, while he intoned the opening chapter of a Balzac novel. Convinced that he was contributing to our pleasure as well as profit, enthralled with his self-appointed task, Sickert soon forgot all about us and became completely engrossed in the lengthy prelude to this story which, to our untutored ears, seemed interminable. All I can remember about this particular work is that it described a young woman who was being followed home by a persistent admirer and that we soon gave up all hope that she would ever gain the shelter of the roof tree. On and on went the reading in Sickert's mellifluous French, while the shadows deepened and the fire burned low in the great gaunt room. Longing to cough or to yawn or to fidget, cramped and weary, we listened; no one had the heart to interrupt him. At last the book was dropped and he demanded tea. So far as we could gather, Balzac's heroine was still some distance from home and alas, with what gusto did we stir the fire and plonk the kettle on the hob!

But next week we did better. Sickert chose a more accommodating Balzac, *Eugénie Grandet*, and gave us such a spirited rendering of Père Grandet, stammer and all, that I was induced to try the book for myself. When I told him how interesting I found it, his face lit up instantly. Enheartened by this tardy sign of literary appreciation, he gave us more readings during the winter of 1917: Sainte-Beuve—'if you read him you'll learn what criticism really is'—the Goncourts, Delacroix and still more Balzac.

I do not recollect his views on German or Italian writers except his fondness for Goldoni, which everyone knows. British writers, past and present, were of course constantly walking in and out of the conversation. Sickert was a fervent admirer of Doctor Johnson; he loved to quote from Boswell, especially Johnson's famous riposte to Bishop Berkeley:

'After we came out of the church, we stood talking for some time together of Bishop Berkeley's ingenious sophistry to prove the non-existence of matter, and that everything in the universe is merely ideal. I observed, that though we are satisfied his doctrine is not true, it is impossible to refute it. I never shall forget the alacrity with which Johnson answered, striking his foot with mighty force against a large stone, till he rebounded from it, "I refute it thus." '

This anecdote afforded Sickert infinite gratification and he too would refute Bishop Berkeley, dealing heavy blows on the furniture with his poker. But I should add, that if any of us were inclined to speak disrespectfully of learned men, Bishop Berkeley or another, the flippancy was coldly received.

Richardson was preferred to Fielding; again, Sickert agreed with the Doctor when he told Mrs Thrale that 'Richardson had picked the kernel of life, while Fielding was contented with the husk'. The great Victorians were all popular, excepting George Eliot, who moralized too much for him, and the placid precincts of Trollope proved a respite from a world that was spinning too fast for his liking. But there are aspects of Trollope which are not tranquil and he declared that he could not read about Mr Slope, 'the most detestable character in English fiction'. Dickens, of course, was a towering genius; 'no more need be said about him', but for all that, Sickert said a good deal. Dickens undoubtedly helped to inspire the Camden Town scenes and his association with Camden Town was one reason why Sickert loved North London. *Bleak House* was the most favoured work; Sickert dreamed of the rain dripping on Chesney Wold, of Sir Leicester Dedlock and Mrs Jellyby and Borrioboola Gha.

Meredith he found too obscure; when I suggested that *The Egoist* was surely terrific and that *Clara Middleton* was a charming creature, he retorted, 'Ah, Meredith knew how to please the women! You all like to fancy yourselves as Clara Middletons.' He disliked obscurity in any of the arts and had little patience with silent people, always excepting his old friend Walter Taylor, whom no one must laugh at but himself.

'If a man never talks it's because he has nothing to say. If there's anything there it will come out and we shall have the benefit of his conclusions, you can take my word for that. And what's more, he will be intelligible. If he has been really thinking, his meaning will be plain.' Which seemed hard on some people, especially youngsters, who were tongue-tied in his presence; as Sir Harold Nicolson has pointed out, if the young are never shy they will become bores as adults. But Sickert found shyness exasperating, no doubt partly because he sometimes suffered from it himself. It would be unwise to take these sweeping observations too literally; like his loves and hates, they were exaggerated, made in the heat of the moment after he had exhausted himself in trying to evoke a response from some unfortunate who, in spite of repeated proddings, goadings and perhaps even outrageous statements from his host thrown off in a final effort to 'stir the porridge', remained dumb.

This passion for clarity may have been one reason why he said little about the work of Henry James. I feel all the rashness of the comparison between writer and painter, one working in time, the other in space, but it has always seemed to me that there was a certain affinity between these men. Both were affected in much the same way by the time spirit; Sickert's best work is literary; Gide's comment on the work of Sickert—'his morose and powerful art'—might have been said of the work of James and the superb answer that James gave to one of his admirers who asked him what life was—'Life, my dear lady, life is the predicament which precedes death'—might easily have been spoken by Sickert himself. While James built up his sombre themes by a multitude of touches Sickert, as painters must, conveyed his meaning in a single sentence; but both men created their especial atmosphere by implication rather than by direct statement; by means of the depth in a shadow, relationships of colour such as ominous reds and morbid darks, even the listless gesture of a hand, Sickert could evoke a visual sense of the treachery of life that lies at the heart of *The Wings of the Dove* or *The Beast in the Jungle*.

But if he seemed curiously lukewarm about James the novelist, Sickert was anything but lukewarm about James the man. He gave unstinting praise to the conversational powers of the great American. 'His talk was unique. One sentence would go on and on and on with endless digressions until most people had lost the thread of the argument; sometimes we held our breath, saying he's lost his way at last, he'll have to give it up this time, he'll never make it ...' but after a tremendous pause James would gather up the reins of his thought and tie them in a neat bow which he solemnly presented to the company with the 'final word, the all-embracing significant word'. This performance was so compelling that no one, Sickert assured us, wanted to listen to anyone else when James was speaking. 'Once, Moore and James were present at the same house party. Nobody took any notice of George when James was there and one night after dinner, when James was receiving more applause than usual, George took to his bedroom in the sulks. Everyone was so entertained that it was some time before George was missed, when I was deputed to go and find him with this message. "Come down, George! We really will listen to you now."'

If Sickert repeated this story with some relish at Moore's discomfiture it will be remembered that by this time the two old friends were estranged. Sickert had never forgiven Moore for his *Conversations in Ebury Street*. But it is doubtful whether the friendship could have withstood the vicissitudes of a life-time, even without this betrayal. Moore fancied himself as an art critic; he wrote a good deal of nonsense about Sickert's work and insisted on discussing it when they met, although he knew little about painting. When he visited the Frith in 1917, Sickert was frankly tired of him; but Moore behaved like a privileged crony, offering advice and reproof and encouragement as if he were the headmaster addressing a favourite pupil. There was something *triste* about his blindness to the fact that the friendship was over.

I only met Moore once, in a large company at the Frith. One knows nothing of people when meeting them in a crowd; they seldom drop the mask unless you see them alone, if then, and Moore was no exception to the rule. But although he wore his public manner he made a good natured effort to take part in the general chatter. He looked ill and forlorn and remembering the pleasure his work had given me, I was anxious to appear interested when he took the trouble to try to amuse me with a long story about a blue-stocking, partly in French, partly in English. It was mortifying to find that I must have missed the point after all and that I had laughed in the wrong place. 'Never mind,' Sickert consoled me afterwards, 'there wasn't any point.'

I felt sorry for this distinguished man when I saw him off, groping his way down the dark street in search of the taxi that was to take him to an empty house and a solitary evening. He was so very deaf at this time, talking almost to himself in his booming hollow voice, oblivious to the cut-and-thrust of everyday conversation; an exchange of ideas was a thing of the past with him. In his heyday he must have been a lively companion, but a handful for his friends when he was in the throes of creation. Once as a young man he came to a full stop in the first chapter of a new novel because he could not find the right setting for his heroine. Somewhere, somehow, he had heard the magic words 'Peckham Rye', which for some reason switched his imagination on the rails; he saw instantly that she must live there and dashed round to his friends to impart this important decision. Here, Sickert would imitate the loud, flat tones of Moore. 'I have never been to Peckham *Rye*; we must all go there at once.' No one else either, it seemed, had visited Peckham Rye or was anxious to repair the omission, but Moore insisted on dragging Tonks, Steer and Sickert from their respective studios in working hours to share with him the voyage of discovery. Without the aid of the efficient Tonks, it is doubtful if they would have arrived, as the others were not very good at finding places; but finally they reached their goal. For Moore, it exceeded his fondest dreams. The cronies were not so convinced of its charms. 'We walked about the streets in a drizzle,' Sickert sighed, 'while George darted all over the place looking for the right house for his heroine to be born in. The rain never stopped and Steer thought he'd caught a chill and we all went back to luncheon at the Charing Cross Hotel.'

The portrait of Moore by Sickert in the Tate Gallery (plate 4) is familiar to everyone. Moore, of course, was the answer to every painter's prayer; that pink complexion which took the light, that round face, those round eyes, chubby cheeks and round lips, all those glorious rotundities must have been a joy to model, but Sickert's version of him is a thought unkind. Moore thought so too. 'You have made me look a silly ass, Walter. And I cannot be a silly ass, for I have written *Esther Waters*!'

Among contemporaries, Sickert did not appreciate the work of Shaw or Wells. He respected Shaw's intellect but found him uninspired; both he and Wells were too concerned with sociology for him. Preaching, proselytizing, prophesying all bored him unless the powder was cunningly masked by the jam. Arnold Bennett was congenial as a man and he read early Bennetts, although he could not refrain from teasing Bennett when he met him.

Bennett, however, could take care of himself. When Sickert walked up to him at a party and enquired, 'Arnold, are you or are you not the navel of the universe?' Bennett confided to him, 'As a matter of fact, Walter, I am.'

E. M. Forster appealed to Sickert greatly; he liked especially *A Passage to India*. 'It's *so* good,' he used to say. Life seen at one remove, as Forster seems to see it, corresponded with his own love of reflections in looking glasses; mysterious characters like Mrs Moore in *A Passage to India* or Mrs Wilcox in *Howards End* touched an answering chord in him. Although Sickert was completely unswayed by fashion, it is curious to look back and see how unfashionable it was becoming in 1918 to stress the emphatic note in painting and how the same tendency was revealing itself in literature; sensibility was all.

Certain plays and books affected him as deeply as a child. Once, years afterwards, I asked him if he had seen *Journey's End*. He shook his head sadly. 'I should have been the first to see it once,' he said. 'Alas, I couldn't bear it now.'

But I doubt if he would have been able to bear it, even as long ago as 1918. Already, life was proving rather much for him. It was unfortunate that at this time he happened to read *The End of the Tether*. Kindly Captain Whalley, struggling for survival in an alien world, is surely the most moving study in Conrad's portrait gallery and there is a curious resemblance to Sickert in his description of the appearance and characteristics of Captain Whalley, even to their common plight, which Sickert could hardly fail to realize. Reading this story in the midst of a bloody war, with old age creeping on and his finances gradually worsening, he began to know that he would not always be able to laugh in the face of poverty. No story had such a disastrous effect on Sickert as this. He considered it to be Conrad's masterpiece and it left him exhausted. For some time after he had read it he could not bear to be alone; deserting the Frith, he followed his friends about in silence. It was days before he recovered his usual gaiety. I believe that Conrad himself disliked this story because he suspected that it was sentimental. But Sickert had none of the prevailing horror of sentimentality, although his own work is so free from it that he was actually accused of coldness in his own day, even by Roger Fry. He found seeds of talent lurking in all sorts of improbable places and people, in many a humble little book or obscure author or, stranger still, in some unfashionable writers whom it required the strongest moral courage to recommend. For instance, he admired Hall Caine, dismissed by literary pundits as unworthy of mention. But Sickert never sought to ascertain the value of anything he fancied by putting it to the fashionable vote; his own judgement stood carelessly alone. And he would hardly have reversed his liking for the work of Hugh Walpole because Walpole is now under a cloud. He and Walpole understood each other. Walpole has written about Sickert with more insight than many of Sickert's older friends. This is curious, as Walpole only knew him as an elderly man with failing powers; in spite of that he has seized the essential Sickert.

His affection for classical poets is well known and he frequently browsed among the Elizabethans. Among the poets nearer to our own day, I think Burns was his favourite. *Mary Morison* and *Tam o' Shanter* he considered to be beyond praise. But he found it difficult to forgive Burns his weakness for the bottle. 'If you have such a gift as that, it's your duty to preserve it at all costs.' Sickert had almost as great a horror of drunkenness as he had of theft, especially as he endured untold miseries himself after evenings with old cronies. After a party with Moore and Max Beerbohm, we found him next morning in a darkened studio wrapped in a monastic dressing-gown, immobile, grey and speechless, clasping his aching head and sighing at intervals. It was odd to see him indisposed, odder still to see him lying quiet for so long without speaking. No doubt he felt the situation called for drama and he enjoyed dramatizing himself immensely, but he had neither the head nor the inclination for heavy drinking.

By lunch time he had revived and was inclined to talk about the party. It appeared that they had raked the universe for subjects and had landed, finally, on an especial topic of Moore's—his favourite kind of woman. I forget Beerbohm's contribution to the discussion, but Sickert was very pleased with his own definition of female charm. 'They asked me what I liked best and I said, my own particular brand of frump.'

One seldom found him reading any modern poetry unless it was the work of a friend, while if Wordsworth was mentioned he would reply in that especially polite detached voice which meant that he would do nothing of the kind, 'Ah, no doubt, no doubt; I must look into him some day.' One would have supposed that he and Wordsworth would have fraternized over their common craving for solitude.

Among women poets, Emily Bronte held pride of place. He felt as most people do about *Wuthering Heights,* that this book soars beyond the frontiers of prose. As A. E. Housman would say, 'Because it is poetry, and finds its way to something in man which is obscure and latent, something older than the present organization of his nature, like the patches of dew which still linger here and there in the drained lands of Cambridgeshire.' Emily Bronte's work as a whole enchanted him. I have a vivid recollection of him when he was painting a favourite subject, a churchyard scene. Shuffling up and down in his carpet slippers, whistling and humming old music-hall ditties under his breath and scratching at his beloved canvas with a derelict brush from which most of the hairs had long since vanished, he would stop at intervals to murmur solemnly:

'Cold in the earth and fifteen wild December
From those brown hills have melted into Spring.'

He was a long time finishing this picture. He lingered over it with such loving patience, squeezing the very last drop out of the subject, that it was almost too late to be included in the spring Exhibition at the Grosvenor Gallery. And he had not made up his mind to send it to the Grosvenor. He rather thought it might do for the London Group. 'Shall I be a dasher among the stuffers or a stuffer among the dashers?' He finally decided to be a dasher among the stuffers and it was hustled off at the last minute to the Grosvenor Gallery. But an S.O.S. soon arrived from a perturbed secretary, pointing out that the canvas had no name. Would Mr Sickert please find a title for it immediately?

Sickert was already forgetting all about his churchyard. As he explained, 'A picture, once finished, is like a married daughter; you take no further interest in her.' But after some thought, his mouth twitching a little as it always did when he was amused, he produced the necessary title.

His joy was great when he received a copy of the catalogue and saw these words beside the number of his picture:

'Forever with the Lord.—Walter Sickert.'

28

Chapter 3

Finance

Having been brought up in a business world where two and two, we were assured, were only four and never five nor three, we were soon bewildered by Sickert's propensity to make them five, or even six or seven. He built castles in the air on the most slender evidence of sales, saw himself relieved of money worries for evermore, his work sought after by queues of discerning collectors, every problem solved by the wave of some mysterious magician's wand. Half mesmerized by the flow of plausible argument that we were privileged to hear when he was in this optimistic mood, lost in admiration for his precise and fluent speech, we almost believed with him that all his difficulties were over. But alas, with a start, we awoke from daydreams. For all his eloquence and conviction it wouldn't do.

His disinterestedness is obvious; he never consciously painted a pot-boiler in his life and he spent his best years following his star, which led him to concentrate on scenes of his youth in the stern worlds of Islington and Camden Town. Here he created perhaps the most interesting of all his works, transmitting his unpopular material into beauty by technique that is a joy in itself and a vision of unsurpassing truth. It may be that he who understood so profoundly the man in the street will never summon response from him in return; with his lonely ironic insight, his severe selections and comparisons, Sickert is worlds away from the dog-fight towards which we are so diligently racing.

Critics were disconcerted because no label fitted him; he eluded all schools and categories, ignoring the temporary prestige conferred by cabals. Official bodies paid him lip service while passing him by, which can hardly be held against them; his erratic attendances at meetings, his invariable practice of resigning from any society whenever its aesthetic values clashed with his own, could hardly further his cause with his colleagues. Adamant where aesthetic standards were concerned, friend or foe alike was sacrificed to them. Above all, his sudden disappearance for unspecified periods from the scene of action lessened his influence in art circles.

'If you really want to get down to work in peace, there's no need to go to the country. People start calling and all that sort of thing. Try Hackney or Edmonton, you'll have the place to yourself there, you needn't speak to a soul except the grocer and the milkman—'

And sometimes he would vanish to Dieppe, where he was completely cut off from his countrymen. Needless to add, that on his sudden returns, unpredictable as his departures, there was lost ground to be recovered and those who were busy launching new styles every year in the name of progress would proclaim that he was 'dated'.

The pundits of the Vale, the backbone of the New English Art Club, respected his work but were jealous for the supremacy of their gifted friend, Wilson Steer. Having formed a trade union with their idol as figurehead, or rather as reluctant chairman, they would brook no rival near the throne. Unhappily, Sickert and Steer were often pitted against each other in the first part of the century, as the 'English Impressionists', although it seems obvious today that their mature work had little in common. Sickert had an almost boyish admiration for the talents of Steer but he found it impossible to enjoy the sweets of intimacy with his old friend any longer, sealed off from the outer world as Steer was by his redoubtable bodyguard, Tonks and George Moore, with D. S. McCall looming watchfully in the background. Steer himself made no attempt to break his bonds. He had not forgiven Sickert for deserting the New English Art Club. Sickert would ask rather wistfully why Steer never visited him in Fitzroy Street; it did not occur to him that his defection was considered disloyal, a betrayal of the companion of his youth or that any artist could put personal considerations before his convictions. He dismissed Moore as an authority on painting and was but mildly interested in the views of Tonks, but found, on his excursions to the Vale, that Steer dozed off while Tonks or Moore took the floor, so that he and Steer became even more estranged. As for Fry, although too good a critic not to appreciate Sickert's work, he was buried beneath the mantle of Cézanne.

And Sickert aroused jealousy in other quarters besides the Vale.

'People were always rather envious of him, even when he was young and unknown,' Sir William Rothenstein remarked to me one day, when we were chatting about him. 'He had so much, you know; wit, talent, looks, charm, it all came so easily to him . . . And he didn't seem to realize how lucky he was. He always thought that everyone could do as he did if they wanted to.'

This aura of triumph and well-being had clung to him so long that he was still regarded, at fifty-eight, as one of Fortune's favourites. But time's wingèd chariot had caught up with him; the long world war, tardy recognition and lack of money were taking their toll at last. It might be argued that in the long run, only his work counts and we should be thankful today for the instinctive wisdom that prompted him to sheer away from social ties and art politics when they were wasting too much of his time. But we are suffering today from those years of public neglect. His own carelessness about preserving his best work was only equalled by the carelessness of the art world. He remained the painter's painter for too long; his best period was overlooked by art advisers and curators until these pictures were difficult to acquire, when they often fell back on inferior examples to fill the important gaps on their walls. One could cite many instances of this; I will confine myself to one. Even the fine Burrell collection at Glasgow has only a poor Sickert, a head of Sir Hugh Walpole, painted in his declining years, when flashes of the old magic were few. Sickert's masterpieces steal on one unawares; his work has a cumulative effect and the simplest way to enjoy him is to see a lot of it. Those who had the privilege of visiting the collection of 1941 at the National Gallery, assembled by Miss Lillian Browse, found it, as he would say, 'one long roll of revelation'. There are fine Sickerts to be seen today, here and there; at the Leicester Galleries, and at Messrs Agnew; the Tate, which has made gallant efforts to catch up with him, possesses several interesting portraits— 'Aubrey Beardsley', 'George Moore', presented by Wilson Steer, and 'Harold Gilman'. The Gilman is one of the best of his portraits, the very heart of the matter. But when students and art lovers ask me where Sickerts are to be found it is difficult to suggest a gallery which exhibits enough of his best work for them to gain a true impression of his powers.

He once told us that he never sold a picture until he was forty. We felt that this must be an exaggeration, but considering how helpless he was in furthering his own interests and his frequent choice of uncongenial subjects, this statement was probably not so far from the truth. He did not complain of his lot. He held that it was absurd for an artist to complain of poverty and neglect when he had deliberately chosen a career that should be a vocation. The joy of painting alone should compensate for the hazards of the profession.

'Our own fault if there's no money, we shouldn't be painters. We know, when we choose to paint, that there won't be any.'

These philosophic reflections however, and his distaste for official ties, conflicted with his desire to have more say in shaping the art policies of his time. He did not share the indifference of the Slade and the Camden Town Group towards the Academy: he did his best for the Group but was not confined by it; he needed a larger scope for his aims than any one society could afford. When Gilman denounced the Academy, Sickert maintained that you were lucky to find even a few grains of good work in any large organization which exhibited every year; that as a national institution the Academy was more useful to newcomers and strugglers than any small society could hope to be. Gilman, who was not interested in small fry and knew only too well what it was to struggle, regarded these contentions as humbug. But the chief reason for Sickert's interest in the Academy was his longing to teach the students and to influence the younger generation as he had hoped to do at the Slade. It was not, however, until 1924 that he was at last elected Associate Academician; too late to make any solid impact on that body. It was Orpen who proposed him and it must have required iron courage and great aesthetic integrity on his part to push Sickert's claims and reflects great credit on the perspicacity of the members. Possibly they took the line that a little of the brilliant and unpredictable Sickert might be more stimulating than a lot of someone of lesser calibre. He would, of course, sooner or later, with or without reason, resign; but many things might happen before then. It must have been a matter of self-congratulation to the members at his death to remember that

31

they had received him in their ranks and brought the pleasure of recognition before it was too late to a life that had been singularly devoid of official encouragement. For strange as it may seem in view of his unfitness for the post and his need for time to pursue his own painting, one of his dearest ambitions, as well as teaching at Burlington House, was to be President of the Academy. He was deeply gratified to become an Associate. All the old optimism flared up again when he received the distinction and he began to hope for the impossible. He came to luncheon with me at this time and I would not for worlds have reminded him that here was another routine job, leading to ties and fresh social commitments that he could never sustain. In any case, the honour conferred upon him had done him a power of good.

'It's almost too good to be true,' he said with shining eyes, too absent-minded to finish his soup. 'I can't believe it . . . but—do you know—I may end up after all as President!'

He had always felt lack of recognition more than his poverty. Mrs Swinton, an intimate friend, has said that Sickert cared naught for money. In a sense, this was true; with all the money in the world he would have chosen to live in Fitzroy Street and Camden Road, he drank little and was only interested in food when he had friends to share it with him, he only travelled in a circumscribed area, from Venice to Dieppe, from Bath to London; although he had lived in Paris, it was not altogether his city. He certainly never seemed to notice money until it was no longer there, and how he contrived immediately to dissipate any little windfall that came his way is one of the mysteries of his mysterious life; there never seemed to be anything to show for his expenditure. Mrs Swinton was right when she suggested that the one thing that really frightened him was the thought of failing powers; not only because he could then no longer maintain his hand to mouth existence but that the distant peaks of art that always challenged him, beckoning him on to fresh endeavour, would never now be scaled. This of course is the common tragedy of uncommon men; one likes to think that Sickert was largely spared the knowledge until he was too old to feel its full bitterness. But he hated analysing himself or others and would seldom confess that he was conscious of the hand of Time on his shoulder. 'Oh, join a debating society', was the usual retort if the conversation became too introspective for his taste. Romantic sentiments about art or anything else embarrassed him; he assumed a practical attitude even when his actions proclaimed his altruism. 'Come now, Spencer, don't be so damned spiritual. Beef or mutton?' he said to Stanley Spencer when they were lunching together, a remark which tickled Spencer so much that he never forgot it. He liked to be thought business-like and stressed the importance of sales for other painters, not only for the necessary cash but because they enhanced the reputation of the artist.

'How can people judge work they never see? Get your pictures out of the studio at any price, into the galleries, into people's houses, where they ought to be.'

But for himself, how differently he might see the matter!

One December afternoon, in 1917, two callers arrived at the studio; Prince Bibesco and his fiancée, Miss Elizabeth Asquith, daughter of the Prime Minister. They came to persuade Sickert to send a portrait to a bazaar in aid of the Red Cross that Miss Asquith was sponsoring. Portraits by leading British artists were to be exhibited at the sale and it was hoped that the public would give commissions to the artists of their choice for future portraits. I cannot remember the financial arrangements but in any case, this side of the bargain would not be of paramount importance to Sickert; if he intended to send a portrait it would more certainly be because of his great admiration for the Prime Minister as a first-rate classical scholar than for the sake of some potential gain or free advertisement. As an old friend of Sickert's, the Prince was hopeful that he might help them, but Sickert immediately raised objections. The lady, misled by his charm, proceeded to exercise her own considerable charm to get her way; she persevered for some time before she discovered that he was adamant. She was pretty and very young and Sickert, who took for granted that young girls should certainly be seen but on no account heard, was somewhat nonplussed when she took the floor as a matter of course. They made a true Camden Town conversation piece as they sat grouped round the fire, the Prince sunk deep in his chair, lamplight playing round the head of the girl, the solid presence of Sickert confronting her across the shadows. The Prince put in a slow word here and there but no more; he knew his Sickert and had already accepted defeat. Indolent, keen-witted, urbane, a gleam of amusement crossed his handsome, closed face and he exchanged a smile with Sickert when Miss Asquith protested that all the other painters whom she had approached had promised her their support and that this was her first rebuff. But after a prolonged tussle she dropped the matter, the conversation became general, Sickert and the Prince recalled old times, the visitors drank their tea and went their way.

Sickert saw them off, infinitely gracious. He assured Miss Asquith of his great regard for her father, deplored the ascendancy of Lloyd George and armed her into the street. Returning to the studio he explained himself.

'I don't approve of charity bazaars. Amateur affairs, one must really draw the line *somewhere*. Pretty child, eh? Quite promising when she's fledged . . . pity she looks round for applause when she's said a good thing . . . Well, they'll be back soon with a more sensible proposition. You'll see, you'll see!'

So far as I know, they never returned. But in a few days Sickert had forgotten the episode.

A large tome could be written on his association with dealers, no doubt with fervent contributions from these gentlemen themselves. Brimming with goodwill though he might be, only too eager to co-operate, full of solicitude for the hardships of their lot, taking up the cudgels in their defence at the faintest breath of adverse criticism, Sickert and his ways must nevertheless have presented them with many a problem.

3—S * *

'Vile life, a dealer's. Walking about in a gallery from ten to five,' (he always recoiled with horror from the thought of clocking in) 'recommending my paintings to someone who doesn't want them . . . they deserve to make as much money as they can out of me.'

He really believed this at the time but as money disappeared from his pockets almost sooner than it went in, he was not always as good as his word. Arthur Clifton, director of the Carfax Gallery, to whom Sickert had entrusted a large consignment of his things, preached economy and a waiting policy, wisdom which was coldly received by Sickert. They disputed about prices; Clifton wanted to see Sickerts selling for the price they should command but Sickert argued that his pictures should be sold to the first comer for what they would fetch and scattered to the winds, which would soon advertise them. What was the use of waiting, year in, year out, for tardy patrons who might only buy a few canvases at Clifton's price and then hide them away for ever in private houses? Not that Sickert objected, in theory, to pictures remaining hidden in private hands; seemingly unaware that many of his best works, especially the Camden Town series, are obviously gallery pictures, he considered that the right setting for them was the home.

His indifference to prices was part too, of his disastrous indifference to his pictures once they were painted. On, on always to the next adventure, the next problem! To Clifton, guarding his Sickerts jealously in his cellars, pulling them out at regular intervals to gloat over them, this lordly negligence was just madness. Worse still, Sickert might create fresh complications by presenting an important canvas to any newcomer who had happened to take his fancy; this, Clifton considered, was the most regrettable caper of all. Waiting patiently for an especial Sickert for an especial buyer, he would find that it had suddenly disappeared and could not be traced. Inured as he was to complaints from collectors that Sickerts could be purchased direct from the studio for less than the Carfax price, this presentation of his work to semi-strangers proved the last straw.

Paul Nash has given us a vivid portrait of his first meeting with Arthur Clifton at the Carfax in his autobiography, *Outline*.

'I was absorbed in a vision of my own drawings hanging next to Johns and Steers when I became aware of a faint metallic footfall and the gradual appearance of a large melancholy head, in slow helical progression from below the floor level. The manager was ascending the spiral staircase.

'A. B. Clifton was a big man rather inclined to be stout. He was eminently flat-footed, but always conveyed a dignified presence crowned by a rather distinguished head. As a personal friend of such personalities as Robbie Ross, Charles Conder and Oscar Wilde he had acquired a very special standing in the art world. He was well known for his shrewd and even generous treatment of artists, but could seem on occasion more discouraging and cold than any man I have ever met.'

This was an aspect of Clifton that seldom appeared but then we were more fortunate than Paul Nash, in that we never had to ask him for a favour. The Clifton we saw was genial, easy, imperturbable, with a keen eye for quality in contemporary as well as traditional painting; as Paul Nash says, ready to support fresh talent where he found it as well as established reputations. When we first met him, he was lunching with Sickert at Number 15. He wore an indigo blue scarf that matched his eyes, the cold innocent blue eyes of the soldier or the explorer and the scarf certainly heightened the purity of their hue. But they expressed more; bewilderment rather, a profound passive sadness, a suggestion of *le temps perdu*, of a spacious leisured polite society that was rapidly retreating before the onslaught of Armageddon . . . Greatly he deplored the lowering of standards, the slapdash habits of the younger generation.

'In my day,' he observed, lifting those mournful heavy-lidded eyes to mine, 'we always called on our hostess on the first Sunday after a dinner party. Now, I understand, the young Yahoos don't even send a thank-you after a week-end . . .'

Chris visited the Carfax with me the following week, when Clifton greeted us gravely in his precise Oxford voice and introduced us to his assistant, Madeleine Knox, whom he afterwards married. As she stood beside Clifton, stroking her fair hair thoughtfully with long thin fingers, I recalled Sickert's description of her, 'a pearly little thing'. Clifton was very proud of her talent for painting and always regretted that she had so little time to devote to it during the war. She was also extremely practical about everyday affairs. It seemed unlikely that this frail creature should be so capable; efficient women were rarer in 1917 than they are today, but Miss Knox tackled the sudden war-time problems that came her way with unruffled ease. While Clifton and Chris were engrossed with a batch of drawings she spoke of etching classes she had conducted for Sickert at his school, Rowlandson House; of her pupils at Dulwich, of gardening, motoring, needle-work and all the various activities which she found time for somehow during her crowded days. Clifton, meanwhile, was trying to catch Chris unaware with a clever imitation of a Sickert drawing, which she promptly recognized as a forgery, to his great satisfaction. One drawing, however, confounded us all when he proceeded to drag up some of his treasures from the basement, a large heavy sketch of a nude in black chalk.

'It's by a great swell,' Clifton declared, enjoying our ignorance. It happened to be a Degas . . .

When he got bored with his expeditions to the basement he began to indulge his favourite pastime—a good gossip about mutual friends and acquaintances.

'Don't be injudicious, Arthur,' pleaded Miss Knox.

'Ah, I am always injudicious,' he assured her.

As a matter of fact, he was not. A long legal training had ironed out any tendency to indiscretions. But he loved to talk about people, especially Sickert, a never-ending source of mystification to him. Why oh why did he do this, that or the other? This inconsequence, this fatal impulsiveness! He lost no time in trying to enlist our sympathies for his business dealings with the Master.

'*No* notion of money,' he pronounced severely.

We suggested that Sickert couldn't help it. Clifton considered this statement and found it a thought presumptuous.

'Please to remember that we are not talking about a simpleton who is not responsible for his actions. We are talking about a MIND.'

The lamentations continued. Difficult to get Sickert to sign a painting; impossible to persuade him to stick to market prices; infuriating when he gave pictures away to perfect strangers. 'Who *are* these people, how do they get access to him, there should be a watchdog at Number 15 . . . Absurd, that he should be exploited by every Tom, Dick and Harry!'

'It's not always Tom, Dick or Harry,' we sighed. 'The other day the poet Davies went off with that lovely painting of Wellington House Academy under his arm. Sickert insisted on giving it to him.'

'I can only repeat,' said Clifton with Johnsonian majesty, 'that the whole thing is preposterous.'

There was a huge shelf, stacked with canvases, running round the walls of Number 15. One of these canvases represented a cherished grievance of Clifton's. 'If he would only carry that picture through!' But Clifton had hinted, hovered round the subject in vain. 'To think that it's hidden up there with its back to the wall, only, no doubt, to be thrown away in the end.' Would we, could we possibly persuade him to finish it? 'It's important. I could sell it immediately.'

I blush for my officiousness. But Clifton was so worried about his failure to save this canvas that I agreed to help him. At first there seemed no chance to interfere. But one day I saw a ladder standing against the wall below the sacred shelf. Under pretext of dusting the pictures I climbed the ladder and brought down the coveted object.

'Have you forgotten this?' I asked, holding the canvas out to Sickert with one or two others, which I hoped might put him off the scent. 'It does seem such a pity—'

Sickert peered at me over his glasses with a malicious gleam in his eye.

'And *when* did Arthur tell you to say that?' he enquired.

I thought Clifton would smile (he never laughed), when I told him of this rebuff; it was so richly deserved. But Clifton was not amused; he looked sympathetic, gloomy, infinitely resigned. 'Well, you know what he is,' was all the consolation he could offer.

If money was scarce in that winter of 1917-18 it was scarcer still in the spring of 1918 when Sickert and Clifton became estranged and Sickert demanded his pictures back from the Carfax. The loss of Clifton made itself felt. It was not until some years later that Sickert settled down to a long and happy connection with the Leicester Galleries which lasted until his death. Other dealers were, of course, showing Sickerts but there was no one at the moment to take the place of Clifton, so that Sickert decided, temporarily, to be his own dealer.

I need not say how soon the novelty wore off. Playing at dealing with friends and acquaintances or presenting them with his work was one thing; advertising himself and enduring prolonged business sessions with strangers who wanted to drag out all the canvases in his studio was another. There were ominous signs, however, that his finances were getting out of hand; loss of spirits, great restlessness, much re-arrangement of the furniture and a marked disinclination for his own company all pointed to a disturbed mind. At this time, in fact, he sought distraction wherever he could find it. 'Oh dear. Must you leave me so soon, *alone* with my genius?'

The Frith was now a more exciting place than ever, filled with canvases, many of the Camden Town period, that had been relinquished by Clifton. Collectors were now beginning to find their way to Fitzroy Street. I have often wondered how they got there. Sickert would have been appalled by the mere thought of a telephone in his workshop or home and he seldom answered letters; indeed, to cope efficiently with his correspondence would have required the services of a secretary, whose constant presence, complete with typewriter, was unthinkable. But when a client was coming he did his best to cope with the situation; the furniture was shuffled about again, little ornaments suddenly appeared from nowhere, the fire was replenished, the kettle filled and ready on the hob. Other preparations, alas, were also made; important canvases were tucked away, one behind the other, with their faces to the wall. But invariably, 'Le Vieux Colombier', a small, dark, very green picture of some logs and a pigeon cote, was placed on his easel in the middle of the room.

'Never give people too much to see at once. One picture at a time is sufficient for them.'

If the collector was to see one picture only we could have wished that it might be something more characteristic of Sickert than 'Le Vieux Colombier'. Doubtless, we failed to appreciate its quality, but I fear it remains a blind spot to this day for Chris and me. Sickert adored it. He did several versions of the subject and finally, as if to get it, once for all, out of his system, one large canvas which cropped up again only a few years ago when I was hanging an exhibition in Scotland. Different versions of 'Le Vieux Colombier' are always appearing from time to time, while Sickerts that one longs to see again have vanished, never to return. Not only was this picture to the fore when collectors were present; it seemed to be always about, as if affording Sickert some inner consolation. He would linger over it with affection, nursing it with his brush, adding thoughtful touches here and there with fatherly pride.

When collectors came, their meetings with Sickert seemed to lead only too often to the same unsatisfactory conclusions. The visitor would arrive, groping his way through the dark house to the door of the Frith, when he still had to cross the ante-room and find the steep stairs at the far end before he reached the main studio. And if this was not intimidating enough, the Sickert who received him was in his most difficult mood. Charming, ceremonious and slightly vague, he left the situation on the hands of his guest. Miss Gosse had told us that Sickert could be shy; now we knew how shy he could be. I do not remember that the visitors were assertive; Sickert's demeanour, the vast room, the creeping shadows, the penetrating silence were nicely calculated to reduce them to submission. Conversation seldom flowed. It became more halting, strained, a crescendo of embarrassment for guest and host.

When the collector did summon up his courage and ask to see some work, Sickert pointed firmly to 'Le Vieux Colombier', but whether this picture pleased him or not, the collector was naturally attracted towards forbidden fruit; he stared longingly at the rows of canvases stacked with their faces to the wall, hesitating to ask that they might be reversed for his sake. After further skirmishing, it became a battle of wills between them, 'Le Vieux Colombier' or nothing. Whenever this contest took place, the collector won. He developed a dumb resistance to the picture by ignoring it and refusing to play at all.

The tea party that followed was not gay. Sickert had by now washed his hands of the affair; he would relapse into a flat, weighted silence, gazing with lofty absorption at a distant corner of the ceiling; he might, however, emerge from his trance to offer some languid disparagement of his own work and ardent tributes to everyone else's. Long pauses were broken by trite remarks from Chris and me. As soon as possible the visitor took his leave, Sickert bowing him off the premises, hailing a taxi with solicitude and further mystifying him with parting words of advice.

'Do you know Gore's work? If you're after English painting you should collect Gore. He's your man! Now there's a *painter* for you.'

When he returned to Frith he could not fail to notice our downcast faces. They would have been still more downcast had we realized how very empty his pockets were at that time. Seeing us depressed, he set to work to cheer us up, relating every entertaining story he could think of, talking sublime nonsense, wasting the wit which could have dazzled the collector, poking fun at us and himself and chattering about everything except the recent disaster, which was never mentioned again.

Business was better if callers came when Sickert was out. He had given us permission to show drawings in his absence; amateur saleswomen though we were, we had some success through the simple expedient of leaving people alone and letting the drawings sell themselves. One diffident, reserved man much enjoyed this diversion; he spent a happy afternoon pottering among the litter of sketches on the great table and selected things at his own pace to decorate his flat in the Albany. When Sickert returned he was full of an exhibition he had just seen, and not interested in buyers. He popped the cheque that we handed him into his pocket without a glance; for all he knew we might have sold the drawings for a few shillings or a few pence.

There was, however, one collector who understood Sickert only too well and managed him to admiration; the Japanese Ambassador. It was a sad day for Britain when this gentleman knocked at his door. How the Japanese discovered that Sickert was no longer under the wing of Clifton and that the bulk of his available work was back in the Frith, I cannot say; but they lost no time in forestalling London. Their ambassador had *carte blanche* from his government to choose as many Sickerts as he thought fit and ship them immediately to Japan. Unfortunately for England he had an eye for painting. It would be interesting to know which pictures he took and what he paid for them.

Their tête-à-tête luncheon was a great success. Sickert informed us afterwards that the Ambassador's English was excellent; they shared a Bath chap, a bottle of Madeira and mutual entertainment. Luncheon over, he allowed the ambassador to see his things, the choice was rapidly made, a van appeared to collect them and the cheque was promptly paid before Sickert could change his mind.

Returning to Fitzroy Street that afternoon, we saw the van at the door, being loaded with the pictures. We wandered round the Frith in dismay. Reluctantly, we had to admit that the ambassador knew what he was about. No wistful glances at withheld riches for him; he had taken what he wanted. Sickert was in high spirits, but cagey. He did admit that the large version of 'Suspense' had gone with the wind, but I am afraid many other important Sickerts were also whisked away before his countrymen were properly aware of their existence, never, in all probability, to appear in Europe again.

The ambassador, I might add, had side-tracked 'Le Vieux Colombier'. It still held its advantageous position on its easel in the centre of the Frith.

Chapter 4

Work

In 1917, Sickert was still a prolific painter. He was also teaching at the Westminster Technical Institute in Vincent Square for several evenings a week, sitting on committees, writing articles, lecturing and trying to cope at the same time with his social activities. It is not surprising that he gave up the contest a year later when he retired to Dieppe, but the last lap at the Frith before he disappeared to France was a strenuous one. Presents did get acknowledged, invitations usually answered, but in the absence of a secretary, correspondence piled up on his desk until it assumed such gross proportions that he lost heart and consigned it to the wastepaper basket. To the casual observer, it would seem that people were making an obstacle race of his life with the express object of wasting his time. No serious painter can have been more cursed with popularity. His indolent good nature made him an easy victim; he drifted along, protesting faintly, until the situation got completely out of hand. I remember a queue outside the Frith one wintry morning in 1917—a group of people staring suspiciously at each other, waiting to pounce whenever he might appear—an indignant painter armed with portfolio, determined to air his grievances because his work had been refused by some hanging committee and eager to point out exactly how the judges had erred by not availing themselves of his talents, a model seeking an engagement, an art student wanting help, a journalist after copy, a pretty lady with her peke, bubbling over with affectionate protestation and assurances of her full and free forgiveness because he had not turned up at her dinner party . . .

'Cher maître, of course I understand! You mustn't ever do anything that you don't want to.'

'After all,' as Sickert remarked when the invaders had been coaxed or threatened, according to sex, to give ground, 'one must paint *sometimes*'.

The work, however, did get done. This was a constant source of wonder to his friends, especially Arthur Clifton, who never ceased to marvel at the amazing, the inexplicable fact. He must have forgotten that Sickert was astir soon after five o'clock in the morning and that when he was engrossed with a picture he would work on it far into the night. Sometimes the idea tormented him until it was resolved; he would seek his bed from sheer fatigue, rise again after a broken sleep, dress himself anew and thresh round the streets until dawn, lost in meditation.

Perhaps all the turmoil of his London life was not entirely destructive in its

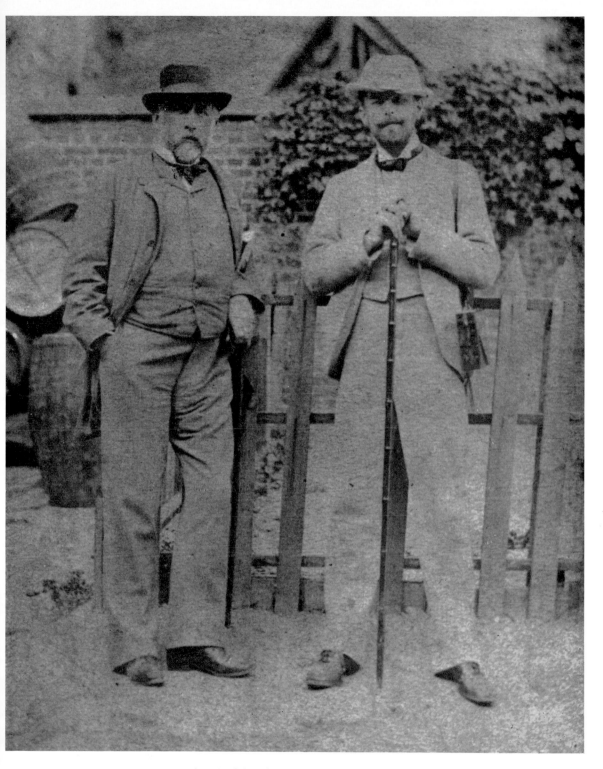

1. Sickert (right) and Degas at Dieppe, August 1885.
Islington Public Libraries (J. A. Hamilton Studios, Islington)

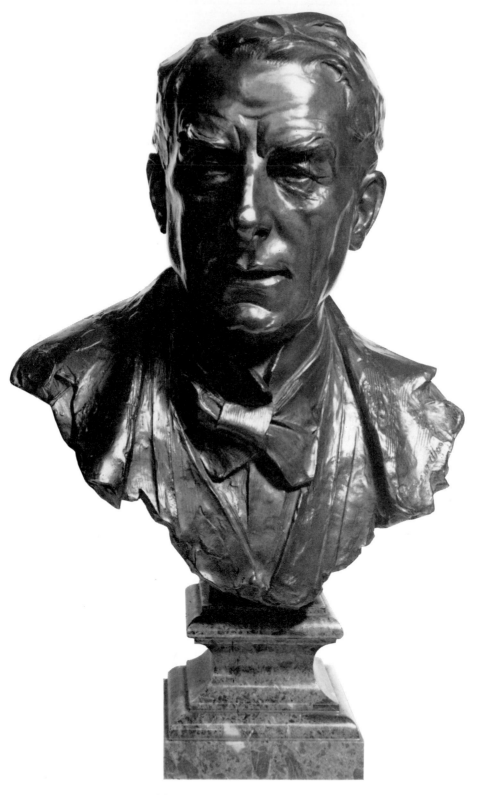

2. Derwent Wood (1871-1926). Bust of Sickert, 1925. Bronze. 18 ins.
Royal Academy of Arts, London

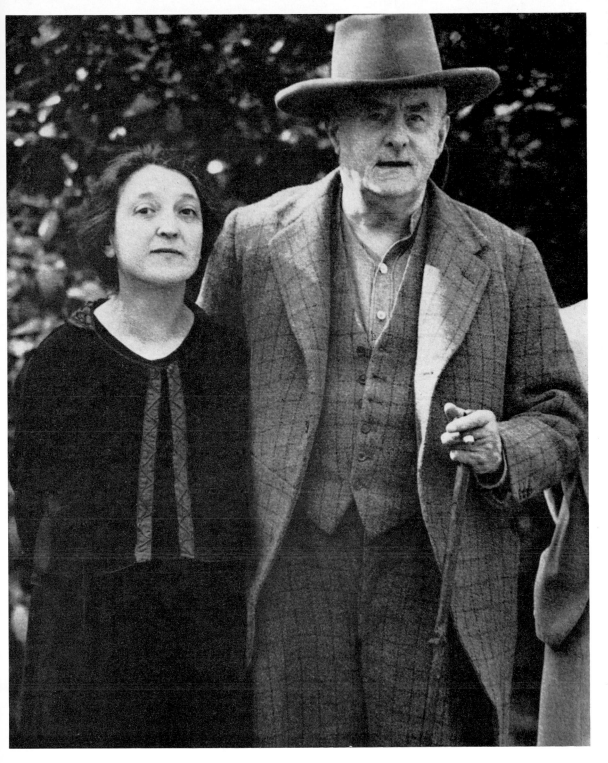

3. Sickert with his third wife, Thérèse Lessore.
Islington Public Libraries (J. A. Hamilton Studios, Islington)

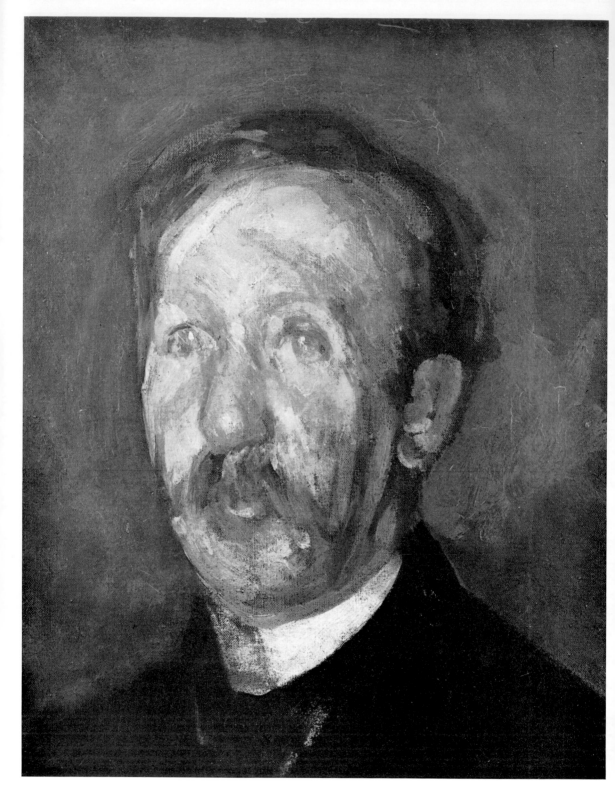

4. Walter Richard Sickert (1860–1942).
GEORGE MOORE, *c.* 1890. Oil. $23\frac{3}{4} \times 19\frac{3}{4}$ ins. *Tate Gallery, London*

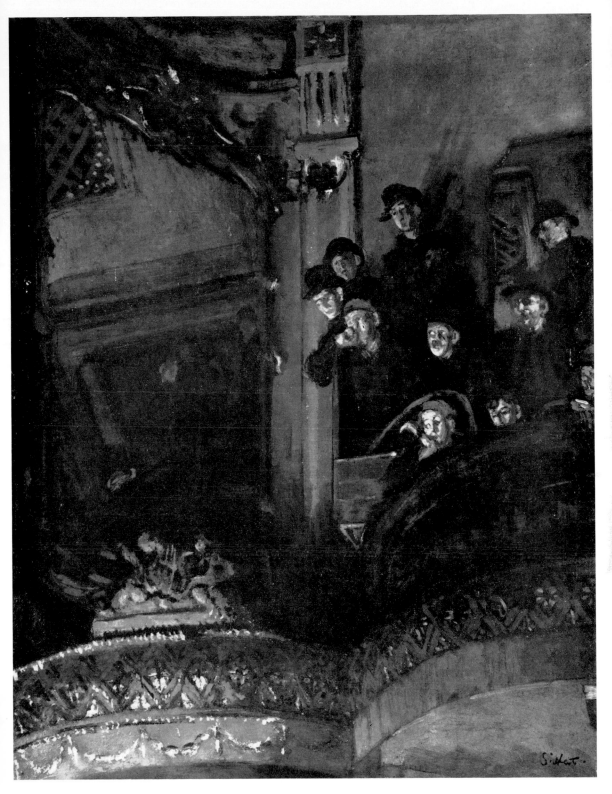

5. Walter Richard Sickert (1860–1942).
THE OLD BEDFORD: A CORNER OF THE GALLERY, *c.* 1897. Oil. 30 × 23¾ ins.
Walker Art Gallery, Liverpool

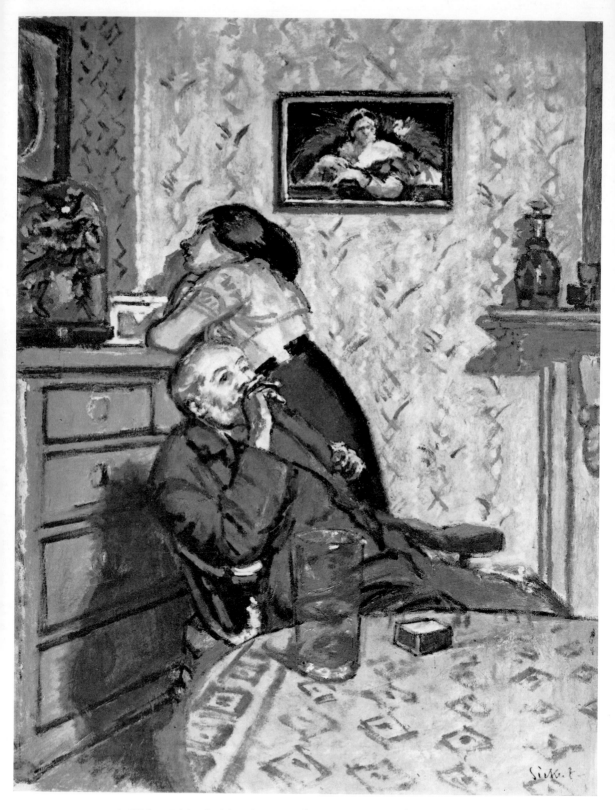

6. Walter Richard Sickert (1860-1942). ENNUI, *c.* 1917. Oil. 30 × 22 ins.
Ashmolean Museum, Oxford

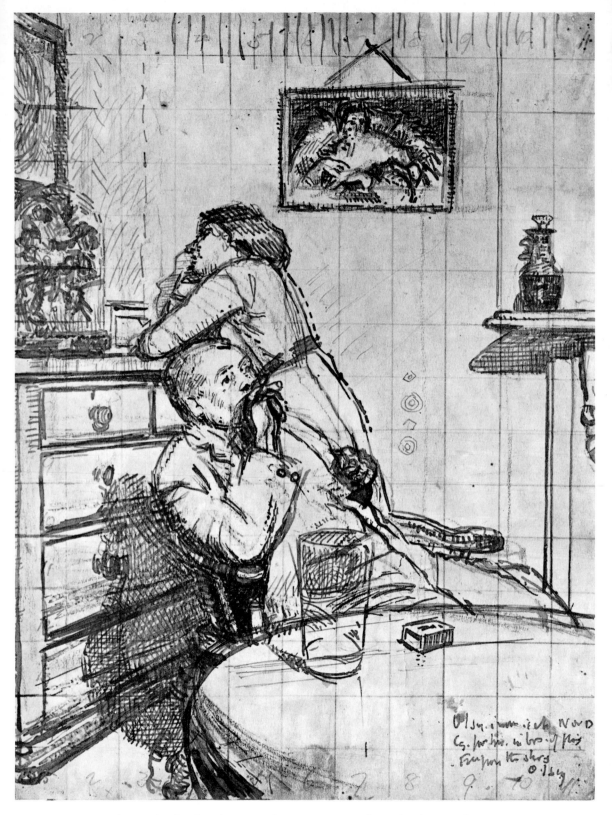

7. Walter Richard Sickert (1860–1942). ENNUI, *c.* 1913. Charcoal and pen. 14⅝ × 10½ ins.
Ashmolean Museum, Oxford

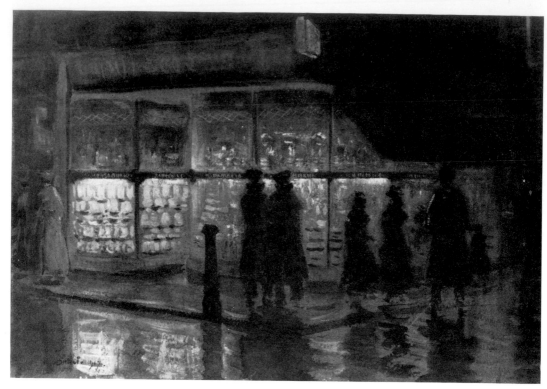

8. Walter Richard Sickert (1860-1942). ISLINGTON, 1917. Pastel. 13 × 19 ins.,
showing the corner of the Pentonville and Caledonian Roads.
Reproduced by courtesy of Miss Violet Hopwood

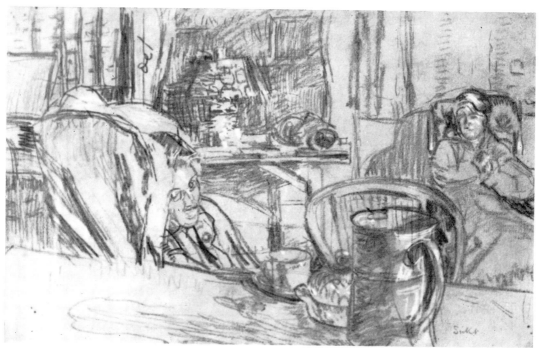

9. Walter Richard Sickert (1860-1942). ALPHA AND OMEGA, 1917.
Blue and white chalk, showing the author (left)
and her friend Christina Cutter in the Frith studio.

effect; in fact, it seemed as if it inspired him to be thus involved, from time to time, with the human condition. He dealt precisely with the daily round and even with the interruptions, talking surface chatter while his real thoughts were engaged elsewhere, a smokescreen that he could always put up in self-defence if necessary; as he moved sedately from one thing to another he was forever meditating about the picture in hand or on the quest for the next one. As for the disturbers of the peace, he could deal firmly enough with them if they became too importunate. In his odd Sickertian way he was arranging his life, amid all the seeming chaos, as he arranged his friends, in cycles; first the multitude, then solitude. And when the dire need for privacy was upon him, all the King's horses and all the King's men could not have kept him from securing it. 'This is a little much,' he would say at last, his upper lip lengthening ominously. One knew then that he was about to escape. His door would shut suddenly and finally; visitors pounded away at the knocker in vain while he took cover in some garret round the corner, giving himself up to solitary contemplation.

He was now fifty-eight; the grand period, which lasted, roughly speaking, some twenty-five years, was nearly spent; from now on we have flashes of the old magic but no longer the even flow of masterpieces that we associate with the first quarter of the century. The strain of a hard life was beginning to tell but he could always rely on his great reserves of technical knowledge, above all on his long experience in the art of saving himself from useless exertions.

'So many years have taught me not to waste time; I know when a picture *isn't there*, and cut my losses.'

An unusual error of judgement occurred in the winter of 1917, when he actually squared up a drawing which was, presumably, unsuitable for enlargement. I refer to 'Alpha and Omega', rechristened years later as ' 'Arf a Pint', a silly title which he must have thought up when he was in vacant rather than in pensive mood. 'Alpha and Omega' (plate 9), which portrayed Chris and me seated in the Frith, was evidently intended to be the working note for an oil of considerable dimensions. On the same evening that he made this elaborate drawing he enlarged it on a big canvas, some three by five feet. The result, however, displeased him; whether the drawing was unsatisfactory as a working note or enlarged on the wrong scale or whether he decided that the picture 'wasn't there' I do not presume to say. It cannot have been the composition which he found wanting, as when the drawing is enlarged on the screen it stands the test as well as other Sickerts; in fact, as is usually the case with his work, the composition is more impressive when enlarged. Perhaps the explanation is simple, after all. He may have lost interest in the subject. Although he was working at white heat with excitement when he did the drawing, 'the fizz may have gone out of it' when it was once drawn. Be that as it may, the project was abandoned; never, so far as I know, to be revived again as a painting. I have often wondered what happened to that canvas. It stood for days in the passage outside the Frith with its face to the wall, then disappeared for ever. Once, when no one was about, I turned it round and studied it at length, wondering why he had not carried it further. There was so much information in it already; he must have worked all night, painting with the utmost speed and certitude, to get thus far; the more I looked at it, the more I marvelled that he should have covered so much ground in so short a time. But 'Alpha and Omega' will always remain a mystery. The oil was never referred to again; he evidently looked upon it as a mistake, to be forgotten as soon as possible. But the idea still detained him as a drawing; he liked the composition and made several versions of it later.[1]

It is regrettable that Sickert did not see his way to carry this oil through; we have so few large Sickerts of merit in this country, although I believe there are some in private collections in France. As Mr Gabriel White has said, 'It is rare that Sickert could not say all he wanted on a modest-sized canvas, in fact some of his loveliest pictures are small by any standard. It is, however, in some of the larger works of his later life that one can detect some of the developments in modern painting which were to influence artists today, especially in their preoccupation with the purely surface quality of the paint.'[2]

Latterly, he went for greater economy of style and thinner painting, becoming sometimes so laconic that his work proved baffling to the layman. In 1926, when he was living at Brighton, he showed one of his sketches to Mr Wood, an antique dealer who was helping Sickert to remove his furniture from one studio to another. Mr Wood looked at the sketch closely, then remarked—'It'll be all right when it's finished.' 'It *is* finished,' replied Sickert.

Was it not Van Gogh who said in order to paint a pair of boots you must *become* a pair of boots? Indeed, Sickert did become his own particular brand of third floor back. He never used these gaunt interiors for work until they had become a part of him. As time went on he seemed to need a fresh garret for almost every picture, as if each one afforded him a separate sharp experience that must be concentrated on a single canvas. This of course was hardly an economical proceeding but posterity must be thankful that he did not allow economy to frustrate his purpose. He generally preferred to take a 'furnished' room, that is, a chance accumulation of sparse and battered relics which had survived the onslaughts of previous tenants, but sometimes he would arrange it himself with, say, a looking-glass, a horsehair sofa, a circular table, a Victorian chair studded with buttons, wax fruits or salmon in a glass case. When he had finished with the room some friend or pupil would take it over from him; he usually made them a present of the contents. An old secondhand shop at the corner of Tottenham Court Road, filled with junk, was a great lure when he was moving into a fresh garret; he would find all sorts of excitements there, especially pictures that no one else wanted. Should a friend be with him, he might be wheedled past the danger but if he was alone, a serpent voice would whisper '*Buy*'. Then he would drag a dusty trophy back in triumph to the Frith, spend hours

[1] The original and best drawing, in black chalk on grey paper with white chalk accents, was recently in the possession of Mr Mark Oliver.

[2] Foreword: *Sickert*, Arts Council of Great Britain, Tate Gallery, 1960.

cleaning it and amusing himself with the notion that it might be a Delacroix or a Rubens, playing his favourite game of 'let's pretend'. After indulging in blissful fantasies about it for several days, holding forth brilliantly on its merits, he had almost talked himself into believing that it was the real thing. But not quite. Alas! sooner or later, doubt set in. Suddenly, we would find him gazing severely at his vaunted masterpiece. 'Do you think . . . perhaps . . . it's not a Rubens after all?'

His famous passion for just one more garret to add to his collection was a source of endless amusement to his friends. As he and the painter Ambrose McEvoy were walking down Charlotte Street one day they saw a notice, 'Studio to Let'. McEvoy grasped Sickert's arm and hurried him away. 'Be a man, Walter!' he implored. 'Pass it, pass it!'

In the spring of 1918 Sickert became increasingly restless. One day, we walked about for hours while he was searching for a new 'hide-out', inspecting first one room then another, finding none that was quite the thing. 'There's an interesting subject,' he remarked suddenly, as we made our way down the Euston Road. I gazed at some roofs and a row of blackened chimneys belching forth smoke, while he stood stock still in the middle of the pavement, oblivious of the crowds surging past us, and delivered a discourse on this arresting combination of shapes and spaces, the substance of which is best summed up in his own written words:

'Much of the world we live in is becoming hideous. But skill and selection may collocate a part of one ugly thing with a part of another ugly thing and produce a third, which is beauty.'

He was happy at first as we pottered about, but when the afternoon wore on and the fickle light was fading, as we rapped on endless doors, dived under greasy curtains in narrow halls, climbed rickety stairs to third floor backs, he relapsed into mournful silence. 'We want Paradise', he explained to the puzzled landladies who showed us their premises. 'A thousand apologies . . . no, I'm afraid this isn't quite Paradise,' he would confide to each of them in turn, lingering wistfully in her dingy apartment, gazing raptly at her photographs and ornaments, so that she, bemused by his charm, was almost as gratified when he bowed himself out as if he had taken her rooms after all . . .

At last, however, he came upon his treasure trove. A crooked room at the top of a crooked house in Warren Street, so rightly named. I fear that I failed to appreciate the significance of this grisly chamber. All I saw was a forlorn hole, cold, cheerless, the ceiling so black and hammocky that I begged him not to go there, foreseeing mountains of plaster descending on his head at any moment. But we were not looking at the same thing. All he saw was the *contre-jour* lighting that he loved, stealing in through a small single window, clothing the poor place with light and shadow, losing and finding itself again on the crazy bed and floor. Dirt and gloom did not exist for him; these four walls spoke only of the silent shades of the past, watching us in the quiet dusk. Here, the psychological and the visual aspects of his art came together; here he could transform some incident, a figure at the window,

43

an inscrutable presence, the listless gesture of a hand, the droop of a head, to the universal.

It would be idle to suppose that Sickert was an optimist; in his heart, he agreed with Yeats that we begin to live when we have conceived life as tragedy. But he could and did rejoice. Unless he was too harassed by shortage of money, he was indeed the good companion. He had the blessed faculty of enjoying little things that came his way, a present of fruit or game, a bottle of Madeira, a sunny sky, a branch of lilac, a new book or play or painting that took his fancy, a tree in bloom. He responded to the merest hint of success. When he had solved a difficult pictorial problem or if he had received recognition from a source that he valued, he would greet us at the Frith with a radiant face. 'I felt so happy this morning coming here, I could hardly keep on the pavement.' With his favourite, Byron, he could have said, 'Nobody laughs more.' And many a time he has kept us laughing too, literally for hours on end, with his quips, his extravagances, his anecdotes, his imitations of our friends, sharpened by the stately and mock-pompous English with which they were presented. The fact that he was still producing good work at this time enhanced his wit and gave him spiritual satisfaction. Indeed, I think it is not too much to say that the fits of depression which have been noted by previous writers, when not caused by fears of failing powers, were almost entirely due to money troubles.

The connection between the man and his work was elusive. Those who had only met him in his buoyant moods might wonder that he could have painted and was still painting what André Gide called 'his morose and powerful' work, especially that of the North London period. When he was gay and witty, all sparkle and abandon, he and the underworld he portrayed so gravely seemed poles asunder. But had they known him when one of these pictures was germinating they would have been baffled to see how completely Dr Jekyll had assumed the mantle of Mr Hyde. In one of his fits of intense concentration, he would enter the Frith through the ante-room, glide through it gravely like a sleepwalker, pick up the tool or other materials that he was searching for and leave at the other door so silently that it seemed as if one had seen a spectre rather than the solid form of Sickert himself.

In 1905, he had left France, where he was gaining recognition, and returned to England. This may have seemed an unwise proceeding at the time but although one must always allow for the capricious streak in him, a deeper urge was driving him home; he turned to North London because his roots were there. His interest in architecture was already apparent in his early work and this strong feeling was now transferred from buildings in Dieppe and Venice to music halls in Camden Town and Islington. Sometimes the audience sang the tune, sometimes the scene was almost pure architecture, but always there is the sense of movement, of an inhabited world. And the city itself drew him; it was still infinitely various. Horses, hansoms (those loveliest of shapes), growlers, gardens, imposing squares, queer byways, parks, cottages, trees, flowers and grass abounded; there were endless reminders of Hogarth and Dickens; the cockneys who were bound up with his childhood had not yet vanished from the scene. He revelled in the soft misty light that he found nowhere else, in the urban blues and greys and umbers.

'London! Like the evening star, you bring me everything . . .'[1]

During the Hitler war, I met two schoolfellows of his at York. They told me:

'He was the cat that walked by itself. He didn't care to do our things, he was aloof . . . but he could be wonderfully good company when he was in the mood. Everyone liked to be asked to walk home with him from school. He never invited more than two of us at a time. He knew North London like the back of his hand, he could tell us endless stories about the little streets and byways as we went along and pointed out pictures that we hadn't seen. It was another world to us.'

One wonders how his especial vein of poetry, melancholy and grandiose, his feeling for the spirit of place, will appeal to art lovers when Camden Town is finally reduced to a dust bowl. Future generations will not know his world as he saw it, there will be no difference between Islington, still so full of character, and any other featureless suburb such as Ealing or Streatham; the variety and contrast that give each area of London its special flavour will have departed. But there is still time for a ramble round the backwaters of North London for those who would like to gain fresh insight into Sickert's work. It should be taken on a November day if possible; autumn was his favourite time of year. Camden Town, in his sense, is almost finished; another few years will complete its destruction. But Islington, brooding on its high hill, still retains the Sickertian atmosphere. Only a native of the place could have the profound intimacy with his subject that he portrays in his studies of North London; but Islington reveals the sources of his inspiration more clearly than Camden Town. He was never tired of pointing out some secret or forgotten crescent, coiled in the labyrinth of the northern slums, or the sad silhouette of old streets near the Angel, transformed by the light of his eager spirit from squalor to romance. Along Duncan Terrace, where he had lived as a child, down Noel Road, by Lamb's house in Colebrook Row or in one of those vast squares which always seem to be empty, black and embattled against a winter sky, the shade of Sickert walks. Above all in Milner Square, reached by way of a dark tunnel from Upper Street. Emerging from the tunnel, the menacing quality of the square strikes the eye with the force of a blow; one is trapped as at the bottom of a well, walled in by those stern rectangular ramparts of stone. Two world wars have wrought their havoc on Milner Square as I knew it in my childhood. The trees have been cut down, the cockney accent replaced by alien tongues; the muffin man no longer rings his bell on Sunday afternoons, the granite walls have been gayed up, the hurdy gurdy has ceased to grind out its single dolorous refrain:

[1] Robert Emmons: *The Life and Opinions of Walter Sickert*, Faber & Faber, 1941

45

'In the swee-eet bye-and-bye
We shall mee-eet bye-and-bye . . .'

Today, it is almost a friendly place; certainly less mysterious since the tall trees
have gone; they formed an impenetrable thicket once, in the centre of the square.
Now, all four sides can see each other, however distantly; there is laughter and
chatter on summer afternoons, women appear at the windows, leaning huge
elbows on sills that are adorned with flowers; the mystery, the strangeness are
gone. But come a winter's day when the light is waning, the windows shuttered,
the great streets empty, and a threatening note, faint but enduring, still lingers in
Milner Square.

Those bleak interiors shadowed by Venetian blinds with recumbent forms on
iron bedsteads were all painted in North London. 'Ennui', one of his best-known
pictures, was inspired by a decayed first floor in Granby Street, off the Hampstead
Road. Visitors to the Tate will remember the man smoking in the foreground,
the woman drooping over the chest of drawers, even the matchbox on the table
exuding boredom. Sickert was so swept away by 'Ennui' that he forgot to eat a
square meal for days together and slept on the kitchen table in the gaunt house
until he had exhausted all the possibilities of his subject. When at last he staggered
to his favourite restaurant the waiter, an old ally, remarked: 'What you want, sir,
is a good beefsteak', and ran off to provide it for him.

The composition of 'Ennui', with its Whistlerian spacing, reinforces the theme;
the high empty walls, devoid of statement save for one picture placed there to
strengthen the design, enhance the feeling of utter blankness that overpowers not
only the protagonists of the drama but the spectator as well. The emptiness is part
of the meaning. And boredom is a great theme; one that Sickert had much at
heart. Nothing shocked him more. Once, when someone confessed to frequent
attacks of boredom, he was distressed beyond measure. 'But it's so *stupid* to be
bored,' he protested.

But he could be bored too, very bored indeed when the fit took him. Ominous
signs of the state that he so much deplored in others were evident at various times,
especially when he was grinding coffee after luncheon. If the guests appeared to be
rooted to the spot, which was but too often the case, he might find the tedium
excessive. And then the rattling of his coffee machine grew louder and louder and
more prolonged, while Sickert thus registered the protest that he was too polite to
put into words. It were well for the company to heed these danger signals and to
take themselves off as soon as possible. Should this appeal fall on deaf ears, and
they proved obdurate, they might find themselves, quite suddenly, alone in the
Frith, their host having disappeared into the blue before their very eyes.

The best version in oils of 'Ennui' that I have seen was shown at Colchester, in
1961. It was the high-light of an exhibition of the Camden Town Group,
assembled by Mr R. A. Bevan, the son of Robert Bevan. This 'Ennui' had been
lent by the Ashmolean Museum, Oxford, with working notes of the same subject,

executed with Sickert's favourite goose quill. The working notes, placed side by side with the oil, were exciting, giving one a peep behind the scenes, showing the alterations, the adjustments, the omissions that the idea had undergone before it reached its final statement (see plates 6 and 7). There is a larger version of 'Ennui' in the Tate Gallery and several others elsewhere, as well as a considerable number of etchings, but the Tate version seems lacking in richness of texture; it is almost as if the whole surface were slightly faded.

'Hubby', who plays the lead in 'Ennui', hunched in his chair, staring at vacancy, was a broken-down schoolfellow of Sickert's, now a casual vagrant who had arrived at Granby Street with a suitcase which he had picked up on Euston station. Another thing that shocked Sickert was stealing; his sense of the rights of property was keen; if this was not firmly upheld he foresaw general chaos. On one occasion, while he still rented the Frith, a young couple stole some canvases and other materials from a room nearby. He was expressing the gravest disapprobation of these thefts when a friend of the delinquents began to defend them. 'After all,' she declared, 'everyone has a right to exist.' 'Not at all,' retorted Sickert. 'There are people who have no right to exist, I'd butter their slides for them!'

Granted that this was just his fun, he was serious enough too; he abhorred looting and pilfering so much that he did not care to hear any pleas for the offenders.

Everyone was on tenterhooks so long as Hubby was about the place, fearing trouble with the police. And he was very much in evidence for a time; this rather genial waster appears in many drawings at this period, notably in 'What Shall We Do For The Rent?' (1909) and in 'Jack Ashore' (1910, plate 10). But Sickert was greatly relieved when Hubby suddenly took himself off, disappearing for good.

'Jack Ashore' also depicts Marie Hayes, a model whom Sickert often drew and was still drawing in 1917. We were rather taken aback by the splendid opulence of Marie, who was considerably larger than life or any model that we had ever seen at the Slade, although we had soon discovered that big women were more interesting to draw than thin ones, suggesting a monumental dignity, as revealed by the mountainous figures of Henry Moore.

'Isn't she rather fat?' we asked doubtfully as we surveyed the contours of Marie, spread before us in all her plentitude.

'Well, what would you have?' said Sickert.

'Something middling perhaps—'

'*Middling*? What a word! I can't abide anything middling. Very fat or very thin but middling, never!' He then referred to a society sculptress who was making some stir at the time. 'I see nothing in her. She's neither dark nor fair, tall or short, clever nor stupid, fat nor thin, in fact she's middling. The woman is *nothing*.' He stretched his arms out as if to invoke an all-embracing emptiness; then he gazed affectionately at his drawing of Marie. 'But I hope I know a fine woman when I see one.'

Number 1 Granby Street is still standing, but only just. Near it, in the Hampstead Road, is another decayed house which was the home of Cruickshank, commended by Sickert for his own sake and also because he illustrated the work of Dickens. One would be reluctant to decide the species of the frail yet indomitable little soot-laden tree which still graces the front garden. Both houses had plaques on them to commemorate the artists who lived and worked there, but they are now undecipherable. The Granby Street house is even more coated with grime than the other; engulfed by the railway, with its peeling walls and crazy doors and windows, it totters on the brink of demolition.[1] But everything passes . . .

Bus rides with Sickert were always an adventure. He would enjoy a mild joke as he fished for pennies: 'When we take a bus it shall be *my* treat, when we take a taxi it shall be *your* treat.' As we jogged down the Hampstead Road, past the statue of his father-in-law, Richard Cobden, he would raise his hat and bow gravely towards it, to the bewilderment of the other passengers. A little further up the High Street, we reached the Bedford Music Hall, which he had now almost deserted in favour of the Collins, at Islington. Here he would attend, night after night, until he knew all the turns by heart and could have understudied all the performers. Sitting in the middle of the box with his wife on one side and Marie Pepin, their French cook, on the other, he so filled it, with the aid of the plump Marie, that the slender figure of Christine was almost extinguished and visitors had to fit in as best they could. They came, of course, to hear Sickert talk; which was just as well, for it was almost impossible for them to see the stage. They were also hoping to be asked round to 'Paradise' after the performance; that is, to beer and sandwiches at one of the little eating houses in Upper Street. In 1917, one could still find hospitality here; a dark cosy room perhaps, with clean sanded floor, rough wooden chairs or benches, a flock wallpaper and a cockney barmaid, 'giving as good as she got' while she pulled the beer-handles. The evening was not complete for Sickert without one of these golden, roly-poly girls behind the counter.

But we took our time about achieving Paradise. He lingered everywhere, darting down side alleys, peering at steep stairs and ancient archways or looking for some house that had disappeared. One corner, that might have come from a Cruickshank drawing, especially took his fancy. I have only a vague impression of it after all these years but I remember the little music shop with old instruments in the window and the general store with its usual assortment of soap and boots and candles.

'Look, Christine! isn't it like Venice . . .' Christine did not think it was at all like Venice but she would agree politely, holding up her skirts from the dirty pavement with calm disdain. She was more ill than anyone knew at this time and she must have felt that the party would never end. But the café was quiet and warm, she could rest there for a little before the journey home.

[1] Now demolished.

Marie enjoyed her evenings tremendously, although she had no English; she had never learned one word since the Sickerts brought her with them from Dieppe. Christine had tried to teach her, to no avail; in the end, she said, 'I got impatient and Marie got distressed', so the lessons were dropped for good. This, however, did not prevent Marie from pitting her wits against the butcher and the baker when she went shopping in Camden Town; often, she struck a hard bargain. She was a familiar figure in the Camden Road with her ruddy face gleaming from constant applications of yellow soap, her black hair shored up on top of her head, her figure like a cottage loaf. Everyone was attached to Marie; her simple kindness was endearing and when she vanished, a little unaccountably, some years after Christine's death, she left behind her a blank which was never quite filled. The turns at the Collins were a great joy to her; she wagged her head with the tunes and watched the dancers with awe. 'Moi, je ne pourrais pas faire cela,' she would announce solemnly, to Sickert's delight, when some young thing was pirouetting across the stage on the tips of her toes.

Weeks might pass before he pounced on his subject—a chance combination of figures flitting across the stage, the spotlight on a solitary performer, the loneliness of a stray onlooker hovering in the great shabby boxes upheld by soaring caryatids, a section of the audience in the auditorium—when with lightning speed he would jot down information in his notebook, registering the rest of the picture in his mind. Sometimes, these notes varied from mere shorthand dashes to elaborate studies; they might be incredibly slight, a smudge here, a blur or a line there, the blanks to be filled in afterwards from memory, scribbles that could convey nothing to anyone save himself. The missing links, however, did not trouble him; his grip of the subject was so complete that he did not need to dot all his i's or cross all his t's on paper; gaily, he would attack the canvas, humming the latest ditty that he had heard at the halls.

It will be conceded that the practical difficulties of picture building in the theatre are immense. The lighting alone is the study of a lifetime; diffused, flickering, inconstant, subtle. Few have mastered it. Sickert found his music halls more exacting, physically and mentally, than any other aspect of his work. When young, he could seldom afford to take a box even if it were the best place available for his purpose; night after night he sat in humble seats with no elbow room, no support for his notebook except his knee, drawing in semi-darkness. Sometimes he stood in the gallery, hemmed in by an unruly and restless crowd. On these occasions he was 'getting the feel of the house' and memorizing almost the whole scene; accurate drawing, however slight, must have been almost impossible. But as he pointed out, he would have had to rough it in any case. Unless he studied his subject in all its aspects he could not extract a picture from it with complete authority. In his youth, he had known the theatre in all her moods, from rehearsals on bleak mornings when the huge auditorium was a cold hollow shell to evening performances when it all came alive in a haze of warmth, light, darkness, movement and colour, when the audience took charge and imposed its personality on the scene no less than the actors. In his maturity, whatever view point he chooses, whether it be from the gallery, boxes, or stalls, we feel that he knows what is going on elsewhere in the great smoky interior, behind the façades, the plush, the caryatids and the gilding, drawing effortlessly on his reserves of experience and memory. Nowhere does his memory reveal itself more poignantly than in his music halls, in his command of space. After a canvas like 'The Old Bedford' (plate 5) the attempts of others to depict the inner life of the scene seem mere surface conscientious transcripts. And the physical atmosphere is conjured up as well; the touch, the taste, the smell of London. This, I think, is especially evident in the drawings.

Much has been made of his passion for paint; he spoke and wrote so frequently about surface quality and the application of paint to canvas that this can prove misleading. Beguiled as he was by beautiful quality of paint, much as he hated to see the medium abused, his main object must not be overlooked, the goal towards which he was striving all the working years of his life. This was, to paint without nature in front of him. Everything else, tonal values, brushwork, colour, drawing, stemmed from that first and final intention. His music halls could never have been painted unless he had used the classical procedure of working from drawings. It was the ideal process to develop his powers. His intellectual calibre was revealed by his ability to architect large pictures from working notes, to unify the colour and sustain the vitality of the sketch in the final version. This ability to foster and transfer the spark of life in the drawing to the canvas is one of the most interesting features of his work. As Lord Clark says, in his essay on Constable:

'The steep ascent between sketch and final composition is one for which the English temperament has shown little aptitude. Insufficiently braced by intellect and tradition, feelings grow cold, passages full of suggestion become empty, bright colour thin, dark colour muddy. Constable is almost alone among English painters in that he was able to preserve on a large scale all the brilliance of his best sketches.'

'Degas, Degas, Degas. Why will people say DAYGAS!'
Sickert has been called the link between French and British Impressionists, which is partly true. France was his second home, his devotion to Degas was deep and lasting. He was in touch with Monet and Renoir and Pissarro in the late eighties and wrote so warmly of their work and aims, especially the new prismatic chiaroscuro which they substituted for the dark and light chiaroscuro of Whistler, that it was easy to suppose he identified himself with them. But he identified himself with no group or school of painting. He absorbed many styles but remained himself; as with Whistler, so with the Frenchmen; he took what he needed from them and passed on. He had little of the pastoral urge of Pissarro, whom he admired deeply, and little in common with the later Monet. Sickert used mass contrasts rather than simultaneous contrasts; he simplified the values and where two nearly similar ones were juxtaposed he saw them as one. There

was no 'all-over' irridescent effect in his work as in the later Monet, no prismatic chiaroscuro.

For all his absorption in the study of light, the quality of paint, these things were merely a means to an end, never an end in themselves. The influence of Degas on his personal vision was not, I think, especially important. Sickert's point of view is already emerging, although tentatively, in his earliest work and his roots, as I have stressed before, were not in France. The influence of the older man on his character was, however, great; fortunately for Sickert, greater even than that of the brilliant and erratic Whistler, to whose feckless way of life Degas provided a salutary counterblast. Even in middle age, Sickert never questioned the supremacy of Degas. On winter evenings at the Frith, beside the tea table, he recalled his mentor; the insistence of the Frenchman on steady work and strict routine, his scorn of fashion for fashion's sake, his relentless devotion to an ideal, the importance of discipline for the gifted painter; in fact, Degas held that discipline was more necessary for him than another. This must have been unusual fare for the mercurial Sickert and it made the deepest impression on him. We got a little restive sometimes with all this austerity, these counsels of perfection. 'But you did dine out a good deal, surely; you seem to have met everybody,' we reminded him. 'That was generally for the sake of the meal,' retorted Sickert. 'I was often so hard up that I was hungry, and had to walk to keep the engagement. When it was raining I changed my wet shoes in the hall.'

Once Sickert had secured the necessary information, he might square up the picture next day or put it aside for an indefinite period. He might need only one or a number of working notes to complete his purpose and might use all or only one of them for the final version. These working notes were frequently obscured by being scored with the red ink squares necessary for purposes of enlargement. George Moore objected violently to this process. When he visited the Frith, his first aim was to burrow among the drawings that were lying about on the big table between the windows, for something that took his fancy. But soon he would be grumbling—'Walter, I can't see a thing. Why must you ruin your drawings with those horrible red lines!'

These protests amused Sickert, who took them as just another instance of Moore's ignorance of technical procedures. But although a faint network of squares could be curiously satisfying in some drawings, the more subtle misty sketches, especially those revealing the vast smoky spaces of music halls, lost some of their poetry, however tactfully the squares were applied. Sickert, however, could be ruthless with his drawings and rather liked the squared-up effect because it emphasized the design; he was surprised by critics who, like Moore, preferred their Sickerts without the scaffolding. Nowadays, however, it seems that squaring up may soon be all the go. When a buyer selected a Sickert drawing recently at Messrs Agnew, it was pointed out to him that the drawing was squared up. He replied, 'That's why I want it.'

During the winter of 1917-18, when I constantly saw him at work, Sickert seldom varied his process of picture building.

First, the canvas was carefully washed to remove all surplus grease.

The next step was to square up (enlarge) the drawing from which the picture was to be composed.

Miss Gosse has described this very thoroughly: 'The sheet of paper with the drawing is ruled in half inch or one inch squares.

'The canvas is then ruled with the same number of squares and the drawing, square by square, is repeated on the canvas.

'Then the underpainting in one, two or at most three shades of any one colour, French blue, Indian red or terre verte mixed with white. Light—shadow—darkest shadow.

'The light and shadow should be settled at this stage once and for all.

'At any stage of the painting the lines of the squares can be reformed in white chalk, the drawing refound in each square. The chalk, when the paint is dry, is easily removed with a damp sponge.'

As Sickert said: 'When we square up a drawing, we are always struck with the added beauty of the design.'

After the undercoat has been scrubbed in as forcibly as possible 'to get a good tooth on it' the canvas was left until it was bone dry. The underpainting once dry, the local colours were then applied, 'butter into granite'. He literally attacked the canvas at this stage, scrubbing on the paint fiercely, using a rotary motion as if he were washing the floor, wearing his brushes down to the ferrule and sometimes, in his excitement, scratching away with the tin. His technique was French in its fastidious insistence on surface quality, a point on which British artists have been, and still are, strangely careless; he abhorred the dull greasy surface which results from licking and teasing the paint. Luminosity was achieved not only by the subtlest gradations between a restricted number of tones but by the nervous, incisive pressure of the brush; he declared that the ideal texture of paint resembled 'the side of a matchbox', rich, brittle, scintillating. If the picture was going well he became more and more agitated, moving backwards and forwards across the studio with a stately bustle, staring at his canvas from a long distance with eyes narrowed to slits of light, his mouth twitching with every stroke of the brush.

Water colour he admired, but feared; he never seemed quite at home with the medium, regarding it, as it were, with wary glances from afar. This timidity seems odd when one remembers how surely he, the born diver, would plunge into other mediums; from oils to pastels, from lithographs to etchings. But there was something about water colour which bemused him. At infrequent intervals he would buy an imposing outfit of little tubes, sumptuous sable brushes, a huge white soup plate from a cheap store for a palette; he put the paints round the edge of the plate and used the middle for mixing them. Every time he ventured anew into water colour he bought fresh materials; this was the part of the proceedings that he enjoyed the most. When he set to work it was not with his usual abandon; one heard faint sighs, he had to force himself to the task. After he had been working for a while, he would stop suddenly to glare severely at the result. One day, this evoked an especially heavy sigh. 'You *do* think I'm right, don't you?' he asked anxiously, as if we had been the professors and he the student.

What his water colours generally amounted to, at least those I have seen, were exquisite stains reinforcing a scaffolding of drawing.

He never used a palette knife except for cleaning his palette. He disliked it as a tool and he generally disliked its effect on the canvas. 'These ridges are *bestial*, they set my teeth on edge. What's the matter with a brush, the tool provided for the purpose?' He used a large number of flat-headed small brushes but he was lazy about cleaning them; pupils were exhorted to wash theirs with plain soap and water but he often dipped his own in a solution of oil and turpentine. This was no great matter, as he bought new brushes even more frequently than Gilman; no brush was ever used again that had lost, even slightly, its spring and resilience—which in Sickert's case often meant after a single spell of work.

Sickert seldom worked directly from the object but we brought him some pheasants one day and he sat down immediately to paint them, without recourse to his usual preliminary studies. 'Here am I, like Elijah, being fed by the ravens.' These birds, he declared, must be the fore-runners of a series of studies of game, all painted on the spot. He would do large panels of partridges, snipe, hares, lobster, poultry, quail, in fact *food*. They should be stately panels with crystal goblets, gilded ornaments, precious china and drapery, like some grandiose Dutch still life, rich in content and richer in colour. Then he would hang them round the walls of his dining room at Camden Road. But Christine discouraged this gastronomical dream. She was satisfied with her dining room as it was, and her home had already suffered so many changes at his hands that he was forced finally to promise that Camden Road would remain sacrosanct.

When painting portraits Sickert seldom posed his models; anything 'voulu' bored him and the portrait of a posed model generally petered out. He waited for a characteristic movement, a revealing look or gesture, then seized and intensified it. He probed the depth of feminine temperament with sympathetic insight; however drab, however sorry, always there is emotional emphasis, heightening the prose to that pitch we call poetry.

But he could never have made a financial success of portrait painting. Character, rather than conventional beauty, interested him and he was seldom inspired by the 'drawing room' type, so beloved of his generation; he could not or would not idealize his women as Gainsborough or McEvoy or Whistler idealized them. Even in the most successful of his refined types, such as 'Mrs Swinton', one misses the total abandon, the fierce vitality of, say, 'Chicken',[1] (plate 11) Hogarthian in its

[1] Lately in the collection of Edward le Bas.

bouncing cockney humour and love of life. But pictures of low life were not popular in Sickert's day and his women sitters who fondly imagined they might appear flowerlike and ethereal must have been woefully surprised to find themselves robustly depicted as down-to-earth, flesh and blood mortals rather than exquisite abstractions. He did not even make them appear younger than they were. Consequently, portrait commissions were lacking. And he was not much more successful at flattery in his portraits of men, although he seems to have been more interested, on the whole, in painting his own sex. Full of character as they often are, these portraits would probably be most unpopular with the wives of their sitters.

He was interested in current techniques, such as Pointillism; he encouraged his students and friends to apply their paint in patches, like mosaic: 'the beans, which must be placed side by side, and not overlap, should be about the size of my little finger nail.' This was not such an arbitrary dictum as it may appear. Sickert was not trying to impose a fashionable formula upon malleable students. 'The beans', a mechanical procedure, were to be regarded merely as an exercise to foster precision and a sense of mass. If he used Pointillism himself it was for a specific reason. He did not allow it to usurp the instinctive handwriting of the artist.

He could, of course, be mischievous as well. The portrait of Harold Gilman (plate 23), now in the Tate, is an instance of this. The head is modelled in Sickert's usual manner but a profusion of black dots cascade over the chin and throat. This, however, is no pointless concession to a current theory. The dots are merely a Sickertian comment on the perpetually unshaven condition of Gilman, which was a standing joke among his friends. Seen at the correct distance from the portrait, they drop into place and suggest the dawning growth of beard that disguised his face so constantly that everyone took it for granted. But this portrait is more than a surface likeness of Gilman. His expression was deceptively mild but Sickert probes deeper. Striking the faint note of *terribilità* that is latent in much of his work, he reveals the formidable Gilman that lies dormant, masked by a bland exterior. Painted about 1912, it belongs to the mature period when the influence of Goya was most profound. The Frith studio was full of reproductions of many masters but Goya's *Desastres de la Guerra* was, at this time, the only book that Sickert carried about with him, from which he was seldom parted; he would walk up and down, studying it and often we found him in his long chair, turning the pages in rapt silence. Goya broods over the North London series like one of his own monstrous bats; we trace his passionate spirit through all the grand period; his hold over Sickert never slackened, even in his last years. We see it everywhere, in 'Summer Afternoon' (plate 16), in the Camden Town murder scenes, in nudes on beds, in portraits such as 'The Blackbird of Paradise' (plate 15) which was partly inspired by the poem by W. H. Davies, 'The Bird of Paradise'. Sickert preferred this poem to anything else Davies had written; its macabre note struck the answering chord in him. It consists of a few short verses about a fevered girl who, in her delirium, sees a bird of paradise at the end of her bed.

'For all her cry but came to this
Not for the world! Take care:
Don't touch the bird of paradise
Perched on the bedpost there.'

And some years later we see the echo of Goya again in the swordlike quality of 'The Bar Parlour' portraits of two cockney girls in the Frith (plate 14). No other master affected him so deeply.

There is good work to come after 1917 but the last period, from 1934, is inevitably disappointing. Sickert was now old; years of struggle had left their mark; it was not to be expected that his health and eyesight could go on forever. But alas, this sad decline has been unduly advertised. It was comparatively easy in 1934 to obtain his latest work but the fruits of the grand period lay buried in probable and improbable places abroad, in this country and in private collections. He was becoming, even in his middle years, the legend rather than the reality. Since then, we have had the fine exhibitions at the National Gallery (1941), at Messrs Agnew, and at the Tate Gallery during his centenary year (1960). These efforts to track down and borrow his best work were magnificent. The projects bristled with difficulties and the wealth of Sickert that resulted from all this research was an impressive display. But inevitably, many Sickerts of the best period are still missing. It may be said of all outsanding painters, that a proportion of their work will be lost to posterity, but we have sustained a grievous loss of the best Sickerts, as I know to my cost when I have tried to trace canvases that I valued at the Frith, nearly always in vain. Lack of appreciation in his own day cannot be entirely blamed for this state of affairs, although more official encouragement would have undoubtedly saved us many important Sickerts that are missing. His reckless temperament had much to answer for; his carelessness about his work, his habit of selling canvases and drawings in batches, his generosity in presenting pictures to friends, even mere acquaintances, his long flittings across the Channel, his unfailing resignation from art societies, his irresistible desire to poke fun at colleagues. He did not become bitter at lack of official support. It was more amusing to laugh at pundits, although his witticisms could be more wounding that he realized; more likely to be remembered than his claims to recognition and resented long after he had forgotten them.

In making these painful comparisons between his mature work and the last period I am deeply conscious of Turner's rebuke to Ruskin: 'When a man weakens in his age, you should not tell him so.' But the reputation of Sickert has been so bedevilled by the constant exhibition of his weakest pictures at the expense of his best, that in justice to his memory one must protest against this soul-destroying practice.

In Sickert's words, 'The beauty of Whistler's painting was that he achieved its force purely by relations, considered as opaque, between a restricted number of tones. This is not only extremely difficult but, odd as it may seem, it is so rare that only the great painters can do it.'[1]

This principle of Whistler's made such an impression on the young Sickert that we may thank Whistler, to a certain extent, for the beauty of Sickert's colour. He disciplined himself severely to attain the same austere distinction of colour values. Unfortunately, there were times when he followed Whistler too closely; both men seem to have forgotten that oil paint darkens and the relations of the tones, balanced on a knife edge, were keyed so low that when we see them now they are darker than their authors intended and the lights are too insistent. There are Sickerts which are now exquisite ruins, still ravishing but disembodied, ghosts of their former selves with darkness encroaching on the light. It is probable that he was using Indian red a shade too freely for his undercoats, or using, without knowing it, inferior paints. I cannot say if he saw any of these wrecks in his lifetime but it is significant that this very dark interlude, when Degas said that everything seemed to be happening at night, did not last long; when we knew him, he was using only the best paints.

His colour was his own, as personal as his outlook on life, although greatly enriched by careful study of the great colourists of the past. It changes from picture to picture as the mood ordains; rarely does he repeat a colour scheme. In fact, I cannot remember a single instance where this has happened; he has given us endless variations on a simple palette which embraced more colours as time went on but remained restricted. Those patches of coffee, chocolate, plum, viridian, apricot, ruby-russet and off-black, pungent but never harsh, remind us that it is not necessary to shout at the top of your voice to be a good colourist.

His love of *contre-jour* persisted all through his life. He practised this poetic form of lighting constantly and loved the other painters who had practised it, from Tintoretto to Rembrandt, Goya, Degas and Whistler. *Contre-jour* demands a sure swift touch and an unerring sense of tone; fumbling, dragging or licking the paint is fatal to the transparency and depth of the shadows and the liquid quicksilver of the lights, that elusive pattern of dark and light which enhances the sense of mystery and awe inherent in his best work. This intricate research into the subtlest degrees of tone as a means of stressing his mood was part of the legacy bequeathed to him by the great Romantics of the past; even in his sixties, it flowered anew in such works as 'The Bar Parlour' and 'Victor Lecour' (plate 33) where he used *contre-jour* in a visual music of his own.

'When Whistler and I went down to Rotherhithe,' he once told me, 'we used to observe the rivercraft and the buildings on the opposite shore. We played a sort of game. We would look for about ten minutes at a given subject, isolating it as much as possible from its surroundings, then turn our backs on it and have a guessing competition, giving each other half marks for remembering the position,

[1] Quoted on p. 239 of *The Life and Opinions of Walter Richard Sickert* by Robert Emmons, Faber & Faber, 1941.

size and shape of the various objects that filled the scene and full marks for remembering the exact degrees of light and dark falling on them.'

Mr Clifford Hall has reconstructed for us the layout of his palette:

> Centre: White
> To Right: Reds and browns
> To Left: Yellows, blues and greens

Three values were mixed up for light, half tone and shadow.

His tools were kept in fastidious order. Separate pools of different gradations of the same hue lay side by side on the palette, the varying degrees of light between each pool so subtle that it would be hardly visible to the untrained eye. There was a different brush for every degree of light in the colour. Unrelated tones always worried him; when he was criticizing pictures he would often remark: 'These colours stick out from the rest like the horns of a snail; I long to push them back with my thumb.'

'Photography is like alcohol; no one should use it unless they can do without it.' This quotation from Sickert is worth repeating, if only because there has been so much talk of his use of photographs.

During 1917 and 1918, when we saw him working constantly, he never used a photograph at all. After his return to London from Dieppe in 1921, we saw him working again at the Frith and I never remember seeing him use a photograph, although a small reproduction of 'Her Mother's Voice', by Frank Dicksee, was now pinned sometimes to his easel, simply because it tickled him. He had, of course, toyed with the possibilities of photography when he was seeing a great deal of Degas; the experiments of the older man with snapshots did undoubtedly interest him, as everything to do with Degas interested him. But it was not until old age crept on that he did begin to use the photograph as a crutch to aid his failing powers.

Confusion has arisen about the titles of Sickert's pictures. If these have been altered since the picture was christened, this was often due to his own carelessness. There are, roughly speaking, two kinds of artists; those who treasure their finished work, frame it carefully, keep a list of all their output and its destination when it leaves the studio, and those others who lose interest in the sketch or picture directly it is completed, being absorbed straight away in future conceptions. Sickert belonged undoubtedly to the second category. Although it would have been unwise to gamble on his forgetfulness; I have known him to ask us suddenly to find a picture or a drawing that he had confided to our care a long time previously. But he could be shockingly improvident about past work, presenting important pictures, as Sir Matthew Smith was wont to do, to friends, or even chance acquaintances, who happened to take his fancy. I am glad say that 'Wellington House Academy' the picture that Sickert gave to the poet Davies turned up again in the collection of Mr Blyth at the Arts Council offices during the Edinburgh Festival of 1956. It has now been appropriately framed; Sickert might have clapped it into any frame that happened to fit although here again, he might not; sometimes, he became choosy about frames and full of schemes for enhancing the picture. But careless framing was the badge of all the Camden Town tribe; their work was often blighted by the frame, financial reasons being generally responsible for this seeming neglect of their own interests.

When Sickert was old he was frequently confronted with past works that had been resurrected from various sources and asked to identify them. On these occasions he might re-christen them with the first words that came into his head. Thus a number of pictures and drawings have been re-baptized, generally for the worse, since they first saw the light. This habit of his must have played havoc with his attributions and confusion must have been worse confounded when he suddenly and perversely discovered his father and insisted on signing himself Richard instead of Walter because his father was Richard too. As brother Bernard also painted, the muddle was now complete. I have seen Bernard Sickerts that were attributed to Walter Sickert, genuine Sickerts that have been questioned because they were signed Richard and others that were suspect because they were signed merely Sickert. Members of the public have asked me wistfully on various occasions, 'Can you tell me if I am looking at a Bernard Sickert or a Richard Sickert or a Walter Richard Sickert or *the* Sickert?'

The Sickert would have replied crushingly, as he always replied when asked if he was responsible for this or that picture, 'My work is signed all over.'

But for the sake of a bewildered public I would add that the grand period is usually signed 'Sickert' in exactly the right place in small neat letters that add a final touch of beauty to the canvas; sometimes, a genuine 'Walter' is not signed at all; 'Richard' or 'R. Sickert A.R.A.' sprawling all over the place, is the signature of his last years, but care should be taken here; many earlier paintings, unearthed long after their conception, were brought to him to be signed in his old age.

Bernard Sickert wrote, as he painted, with a quite different, flowing hand.

Another factor which makes for confusion today is that Walter has suffered greatly, even in his lifetime, from forgeries.

In 1917, he told me that he had been dining recently with a friend in Manchester. When they entered the dining room his host said proudly: 'You see, my walls are hung entirely with your work.'

Sickert put on his pince-nez, went round the pictures and replied, 'Not one of these pictures is by me.' He added, when he related the story, that there were at least eight so-called Sickerts in the room.

'Couldn't you have told him *after* dinner?' I asked. 'Or perhaps, have written to break the news next day?'

Sickert stared. 'Why should I? The pictures were not by me and I said so.'

When he told me this I was so sorry for the misguided buyer that for the moment I forgot the loss that Sickert had suffered too; then I realized that he was even more sinned against than the collector. This spate of forgeries had affected both his pocket and his reputation; here at Manchester alone were eight pictures for which he had not received a penny, and to crown all they were impudently signed with his name.

Although Sickert seldom thought about money until it was no longer there, he minded very much about his reputation and he was appalled to discover how easily people could be deceived about his work. I should add, that he also said how good these particular forgeries were; good enough to deceive all but the most experienced eye.

Sometimes, all through his working life, he produced sketches on canvas to reinforce his impressions of the subject in hand before he attacked the final version. These were generally slight, more carried through if necessary, but not completed; with age, a habit grew on him of tracing merely a few lines on a canvas and throwing it aside to be worked on another day. This might be stolen or mislaid; when it is remembered that he also had the fatal habit of selling his work in bundles, direct from the studio, it will be seen how he himself contributed unwillingly towards the production of bogus Sickerts. I have seen, alas, only too many of these faint adumbrations of a picture which have been plastered over by alien hands; gayed up with crude meaningless accents, defaced by leathery shadows, travesties of the real thing.

It is not easy to advertise Sickerts. His oils reproduce badly; the contours become blurred, the values just off key, the rich vibrant surface flat and dull, the whole thing woolly, unclear. It is so difficult to register his sureness of tone that a good reproduction of his best work has seldom been attempted; he eludes the process. It should not, however, be impossible to reproduce one of his best drawings or portraits sufficiently well to benefit schools and colleges and to form an addition to the everlasting Monet and Van Gogh reproductions that hang on their walls, whose beauty is in danger of being dulled by too much repetition. It could, surely, do the students no harm to realize that Britain too, can produce a master. Had Sickert been a Frenchman, one feels that Paris would have rectified the omission long ago. It is odd that we have no good reproduction of a Sickert of his best period, not even a good postcard. And there is no plaque on Number 8 Fitzroy Street to remind us that no less than four interesting painters lived and worked there; Whistler, Sickert, Augustus John and Duncan Grant.

He has been labelled a social reformer by some of the younger generation which is hardly surprising when he used titles such as: 'What Shall we do for the Rent?' But Sickert had no interest in social reform whatever. The subject did not exist for him in spite of his early hardships and his hand to mouth style of living. And he deprecated especially the error of trying to do too many things at once; himself he kept clear of politics and good works and concentrated on maintaining aesthetic standards so far as he was able. No man was more generous to models and dependants, but equality would have struck him as a meaningless word. Although he sympathized with extreme poverty as only one who has experienced it can sympathize, he had no pity for those who dwell in slums. He would have retorted that he did the same thing himself; why should it be a hardship to live in such an interesting place as Camden Town? He was genuinely unable to understand why anyone should deprecate his beloved North London. He was there from choice, not necessity; had the wide world been open to him he would have preferred Islington. It might be poor, grimy, struggling, but it had the spark of life that he valued; the struggle made it all the more significant, he revelled in its vitality.

Another aspect of Islington he valued was the absence of snobbery. Everyone, more or less, was poor and too busy wrestling with realities to bother about social status.

When I was younger, I was absorbed in the Camden Town series and saw these pictures constantly in the setting in which they were painted. It was not until late in life, owing to the enthusiasm of Miss Gosse, that I appreciated the Dieppe series more fully; I had also seen Dieppe by then and walked its streets and the Dieppe paintings were beginning to turn up more frequently in the salerooms as Sickert's prices increased. Even now, however, their appearance is rare; if it were not for Miss Lillian Browse, many people would have missed them altogether. But she has given us some beautiful reproductions of the French period in her book, *Sickert*;[1] I think 'La Rue Pecquet, Dieppe' must be one of the most beautiful of all. It portrays the south side of 'St Jacques' looking down from the Rue Pecquet, and is reproduced in colour; happily, a version of this picture is in a public collection owned by Birmingham City Art Gallery (plate 28). A little withdrawn, it is poetry at its most august and tender. One calls to mind sacred buildings by other masters, often imposing and powerful, but Sickerts' 'St Jacques' is holy. It is a quality that he shares with Rouault.

> 'The Tumult of the time disconsolate
> to inarticulate murmurs dies away,
> While the eternal ages watch and wait.'

'The Visitor' (plate 17), in the possession of the City Art Gallery, York, is singularly interesting. It may be objected that it is 'literary' although Sickert himself had no qualms about being literary and begged Virginia Woolf, when she was writing the foreword for a Sickert exhibition at Agnew's, 'to be the first to say it'. And as Lord Clark has pointed out, 'we are a literary nation and should not be surprised when our art reflects this aspect of our character'. But literary or not, it is difficult to see how this picture could be transposed into the medium of words and not lose its effect.

At first glance, one sees an elderly woman advancing into a room; just that. But one is held by the atmosphere of menace, of foreboding, heightened by the note of red smouldering in the background that Sickert used again when in this sombre mood, as in 'L'Armoire à Glace' (plate 18). She is an evil image and she brings evil tidings. The futility of words to render the disquieting effect of this quiet picture cannot be realized until one has seen the original. It will then be obvious that

[1] Rupert Hart-Davis, 1960.

words have nothing to do with this intense visual sensation. It has the haunting trance-like quality of true surrealism.

Steer had some interesting things to say about displaying pictures, especially those of his own and previous periods. He lamented the supersession of the old ruddy flock-paper background at the National Gallery and thought Holmes, whose appointment as Director he had welcomed, had in this gone astray, 'turning the place into a lavatory'.

One of his sitters, Mrs Thomas Lowinsky, has furnished an interesting account of Steer's advice about hanging.

'My husband and I consulted Steer about the hanging of the picture in our house.

'He advised that we should place it on the wall of the room where the prevailing light came from the same side as that depicted in the picture itself. He further instructed us to avoid white or light walls. To stress this point, he declared that picture dealers, who knew their business, invariably displayed their wares on deep red velvet or damask.'[1]

Steer, it will be remembered, was a contemporary of Sickert's. What would be a sympathetic background for his oils would generally be effective for Sickert's work as well, although their outlook was so different in their middle age.

Visitors to Agnew's Gallery will remember the famous mulberry-russet walls, carefully cherished and patched, with the mellow depth that only age can give. There was a lovely puce damask on the walls of the National Gallery, Edinburgh, which has been replaced by a fairly good imitation of the original, although the velvety richness is lacking. But only too often the splendid old papers have been stripped, only to make way for 'magnolia', that deadly hue for most oil paintings. Sickert is seen at his best against strawberry or muted crimson or soft terra cotta walls, or if it is objected that this range of warm colours might become monotonous if constantly used, a good flock paper might show him to advantage.

Perhaps some day we may have an entire room devoted to Sickert in one of our leading galleries, for the benefit of foreigners who flock to these places as well as for the natives, with a suitable background for his oils, the pictures well spaced and lighted and carefully chosen to display him at his best. If it is feared that this might become a sort of Sickert shrine, therefore stagnant, it would surely be possible to borrow Sickerts from provinicial galleries from time to time and thus vary the collection.

I have only too poignant memories of some Sickert exhibitions in the past outside the West End of London, which were thrown together anyhow; the pictures huddled in rows, almost touching each other, tier upon tier, crammed in one small room, many of them excessively dirty, with crumbling frames.

It would be a joyous revelation to Sickert lovers to see his things, at long last, in good condition in a setting specially chosen for them.

[1] Quoted on p. 104 of *Life, Work and Setting of Philip Wilson Steer* by D. S. MacColl, Faber & Faber, 1945.

Chapter 5

Teaching

If he were famous for no other reason, Sickert would be famous as a teacher.

Partly because he liked teaching, but also because he made his meaning crystal clear and enjoyed the confidence of his students. He soon knew what their limitations were and how far they could push their talents. Towards those who lacked even a grain of promise he could be as forthright as, if less ruthless than, his colleague Tonks, or as candid as his own brother Leonard, professor of singing. He questioned the wisdom of Leonard, who dismissed several pupils on the grounds that their voices did not justify serious training, but in his own way he could be just as severe. The problem, he thought, usually resolved itself; those without talent got bored with the discipline of constant drawing, and even playing with colour failed, after a time, to seduce them; they petered out of their own volition. Sickert politely hastened their departure. He told a friend of mine that she was wasting her time at the Westminster; she took his advice and left after twelve months.

'He gave me a good run for my money and tried to help me,' she said, 'but in the end I saw his point.'

He would say that there were far too many art students in England and that for one dubious specimen who should be given a long rein there were plenty of others who should be weeded out at the end of their first year. But the difficulty, of course, would be to decide whether the unsatisfactory beginner was merely a slow starter or a dilettante. The weeding out must, of course, be done with the greatest care and discretion. Like Tonks, he favoured the hard worker even if little facility was shewn; he held that if there was a steady urge to paint, talent was dormant somewhere, and he was most suspicious of those who although gifted, did little or else worked in fits and starts.

Facility for drawing and painting was not enough; other qualities were also needed for success. Concentration was all-important; it will be remembered that Degas said, 'I am more interested in talent at forty than in talent at twenty,' a remark that had made a great impression on Sickert, summing up as it did his own experience of the results of teaching after a number of years.

He had two main objects in view. One was to encourage the student to paint without nature in front of him; the other, which should follow as the night the day, was to help him to become independent of the schools as soon as possible and find his level in a wider world. He had seen only too many 'professional art students' who relied more and more on direction and less and less on themselves. He often spoke of the bewilderment of those who have been sheltered too long in the incubator and were at last attempting the steep climb between amateur and professional status in their own workrooms, lost without the stimulus of professors and classmates and the yeasty flavour of competition.

His prospectus for classes at Number 8 Fitzroy Street is well-known, but I am quoting it here for those readers who may not have happened to read it before.

Bath, 1917.

'Mr Sickert retains the option of accepting such students only as he believes are likely to profit by his method of training. To avoid correspondence, it may be found convenient to state the principles by which Mr Sickert would be guided in his acceptance of students. Unlikely to be benefit would seem to be: (i) painters whose practice is already thoroughly set in methods (sic) its continuance in which Mr Sickert would be unable to encourage and indisposed to check; (ii) students who have already studied with him long enough to have absorbed—or failed to absorb—the little he has to teach. An intelligent student who cannot learn whatever is to be learnt from a teacher in three years will learn no more in thirty. Mr Sickert prefers not to be a party to the creation or perpetuation of what may be called the professional or eternal student, with no other aims than to haunt the art schools as an occupation or distraction in itself.'

The weeding out process can hardly have been acceptable to the authorities at Vincent Square, who wanted quantity as well as quality, but his reputation as a teacher and his own brilliant work reconciled them to his frankness; they were glad enough, when he returned from Dieppe during the war, to claim his services again for their evening classes. It had become, too, rather the thing to be amused by Sickert and his whimsies; he was the *enfant terrible* of the arts, there was no knowing what he would say next, although the sudden squibs that he delighted in letting off at intervals did not affect the solid basis of his teaching.

An instance of the indulgent attitude of the authorities towards him occurred some years later, when I was being interviewed by the London County Council at County Hall. Having understudied for some time for a friend of mine who lectured on painting for the Council, I thought I should like to join the permanent staff, and found myself sitting on a penitential stool to be questioned by a large committee. They were an agreeable lot but bored and wearied by a long stream of applicants by the time they reached me. Some of the questions, such as, 'why do you want to lecture? why not leave that to the men?' I found disconcerting. Conscious of my failure to impress them, in the defiance of despair I threw caution to the winds in spite of the preternaturally solemn faces of the examiners and quoted some of Sickert's more flippant sallies about lecturing. The sudden reaction of the committee surprised me; everyone cheered up at once and his quips went down to admiration. I retired sadly from the fray, convinced that I was ploughed on my earlier showing, but the committee were so tickled by Sickert's views that they included me on their panel after all, as a present for brightening their afternoon.

Although he had not the dynamic approach of Tonks, Sickert had his own equally devastating method of dealing with offenders. Unlike the fiery Tonks, when he was angry he became as bleak as the north wind. When he reappeared at the Westminster, there were many heart searchings; those who had been indulging in feasts of colour under Gilman bitterly resented being demoted to a diet of four colours and told to explore those thoroughly before they enlarged their palettes, and were only too ready to rebel against such drastic discipline. One youth gloried in flouting Sickert and his instructions; but one evening Sickert stopped suddenly at his easel, saying:

'Do you remember what I told you last week?'

'Yes, but I prefer to do it this way.'

'What fee did you pay for this term?' asked Sickert, feeling in his pockets. 'Here's your money and I don't want to see you again.'

With the dullards he was more patient, although one day he was goaded to enquire:

'Didn't Tonks teach you *anything* when you were at the Slade?'

The student thought for some time, then replied:

'He said that my drawings made him sick.'

'Ah,' sighed Sickert. 'He should have analysed the vomit.'

When he leaves the incubator the student is supposed to have acquired enough knowledge of the language of paint to say what he has to say, but often he has not yet found himself. He is not sure what aspect of life excites him most, what he is best fitted to do. Some, of course, develop early; they produce interesting work because they draw on early memories like the Spencer brothers, Mark Gertler or Lowry, but this pre-supposes an unusually powerful visual memory which may eat itself up in time if no new experiences take effect. Some are late starters like Matthew Smith and Van Gogh, a few, like Charles Ginner, work their passage through several influences and evolve their own handwriting after years of dogged persistence.

Meanwhile, here is our potential painter, still struggling in limbo. He sends to exhibitions and is refused; he does not know why and he has not the useful experience of seeing how his work looks when surrounded by other people's. He cannot 'finish' his canvas; he worries it and mauls it, unaware that the impulse which provoked its inception has died away and that he should put the picture aside until the desire to carry it through has gained fresh momentum. Meanwhile, expenses are mounting, production is low and his things are generally suggestive of a variety of styles, according to the master who is influencing him at the moment, rather than a deliberate advance in a chosen direction. He is told by didactic friends that so and so is the man to follow; if he timidly quotes some other master who means something to him, he cannot quite say why, he is met with the crushing retort that his choice is 'dated'. His confidence, never too sure at any time, is sapped at every turn.

There may, of course, be other reasons why he is getting nowhere. He may not have the physical stamina that is required for the job. But given the necessary combination of physique and talent, Sickert claimed that he could help him to acquire professional status. He never pretended that he could present his followers with his own imagination.

'I am a skilful accoucheur but I cannot produce the baby if it isn't there.'

Drawing was as important to him as it was to the Slade professors. Degas had said that the future of art lay in drawing. But the ultimate object of so much drawing was lost on some students, who were inclined to make it an end in itself, whereas with Sickert it was a means to an end. From the word go, from the minute he entered the school the student should be studying composition *through* drawing, not *after* drawing. 'From the first stroke of his pencil he should be making studies for pictures of his own.'

The single figure against vacancy could hardly stimulate the faculty of composition; two or more figures were necessary, which should be related to their surroundings.

Much information can be obtained on a small scale with a hardish pencil.

Only experience will determine the right scale on which to enlarge the working note. Henry Moore has described size emotion most clearly; it will be seen that his views on sculpture apply equally to painting:

'There is a right physical size for every idea. There is a size to scale not to do with its actual physical size, its measurement in feet and inches—but connected with vision.

'A carving might be several times over life size and yet be petty and small in feeling—and a small carving only a few inches in height can give the feeling of huge size and monumental grandeur because the vision behind it is big. Example: Michaelangelo's drawings or a Massacio madonna—the Albert Memorial.'

When the undercoat is dry and the final colours are applied, the student meets his Waterloo. In this damp climate, drying takes time. Sickert liked to put his canvases with their backs to the sun but with our scarcity of sun this may take months. It requires a highly trained and retentive memory and the power of recalling the original emotion which inspired the working note to continue the picture after so much delay. Many students find that all these preliminaries have killed the picture for them; they must strike while the iron is hot and finish it before their excitement wanes.

With all his keen interest in the younger generation, one feels that Sickert was too advanced for most of them; he could not always realize the gulf between the average or even good memory and his own, which was so precise that he could

65

keep several pictures going at the same time, retaining them as it were in separate compartments in his brain—like lantern slides in a box, one behind the other, to be extracted at will. With this powerful engine at his disposal whenever it was needed, he could hardly be expected to realize what he was asking of lesser mortals. Even very gifted students might find that one picture became confused with another in their minds, that whole gaps would occur on the canvas which the working note did not explain, where they could not remember exactly what was happening. Local colours present further difficulties; if the degrees of light on the colours have not been precisely memorized, the tones are all over the place and the final result resembles a patchwork quilt rather than a deliberate build-up with the ensuing stages *amenées*, as Degas advised, from beginning to end.

But the classic, deliberate build-up from drawings is a counsel of perfection. Sickert was so firmly wedded to the views of Degas which chimed so well with his own inclinations, that in his enthusiasm he may sometimes have pushed his theory too far for his followers. He even toyed from time to time with the idea of using only pencil notes for squaring up the picture and no colour note at all. If the student rebelled, he reluctantly allowed a *pochade* (an oil sketch for purpose of enlargement) to be painted as a crutch for the memory. This, he maintained, should be small, about eight to ten inches or less, and executed in small patches of colour *with the brush only*. But he much preferred the student to memorize the local colour entirely, aided only by pencil notes on the light and shade.

In short, he was a godsend for the brilliant pupil, but pupils were not always brilliant.

At his own school, Rowlandson House, which he had given up before I knew him, Miss Gosse came to the rescue and took the beginners off his hands. She had the patience of Griselda and great insight into their difficulties, but I suspect that many students fell by the wayside afterwards and reverted to painting on the spot. Several successful and interesting painters, Gilbert Spencer for one, have told me that they can only work from nature and would lose all interest if they were pinned down to enlarging their notes. But I have often seen Sickert working from nature in the studio, especially from still life.

The most illustrious pupil of all was Winston Churchill. When he was Chancellor of the Exchequer, Sickert used to give him lessons at Hyde Park Gate. The studio was upstairs and although Sickert assured me that his teaching was as drastic as usual, the peals of laughter that the family heard from below seemed to indicate that they were managing to amuse themselves as well as serving their stern taskmistress, Art.

Sickert found it difficult to induce Churchill to draw. As the teacher brooked no compromise and made no difference between advising professional painters and trying to steer a mettlesome amateur who was tremendously committed elsewhere, they argued freely. Churchill always chafed at the discipline of the pencil and found it terribly irksome to build up the foundations of his picture with sufficient care, and when Sickert returned for the next lesson, he invariably complained that the drawing had been scamped and that Churchill had indulged in his usual orgy of colour. I fear that this obstacle was never really overcome. Sickert could not teach by halves and Churchill was really happier afterwards with more pliable instructors, but he and Sickert engaged each other's society and spent many hours in art appreciation, especially when the Sickerts stayed at Chartwell. Pilgrims to the shrine will recognize a photograph there of the Churchills and Sickert during one of their weekends, with Thérèse Lessore. And quite recently, on turning out a drawerful of old papers, I came across a telegram from Amsterdam that Sickert must have given me; I do not remember how it got there.

'I am bracing my eye on Rubens and Rembrandt—Churchill.'

Sickert always enlarged at length on the importance of setting up a picture on the right lines. With Matthew Smith, he held that 'a picture should be finished from the start. In painting,' said Smith, 'the gravest immorality is to try to finish what isn't well begun. But a picture that is well begun may be left off at any point. Look at Cézanne's water colours!'

Churchill, it appeared, listened gravely as Sickert quoted Smith's words and seemed to be converted. When he was out of office he did persevere to adapt himself to the importance of setting up composition as a whole once for all, from the earliest stages. This, I think, was the chief benefit he derived from Sickert's tuition. It was quite a feat on his part; his sense of colour was ingrained and holding himself back from plunging into paint must have required a stern effort of will. I do not know if he saw the picture in its completion in his mind's eye before he began, but the marvel is that he achieved so much when painting for him was necessarily a sideline rather than the work of a lifetime.

When I first met Sickert he had a craze for gouache painting (I say 'craze' advisedly; it would be more precise to suggest that whenever he made fresh discoveries about a particular aspect of art he would confine himself entirely to that aspect for the time being until, 'that orange was now sucked'.) His interest in gouache was stimulated by the brilliant studies produced by his pupil and friend, Wendela Boreel; Miss Gosse, finding the accent was all on gouache at Number 15, decided that she was not going to be outdone and in no time, she too contributed some first-class examples in this difficult medium. Difficult, because gouache as understood by Sickert was extremely difficult. It is usually defined as water colour with body colour added, thus rendering it opaque. I believe many people use it now with a dry brush, a method which he would have condemned as cheating.

First, a drawing board was covered with oilcloth which was stretched as smooth and taut as possible, then saturated with water. Paper was pressed tightly over this, also damped with water, and the opaque paint dropped adroitly on the wet surface so that the edges of the forms ran slightly, but not too much. The object of all this moisture was to produce a rich, velvety tone, a rhythmical succession of shapes echoing each other with faintly blurred shapes which could be exquisitely lyrical. Wendela Boreel achieved such control of the medium that she even modelled figure studies on this shifting surface. I think the exponents of gouache who pulled off something were those who did not take Sickert's advice too literally but who experimented for themselves, reducing the prescribed amount of water to more manageable proportions. Those who followed him too blindly found themselves dropping lumps of paint into a pond of water, lumps which drifted about and took no shape whatever.

Sickert himself was not too happy about it all. He was always inclined to be uneasy about any form of water colour, a medium he regarded with awe; he did not even seem satisfied with any of his own stained drawings. Certainly, he had doubts about his approach to gouache. 'You *do* think I am right, don't you?' he would ask earnestly; as he ruefully surveyed the casualties that sundry friends had scattered about his studio. One hesitated to presume to prick the bubble of his enthusiasm by suggesting that perhaps a *little* less water . . .

He also had a craze for flower pieces at this time. But his own flower pieces are extremely rare. I only remember two, of white flowers; these especially appealed to him, white lilac most of all.

Drawings of roses by Fantin la Tour decorated the walls of Number 15; Sickert greatly admired these and would have liked us to square up our flower notes as La Tour did. But in this vale of tears we avoid one difficulty by falling into another. If one paints flowers from drawings in the Dutch seventeenth-century manner, one can compose the picture as one wishes, set up a counter pattern of light and shade and suggest great complexity of detail. But for some reason or other, when one comes to memorize the colour it is generally monotonous. One observes this even in the best Dutch flower painting. It seems that the infinitely subtle variety of colour in fresh flowers can only be suggested by painting on the spot. But unless the picture from nature can be finished in one 'wet', which is unlikely, the whole subject will have altered next day. Flowers droop or turn towards the light, petals curl or fall, the painter is confronted with another composition. Few have given us satisfactory flower pieces; it is rare that the difficulty of combining good composition with good colour has been surmounted, seldom indeed that one enjoys such unalloyed bliss as the vision, for instance, of a bunch of roses 'blown on the canvas' by Renoir.

Sickert was extremely fastidious about the use of his materials. Students had then a regrettable habit of smearing the backs of their canvases with paint that was left over after the day's work. I do not know why we practised this odious habit but it was fairly general at art schools. '*Bestial*, quite bestial,' he protested. He could scarcely bring himself to touch the offending canvas, viewing it with horror and dismay.

He always advised students to copy his own extravagance about materials and order quantities of the best paint, as 'one cannot learn to paint without wasting pigment'. In his own case he could hardly have done otherwise, as his impetuous yet precise technique did not allow for cheese-paring.

When Professor Brown resigned from the Slade in 1917, Sickert showed me a letter that he had received from Tonks, warmly expressing his gratitude to Sickert for standing aside and leaving the coast clear for him. Sickert greatly coveted the post of Slade Professor; apart from having studied there himself for a short time when he was very young, he was always attracted to Gower Street and felt that it was, from a teaching point of view, his spiritual home. It is of course unlikely that he would have been appointed Head of the Slade, even if he had applied for the post. He was known to be erratic, and Tonks, the idol of the students, had given of his best for many years. But although Sickert recognized the claim of this old friend, he never ceased to hanker after the Slade; it would have provided so much more scope than the Westminster.

When I attended the Slade, we usually worked on one model from ten to four, often on the same drawing. Senior students arranged the model; the pose might often be stereotyped and listless, seen in a uniform light against a stretch of empty curtain. Tonks would tell us not to fiddle about too long on one drawing but to do several, concentrating on movement and direction, but this precept was seldom observed. It was so much easier to go on piling up detail than to keep on beginning again to search for essentials; 'stop-go' is always exhausting. 'You wanted to get on with the treat, didn't you,' Tonks would say, with his sour smile as he glowered at a highly upholstered, glossy drawing that had been worked over until the last spark of life had been extinguished.

At four o'clock, we had an hour for short poses. Few people stayed for this; most of us were tired and needed a change of occupation. We did little with our drawings, except retaining the best for summer competitions; usually, we fell into the habit of destroying everything and I was surprised when Steer advised us not to throw away a single drawing. You never knew, he said, when it might provide some useful information. I wondered why I should ever want my efforts again; apart from being overworked, they generally portrayed the same subject, a model against vacancy. Few people of my first year were reinforcing their Slade studies outside the school with explorations of their own, such as looking for subjects in everyday life, carrying a sketchbook about with them, making notes on the spot and memorizing as much as possible. This side of our training was not stressed, I think for the very good reason that we were supposed to be enthusiastic enough to do it for ourselves.

In spite of our rigorous daily routine, I should add that most people were happy and stimulated at the Slade. That is, all those who really wanted to learn to draw. Ideas were in the air, there was bracing competition, exchanges of opinion, work of the more gifted students constantly on view, inspiring lectures, windows opened everywhere to a wider world. Above all, there was little of the class consciousness which is so tiresome today. There were angry young men then as now, but they wasted their sourness on the desert air; it was taken for granted that we were a mixed bunch and this only added sauce to the dish.

A few, of course, were incapable of enjoying this strenuous yet exciting

69

atmosphere. A serious disaster occurred about 1916, when no less than three men students committed suicide because of their love affairs with the same young woman, a model who used to pose in the Life Rooms.

Sickert was aghast when he heard of this.

'If they had only come to me!' he would repeat, as he brooded over the tragedy. 'I could have shown them how interesting painting can be, they would never have thrown their lives away for a chit if they had only *known*!'

At teatime in the Frith, he would hold forth on the changes he would have effected at the Slade.

The mornings should be devoted to drawing from the life, preferably from two or more models.

The afternoons should be spent in squaring up the best of these drawings. He assumed that after a really hard morning's work most people would be thankful for this technical procedure and mere manual dexterity.

Light and shade was of the utmost importance but 'of course all this camaïeu business is only for painters who conceive in terms of light and shade, delicate or violent but always light and shade'.[1]

This qualification of his theories is, I think, characteristic of him; he always agreed that there were other approaches to the problems of painting than his own.

The following are some sayings of Sickert:

1. 'Never destroy the idea sketch for a possible work.'

2. 'You must have one more or less conventional clean and more or less reposeful studio as a matter of business and a pigstye as much as you like for private use.'

3. 'A sure technique because the vision behind it is sure.'

4. 'Where there is a constant urge to paint there is probably also latent talent.'

5. 'Conjure up magic with your brush.'

6. 'Do not seek advice about a picture while you are painting it. Each of your friends will find a different fault in it and between them they will talk it to death.'

7. 'A little work done regularly will be more fruitful than working long hours by fits and starts.'

8. 'Don't put on your brush strokes *with* the forms but against them, so that your work will never be slick, but subtle.'

9. 'There are passages in your early work which are as good as anything you will do. For the rest of your life you will be trying to raise the general standard of your work up to the level of those passages.'

10.. 'Win a victory on each canvas.'

11. 'Never mind about the bad drawings; the good ones will carry them up with them like balloons.'

One is a little doubtful about this last piece of advice. It would seem advisable

[1] Letter to Nina Hamnett, 1917.

for the artist to destroy any of his work that he genuinely feels is not a credit to him, as his best work is apt to disappear for good most rapidly into private collections and that which is left will receive more publicity than he intended.

I will conclude this chapter with a description of Sickert when he was teaching at the Royal Academy Schools, by the artist Mr Clifford Hall. He gave me carte blanche to cut it if necessary but I feel it is too valuable to be abridged and the reader will be interested to see how much it repeats my own experience of Sickert's teaching.

'9 Chelsea Manor Studios,
Flood Street,
Chelsea, S.W.3.
24.12.1957.

'Dear Miss Lilly,

'Before Sickert's visit to the Royal Academy Schools, sometime in 1926, Charles Sims, then Keeper, called the students together. He told us Sickert would be the next Visitor, that he was not only one of the greatest painters we had but was also one of the greatest teachers. He proposed to give him an absolutely free hand and we were to co-operate in every way.

'Sickert arrived the following Monday morning at 10 o'clock. He asked a few pointed questions about methods of work, posing of models and so on, and then he proceeded to reorganize everything. It was done quickly and efficiently and his way worked smoothly from the very first day.

'He had great authority and great charm. The three models who normally would have posed singly in three separate studios he posed together in a group. This group was placed in the centre of the studio. We had been used to having the model placed against a drapery background; now we were told we must relate this group of three to whatever happened to come near or behind them—other students, or a corner of the studio, maybe.

'The insistence was on Drawing, and still more drawing. Drawings were to be considered as 'documents'. They must contain as much information as possible.

'Colour sketches, in oil colour, were to be made, painted in one sitting, on canvas or board "primed the colour of a cigar box". These colour sketches to be as coloured as was consistent with fine tonal values; and they were for use in conjunction with our drawings when we were ready to paint the finished picture—away from Nature.

'Because one of the girls in the group found her pose too difficult a man was engaged in her place. He was made to wear a woman's dress and Sickert bought a wig of long black hair for him.

'This model, I remember, was Mario Mancini, a brother of Alf Mancini the boxer.

' "I am not," said Sickert, "going to stumble in and out between easels whilst you are working." He told us how he wanted us to work and at the end of the

71

week, and the models not being present, he expected us to show him all we had done. Each student then received an individual criticism. He was told what applied to his particular needs, yet the criticism was full of advice that was needed by all of us and one gained immensely from listening to the criticisms, indeed Sickert expected us to do so.

'We were told also to write down what he told us and post our notes to him.

'This method, the master posing the models, giving the students a talk on the various possibilities of the motif, leaving them to get on with it and at the end of the week's work giving each a searching and constructive criticism of their efforts is, of course, not the English method of teaching, at least as I have found it in our Art Schools.

'Later, when I studied under André Lhote in Paris, his was the same procedure as Sickert's.

'In our Art Schools the students used to be given too much attention *all the time*, and tended to rely on the master whenever a difficulty arose. In recent years, however, the climate has changed and the majority seem to prefer to be left alone "to express themselves".

'*Commencing a Drawing*
'We could begin with whichever portion interested us most. We must proceed to relate the shapes immediately next to the one we had started with and so on, constantly relating shape to shape, "with no jumps", until "the drawing bumped up against the four edges of the paper".

'The drawing must be commenced with a faint "tentative line". Next the values were put in, starting with the darkest, "to give the map solidity", and finally a firmer more searching "line of definition" was added.

'These were the three main stages although naturally they could and did overlap according to the ability of the student.

'Pencil or black chalk, not too soft and with a good point had to be used and india rubber was not allowed.

'Corrections, that is to say several outlines in the search for the true one could be made and when the corrections became confusing, as they often did in the pencil stage, further corrections were put in with ink.

'A number of drawings from the same viewpoint was advised for each could contain some extra scrap of information and might play its part in the final building up of the picture.

'When it came to deciding on the design of the picture, Sickert advised which drawing would work out best. Design was not a word he used but like Degas he was a master of the *cut*. "Add a piece here, take off some there," and the result was usually a piece of good placing, even of good design, in spite of this somewhat chancy procedure.

'The drawing was then squared up and a full-size cartoon made, in clear outline. A tracing was taken of this, Indian Red being then lightly scumbled over

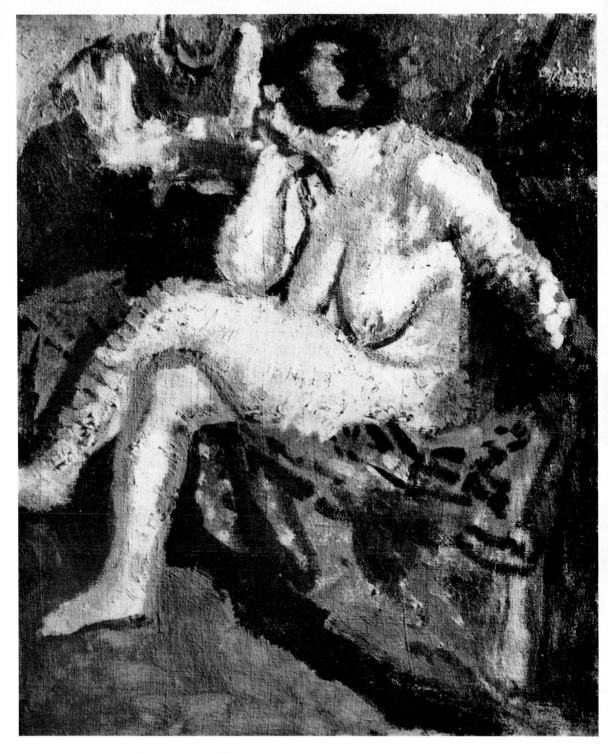

10. Walter Richard Sickert (1860-1942). JACK ASHORE, 1911. Oil. 13 × 16 ins.
Collection S. Samuels

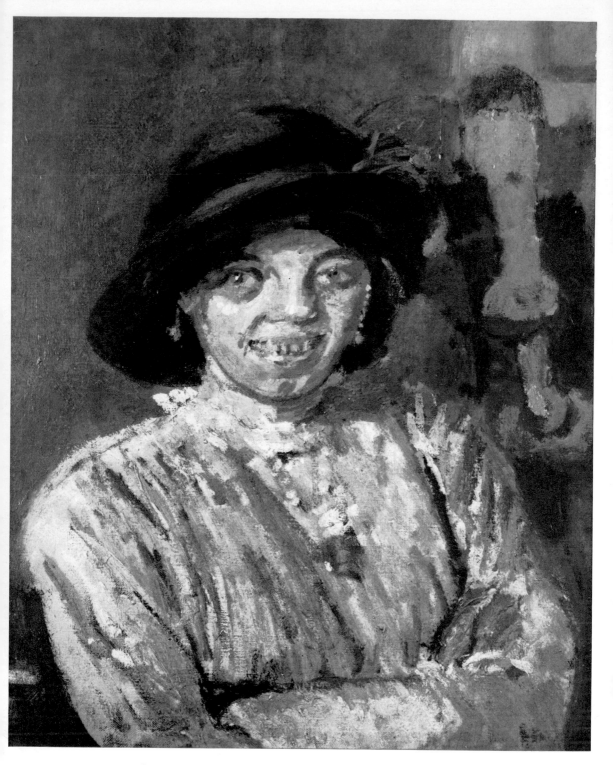

11. Walter Richard Sickert (1860-1942). CHICKEN, exh. 1911. Oil. 20 × 16 ins.
Edward le Bas Collection

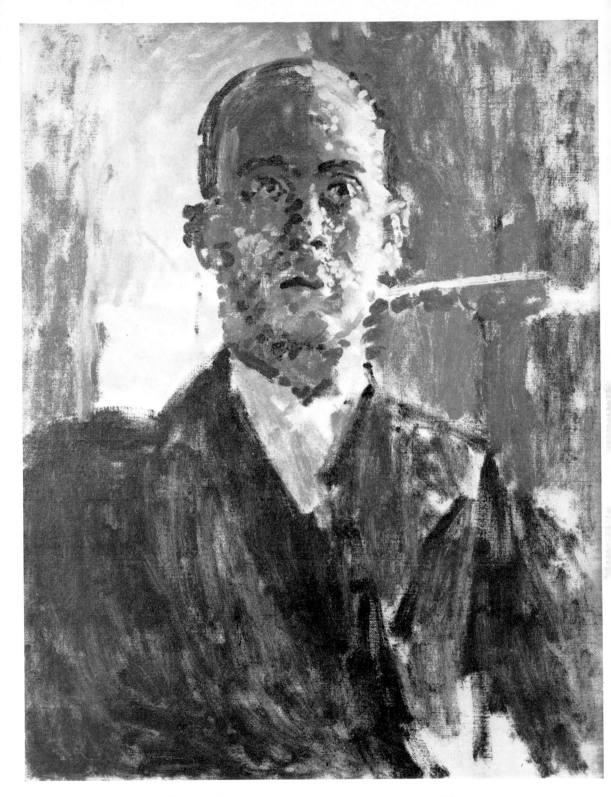

12. Walter Richard Sickert (1860-1942). HAROLD GILMAN, *c.* 1912. Oil. 24 × 18 ins.
Tate Gallery, London

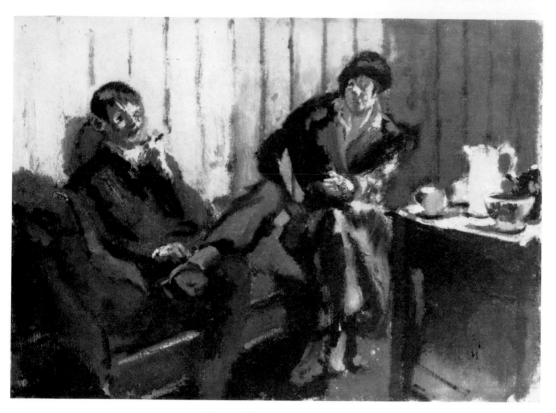

13. Walter Richard Sickert (1860-1942).
THE LITTLE TEA PARTY: NINA HAMNETT AND ROALD KRISTIAN, 1916.
Oil. 10 × 14 ins. *Tate Gallery, London*

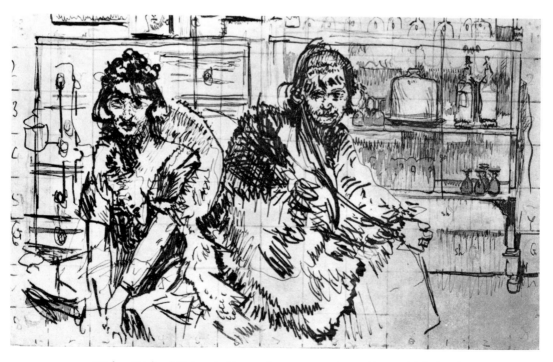

14. Walter Richard Sickert (1860-1942). THE BAR PARLOUR. Pen and ink drawing.
Aberdeen Art Gallery and Museum

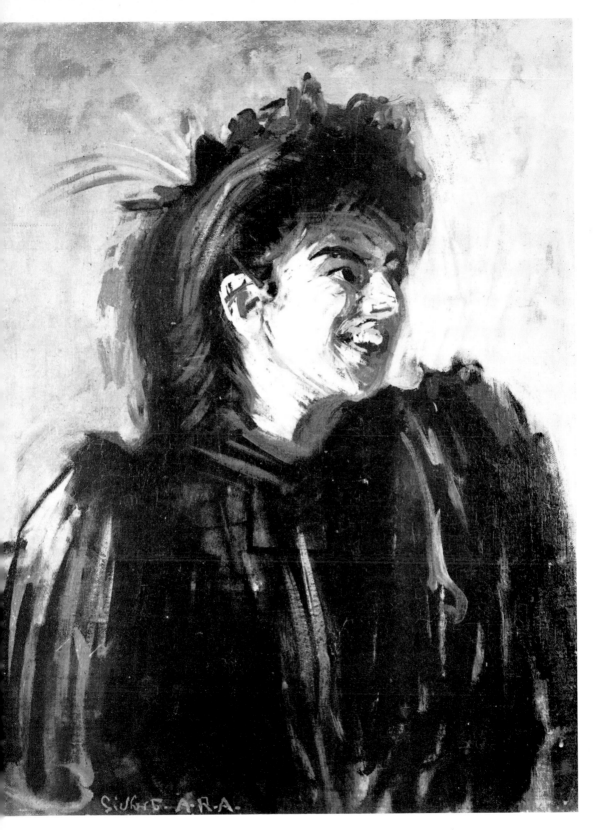

15. Walter Richard Sickert (1860-1942). THE BLACKBIRD OF PARADISE, *c.* 1904. Oil. 26 × 19 ins.
Leeds City Art Galleries

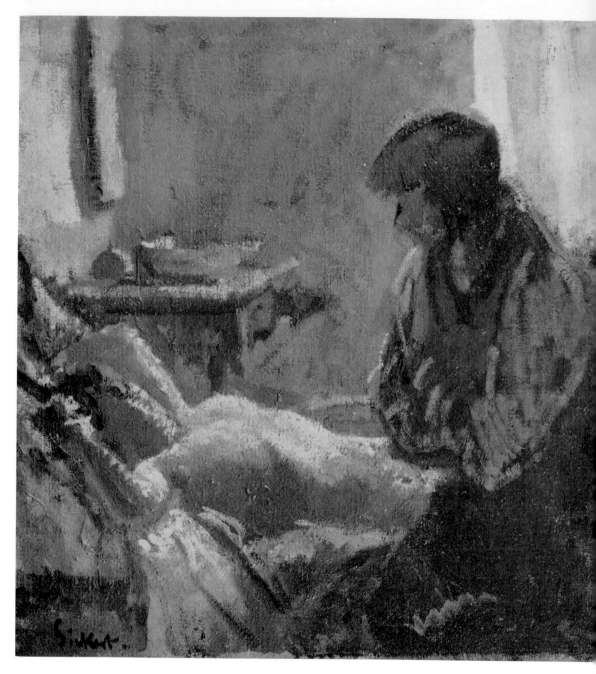

16. Walter Richard Sickert (1860–1942). SUMMER AFTERNOON, 1910. Oil. 12 × 17½ ins.
Collection Mr and Mrs Ronald Simon

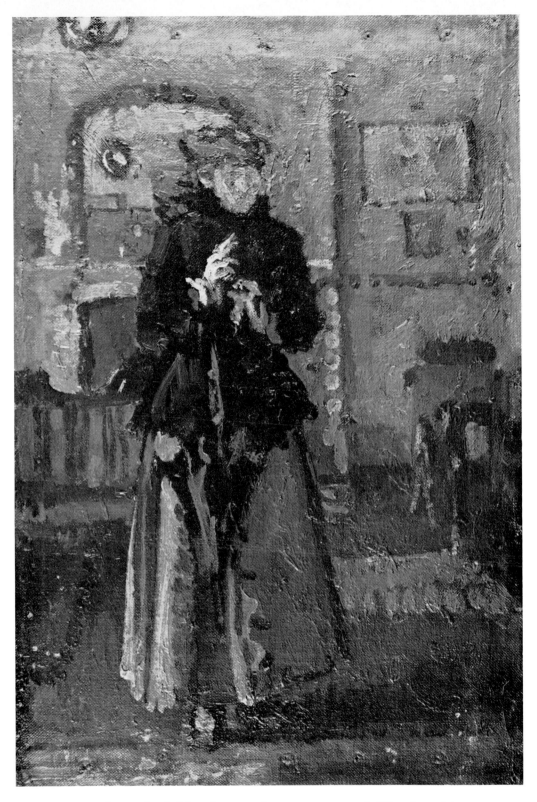

17. Walter Richard Sickert (1860-1942). THE VISITOR, *c.* 1908. Oil. 14½ × 9½ ins.
City Art Gallery, York

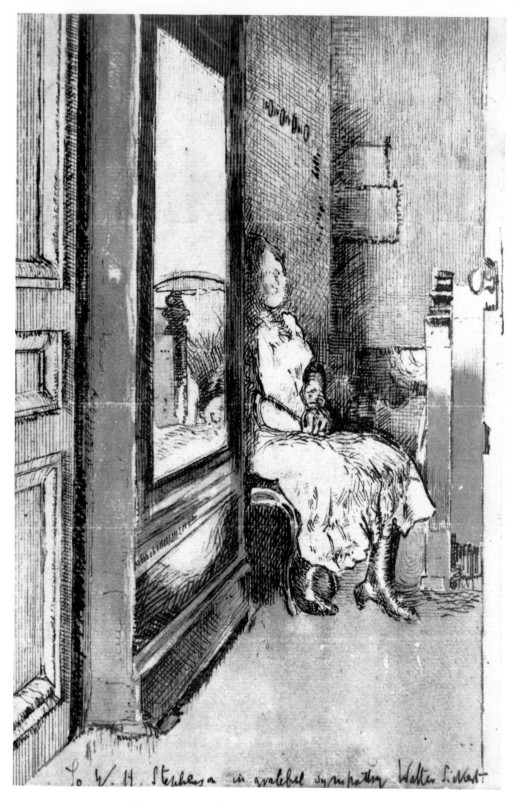

18. Walter Richard Sickert (1860–1942). L'ARMOIRE À GLACE.
Pen and ink drawing dedicated to W. H. Stephenson.
The sitter was the Sickerts' housekeeper, Marie Pepin.

the lines as they showed through on the reverse side. The tracing was laid face up on the prepared canvas and the lines gone over carefully with the blunt end of a thin brush handle.

'Sickert carried an agate mounted on a wooden handle and he used this for marking through.

'Now the picture, on a white canvas from which surface grease had been removed by sponging gently with warm water and Castile soap and sponging again with warm water before careful and slow drying, was under-painted in three tones of Indian Red and Flake White; but *very high in key*. No medium was used.

'This under-painting must be put away to dry, for 12 months if possible, before it was ready for colouring. We "must" continually prepare and lay down under-paintings "as some people laid down wine", taking them out to work on as they became mature. The date of preparation was to be written on the back of each.

'Sickert painted a colour sketch from the model, as a demonstration. Before touching the panel he mixed up all the necessary values on his palette.

'He worked vigorously and quickly rubbing the paint well into the surface and finishing with slightly more gentle touches with a fuller brush. He borrowed my brushes and when he had done with them, after an hour or so, they looked like miniature chimney sweep's brushes, the hairs standing out at right angles to the ferrules. He said "he was sorry but he always treated brushes roughly".

'And talking of right angles his definition of drawing was "the relation of all the angles that occur within the 180 degrees of two right angles". And according to him, if one did this correctly, the problems of perspective were automatically solved.

'Some time later he chose a drawing I had made which agreed with his colour sketch and told me to square it up enlarging it about 2½ times, and underpaint it. This I did and at another demonstration he coloured my underpainting using his colour sketch and my drawing. He also painted a monochrome from a *Daily Mail* photo of a wedding which he had previously squared up. The brush strokes were crisp and went across the form. He often said all he told us could be found in William Hunt's *Talks on Art*, long out of print, and this is largely true.

'He came into the Evening Drawing Class only once and looked at the drawings. This was on his first day at the Schools.

'Ernest Jackson, the Professor of Drawing, asked him what he thought of the work. Sickert was not enthusiastic. At last he told Jackson he liked best my drawing and one by Morland Lewis. These were not, he hastened to add, particularly good drawings, but we two had at least drawn the whole figure whilst the other students only appeared to be interested in highly finished portions—shoulders and arms without hands, legs minus feet and bodies lacking heads.

'The Drawing Class contained, in those days, a number of little figure studies by Thomas Stothard, some in pencil, some in ink, many highly finished. Sickert admired these greatly and sometimes went in when Jackson had no class to take another look at them.

'Jackson professed a low opinion of Stothard.

'Sickert had little time for students who did not work and his remarks to a girl student who brought her pet dog to the Schools were withering.

'He told a student who showed him drawings in bright blue chalk that he was "playing with loaded dice". Black on white was what he wanted and he would make large crosses on empty spaces where he knew something had been omitted, demanding: "What happens here?"

'He divided pictures into two sorts. The ones in which something was going on and the pictures of "yearning" in which nothing happened.

' "Let us have people doing something. Working, making love, misconducting themselves, but *doing something*", and figures or groups of figures must not be shown as in a vacuum, always they must exist in relation to their surroundings. One could build up a picture by starting with a table or a chair or a bed.

'He had little use for studies as such. From the start we were encouraged to paint pictures and to make drawings to be used for that purpose.

'I could go on and on although doubtless much of what I am saying concerns many points we have already discussed.

'I still have some of the drawings I did under Sickert, at least one of my colour sketches and a painting I worked out from these studies.

'Sickert's insistence on good craftmanship is something one seldom comes across now. The lack of method too often encouraged in many art schools of today would horrify him, as it would all painters trained in a sound tradition.

'I have never known a master who gave so much, who was so inspiring to his students.

'I am continually reminded that Sickert's methods of work were so basically right, that they could be applied to almost any point of view. Of course all he taught was absolutely traditional, and he would have been the first to admit this.

'Yours sincerely,
Clifford Hall.'

PART TWO

Chapter 6

Le Quartier

In 1917, Sickert and his wife received his friends and followers at the Frith on Wednesday afternoons. Visitors had to thunder loudly on the ponderous front door if they wished to be heard from the distant fastness of the Frith and once admitted to the house, their pilgrimage had only just begun. Now they must cross the hall and the passage beyond, go through Sickert's door and the ante-room, mount some steps and proceed for what must have seemed an endless journey between groups of people in the dark straggling studio towards their host and hostess, lost at the far end in a cloud of smoke. Timid souls, visiting Sickert for the first time, found this rather an ordeal. Sickert might have forgotten both invitation and guest for the time being or he might be sitting with his back to the ante-room, absorbed in conversation with someone else, so that he did not see the new arrival struggling to catch his eye until the visitor was actually upon him. But whether he remembered the invitation or not, he always pretended to do so. A friend of mine, calling for me one Wednesday, was highly amused at the warmth of his reception, as Sickert hailed him fervently, swept him into the chair next his own and plunged into chat, although they had never set eyes on each other before. Outsiders were not always so fortunate; they might fail to claim their host's attention immediately and find themselves instead at the mercy of the *quartier*. These old stagers had a habit, as the fancy took them, of staring into the fire in dead silence for prolonged periods; the effect of their motionless, brooding forms, half obscured by shadow, indifferent to all around them, could be as daunting as the effort of trying to burrow one's way into the Frith. Even if they happened to be speaking when the interloper appeared, they closed up instantly at the advent of a stranger and remained dumb, while he had the added embarrassment of having broken into the sacred circle. Once shepherded to a seat and provided with tea by his kind hostess he was then passed over, with piercing glances of dispraisal, by the rest of the *quartier*. It was best that he should insinuate himself by degrees if he wished to gain a hearing; unfortunately, through nervousness he might begin to talk loudly and incessantly—alas, about painting— into a devastating silence. Finding him with the situation thus left on his hands it was again Christine who rescued him, leading him gently from the pitfalls of art to general topics in which he would be more likely to ingratiate himself with the company.

Sickert became restive if his Wednesdays were too much dominated by the *quartier*. He liked these afternoons to be as mixed as possible, to remind us of the world beyond Fitzroy Street. On a good day there might be Spaniards, Americans, actors, old pupils, dilettantes, the world of Mayfair, a sprinkling of French, besides the *quartier* and a never ending stream of khaki. One afternoon, hearing a faint scratching at the door in the ante-room, I opened it to find a handful of French painters who had braved the wintry rigours of the channel to salute Sickert and other sights of London; they were arguing as to who should enter first and deliver the little speech that they had prepared. It was some time before they could be persuaded to take the plunge but at last the leader was chosen and they advanced gravely in single file, with outstretched hands. Their welcome from Sickert was uproarious, but they declined to sit until the leader had said his piece, accompanied by bows and flourishes.

Walter Taylor who had a studio in Fitzroy Square was an old friend of Sickert. Sickert told us 'We first met when Taylor came to my studio and bought six pictures straight off. I thought I was made for life.'

He was generally known as Old Taylor, although I suppose he was no older really than anyone else. Only Sickert referred to him as 'My Taylor', 'My' being the prefix he reserved for his intimates. But that Taylor created an impression of age is indisputable. Sir Osbert Sitwell says:

'Sickert often spent his holidays in the company of his friend and contemporary, Walter Taylor, contemporary, I write, though to me Taylor, with his red face and white imperial, his prominent nose, slow movements, leisurely gait, and with a little of the air of a seaside dandy, appeared always to be elderly.'[1]

When we first knew him, in 1917, he lived in Oxford Square and also had a house at Brighton. He had an especial flair for creating a domestic setting which was at once stately, luxurious and comfortable; he merged the old with the new and one could always count on finding some fresh and exciting purchases whenever one visited him. As befitted the solid old house, his furnishings were rich and sober; thick curtains and carpets, capacious armchairs, lavish ornaments, pictures and flowers in abundance. On the table in his sitting room all the very latest novels and biographies were arranged in colourful sequence; he prided himself on keeping up to date, even in advance of the times. I once recommended a novel to him that I thought he might enjoy; he asked when it had been written. 'Some years ago,' I said. 'Oh,' replied Taylor with the world of pregnant meaning that only he could put into his Oh's. 'But I don't read old novels.' He was a prey to the rage for the day after tomorrow which was already bedevilling the arts in 1917, although it had not developed into the definite neurosis, the worship of change that afflicts us to-day when one painter after another is dismissed as 'dated' almost before the paint is dry on his canvas. In his efforts to keep abreast of

[1] *A Free House! or the Artist as Craftsman, Being the Writings of Walter Richard Sickert,* ed. Osbert Sitwell, Macmillan, 1947.

contemporary thought, Taylor's collection of pictures was in a constant state of flux but he was, however, a shrewd buyer, even if he did sell off all his Sickerts one fell day in favour of new gods. Fred Porter objected strongly when he found that the stately Sickerts no longer adorned the dining room at Oxford Square and what he considered to be some rather pert squibs were usurping their place. 'Surely, Taylor, it's not a question of new or old, up to date or out of date, fashionable or not fashionable, there's simply good or bad painting.' 'Oh,' said Taylor.

Looking back on our visits to him, it always seems to have been autumn. Memories of him are tinged with the season of mists and mellow fruitfulness; of cool October sunlight slanting through the windows, scent of woodsmoke from the blazing log fire, whiffs from his cigar and massed chrysanthemums. Taylor himself was generally sitting in a great crimson-hooded chair when his guests arrived, rising to receive us with what Sir Osbert calls his leisurely gait. We never saw him in disarray; he was always nobly dressed. Fortunate in possessing a figure which was the answer to every tailor's prayer, he wore his suits like vestments, yet with casual grace. They were immaculate, distinguished and they never looked too new. For parties, he donned a slightly unusual kind of evening dress, rather like a *soutane*, with a high black stock secured by a pearl pin. When contemplating this severe elegance one realized that whereas most of us merely were clothed, Taylor was attired. Only England could have produced him.

The house at Brighton was a favourite week-end retreat for the Sickerts. Here, he and Taylor reversed their roles, Sickert assuming the part of host, planning the day for everyone, Taylor subsiding into the part of the accommodating guest. Up with the sparrows as usual, Sickert would return to breakfast after his early morning walk, saying, 'I saw some delicious mushrooms at the greengrocer's.' 'Oh,' said Taylor and the mushrooms duly appeared at the next meal. Or, it might be after breakfast, when Sickert would choose a subject for his host to paint, usually from Taylor's own balcony. 'Now Taylor, this is just the thing for you, you sit just there.' Taylor politely yielded, but as he remarked afterwards to me, he would stay outside until he could put up with it no longer and then, aching to join the merriment and laughter that he heard from within, he would slink back to his own sitting room. But he greatly enjoyed being ordered about by Sickert and no one was more distressed than he when, years later, Sickert was too tired to tease him any more. Their last meetings in the thirties were melancholy. Sickert would sit brooding, the ghost of his gay self. He took violent exception to Taylor's butler and remained uneasy until the poor man left the room. Convinced that this harmless functionary was a dangerous character, he would warn Taylor severely: 'I see, Taylor, that you are still harbouring your assassin.' At the Frith, in the midst of his sallies over his bowl of tea, he would suddenly break off as Taylor's plight struck him anew and say: 'I wonder what *that man* is plotting now.'

In his search for novelty, Taylor sometimes collected some very queer fish indeed. Everyone was interested in the antics of one particular fish who descended upon us from theatrical circles; this was Haraldur Hamar, the Icelander. Haraldur arrived in London with a play which I believe he had written in English, then translated back into Icelandic and then again into English. One wondered why all this backwards and forwards was necessary; I had always supposed that writers selected a language, preferably their own, and then said what they had got to say in that. But Nina Hamnett assured me of my mistake; it appeared that all this translating was most important from a literary point of view and she explained its purpose to me carefully several times, although I am afraid I never really took it in. The cast of this play numbered some three hundred characters, so that when Haraldur was hawking it round London, he found it difficult to attract the notice of managers. Ellen Terry, then a very old and impetuous lady, was most indignant about the cold reception Haraldur received at their hands. 'A *play-wright*!' she exclaimed indignantly, 'to be treated in this fashion!' She declared that it was a disgrace to the profession. I never discovered anyone who had read the play quite through and it is doubtful whether Miss Terry had done so, but Haraldur Hamar lunched and dined out on the strength of it; he was always to be seen with his brain child, tucked in a folder under his arm.

Sickert admired Taylor's water colours; he was impressed with water colour if it was any good at all, although strangely, his own lovely stained drawings, conceived generally as working notes, did not appeal to him and he was inclined to be apologetic about them. He never did stereotyped water colour but neither did Taylor, whose use of the medium was very personal, his technique simple but effective. The subjects he preferred were interiors with plenty of light; he worked on a large scale for water colour and was not frightened of big washes, rendering them with freshness and ease. Pre-war Michallet, made with linen rags, was his favourite paper, of which he had an enormous stock; slightly ribbed, it dried with a faint bloom if worked upon by expert hands. He used charcoal to outline the colours, which he painted in large flat masses like a stained glass window. This sounds a simple procedure but the difficulty lay in its very simplicity, as many students found when they started to do a 'a Taylor'.

Soon after we met him he began to show signs of the restlessness that overtook him in his later years. He sold his house at Brighton and rented the first floor of a mansion in Fitzroy Square which had once belonged to Ford Madox Brown. Here he gave large tea parties which Christine Sickert enjoyed, although one afternoon her pleasure was marred by an unexpected incident. She was admiring the effect of the room, sober and splendid as Taylor's interiors were wont to be, when she saw a pair of fine Venetian candlesticks adorning the tea table. 'Look!' she whispered to me, 'there are *my* candlesticks!' It was too true; they were indeed the candlesticks which Prince Antoine Bibesco had given the Sickerts for a wedding present and which Sickert, unknown to her, had presented to Taylor.

But if Christine had a grievance about her candlesticks, Taylor had a grievance too. Sickert sometimes employed a Negro model, an unnerving creature who spoke no English, rolled the whites of his eyes and hid himself behind the curtains, where he indulged in prolonged fits of giggling. I think the poor man was desperately hard up, he looked pitiably thin and shivered a good deal; London winters were evidently too much for him. One morning Taylor put his head round the door of our little room; he seemed preoccupied.

'Is anything wrong?' we asked.

'M'm. I'm just wondering about that overcoat I gave to Walter.'

He was referring to a very beautiful dark blue overcoat made to measure by his own tailor which he had just presented to Sickert.

We were immediately apprehensive, surely, the overcoat must be safe on its peg! Sickert had never looked better than when he was strolling up and down the street in this sumptuous garment.

'Because,' continued Taylor in his flat quiet voice, 'I've just seen that Negro wearing it.'

W. H. Davies used to say that the silences of Augustus John were terrible but he agreed that the silences of Taylor were comfortable, even sympathetic. Dining with him was most enjoyable. Not that he really ever said anything much but 'Oh'; his 'Oh', however, conveyed as much as most people's sentences. He paid his guests the subtle compliment of appearing to ponder their words and he might bring out some careless statement that they had made weeks ago and since forgotten. 'As you were saying last time you were here'—which was of course most gratifying. One could lounge submerged in one of his deep chairs, stare into the great fire and muse at will or chatter to the accompaniment of his Oh's, placed at intervals. Often, good easy man, he led one on into murmuring all sorts of trivialities; he had the faculty, like Thérèse Lessore, of inducing talk in others. And there was so much to see; pictures, books, portfolios and Taylor himself, the perfect portrait, with his rosy oval face, beaky nose and expressive hands, looking as if he had just emerged from a Turkish bath. A slight cast in one eye masked his thoughts; it was impossible to tell what he was thinking.

There had been tragedy in his life. His wife had died on their honeymoon. He never spoke of her and there were no pictures or photographs of her in Oxford Square.

Taylor was fortunate to live in a period favourable to the collector. Given time and a discerning eye, even a man of moderate means could build up an interesting collection of modern pictures in 1918. Art lovers today owe more than they realize to the pioneers of the past, especially the dealers. Some timid souls, feeling the first faint stirrings of the power of art, found it easier to cope with a few pictures in an intimate setting than to see too much at once. If they began their quest by venturing into great halls replete with splendours such as the National Gallery or the Louvre they emerged exhausted rather than refreshed, as if they had been wandering about in a forest without a signpost.

The Leicester Gallery in Leicester Square was especially popular with the West End public and there Messrs Brown and Phillips steered their way calmly through the vagaries of fashion, giving varied, copious but not overpowering shows of leading artists, modern and traditional, for many years before they went to their present home in Cork Street. Until quite recently, one could buy a charming water colour or drawing for a very modest sum; all up and down Bond Street, bargains in mint condition were available to the buyer with a sense of quality, from the Fine Art Society to Colnaghi's and that majestic last outpost of civilization, Agnew's. Even today, prices are surprisingly reasonable for many pictures, although they have necessarily risen with the growing shortage of good painting.

Partners for many years, Oliver Brown and Ernest Phillips of the Leicester Gallery were utterly different personalities. Phillips was quiet, reserved, yet gracious and always ready to help if one went to him with a problem. Brown was lively, spontaneous and enthusiastic, although when young he too was quiet, owing to shyness. The first time I saw him was in the autumn of 1917; he was wandering round the vast hall of Number 15, looking for the Frith, where he was breakfasting with Sickert. I showed him the way to Sickert's door and I remember being struck by his youthful appearance. He was unlike other dealers I had known, he seemed so slight, so boyish, a little lost. He had never met Sickert before, as in his lifetime his father, Mr Ernest Brown, had always managed the elderly and the eminent, and it was with some apprehension that the young Oliver had taken his place and was faring forth to tackle the master in his fortress.

Years later, he told me how that visit had disappointed him.

During breakfast, to use his own words, no opportunity to talk business seemed to present itself. Sickert was rattling on about everything except his own work and was so flippant that Oliver Brown could not feel he was taken seriously. Like so many before him, he gazed longingly at the famous shelf, crammed with canvases; time was slipping by, soon he must take his leave and he had not yet referred to the object of his visit. In halting tones, he took the plunge and wondered if there was anything for sale; he would be so happy if Sickert had some work to spare.

Sickert waved his arms in a sweeping gesture round the gaunt room.

'Take the lot, my dear boy,' he said.

He then named an absurdly small sum as payment for the whole row of canvases.

When Oliver Brown repeated this story to me, he added that his father would not have been surprised at this sally; old Mr Brown knew his Sickert, had battled with Whistler and was hardened to difficult artists of every nationality. But Oliver was unused to the species, diffident and totally bemused.

'I thought I was being laughed at,' he explained. 'Sickert made no effort to show me the pictures and I didn't know what to do, so I went.'

It was a sad instance of Sickert's ill-timed displays of temperament whenever the question of business cropped up, and Brown's own inexperience. They might have traded together to their mutual benefit had it not been for this unnecessary misunderstanding. However, some of the pictures were rescued years later by the Savile Gallery, who held a fine exhibition of them in 1927 in Stratford Place, and in Sickert's old age the Leicester Gallery was among his best friends, helping him when he badly needed it on many occasions. Sickert admired the pluck of Brown and Phillips during the Hitler war; although Leicester Square was heavily bombed and the building often rocked under their feet, they never closed down.

The business is now being carried on by their two sons.

Since the Hitler war, Messrs Roland Browse and Delbanco have continued the tradition and produced exhibitions which are often a joy to behold, and we have Miss Browse to thank for valuable books on various painters, full of information which might have been lost for ever, had it not been for her careful research. She was also largely responsible for the Sickert Exhibition at the National Gallery in 1941, which introduced the public to a collection of his best work.

'You are young and can stand a lot but you won't always be. Save your precious nerves. You must not be perpetually in a state of nervous excitement. The grounds must be allowed to settle and the coffee to clear. The one thing in all my experience I cling to is my coolness and leisurely exhilarated contemplation. If I could influence you to achieve that je t'aurais rendu en peu service. Si tu savais comme j'y tiens! Let this advice be my perpetual and most solemn legacy to you.'

This was Sickert's message to one of his favourite young painters, Nina Hamnett.

Nina was a true Bohemian. The word Bohemian seems as dead now as last year's fashions but once it was often used to describe the sort of person we call a hippie today. Your Bohemian, however, was not quite the same thing as your hippie. He was not a layabout; he might have a capacity for work, he might and often did observe the daily routine of the bath. But like the hippie, he ignored public opinion and lived in a world of his own. So that Nina Hamnett, although brought up conventionally, found the convictions of her own father bewildering; she was hurt and surprised because this gentleman, a soldier of pre-1914 vintage, was horrified to meet her coming out of the Fitzroy Tavern with bare head and a jug of beer in her hand. In 1917, it was unthinkable for a woman to appear hatless in the street. The Colonel could hardly believe the evidence of his eyes; the jug of beer was the crowning misdemeanour. Her talents, her generous nature, her great charm did not console him, which was not altogether surprising as even Sickert, inured to the sights of Fitzroy Street, was shaken by this proceeding. Both gentlemen took a grave view of the matter; it was felt that Nina was sapping the foundations of society. Her mother was frankly alarmed with her unexpected progeny with whom she had absolutely nothing in common, and her brothers were equally disturbed; but what distressed Nina was the attitude of her sister, who was not bemused or frightened or angry but merely indifferent. Nina was attached to her sister, and unhappy when her overtures were coldly received. She was not estranged herself by their differences of temperament, although filled with wonder. 'She *likes* clocking in,' Nina told me, with awe. 'Can you believe it? She gets to the office by nine and leaves at six.'

When her mother and brothers came to the Frith on Wednesdays, Nina was anxious that they should enjoy themselves. She would take pains to find someone congenial for them to talk to, whose conversation would not be too startling for them. She always wanted people to get on together and when she introduced her friends to each other she would whisper any clue about them which might prove helpful, such as 'he's Slade . . . second year' or 'he's F.O. . . . . very cagey' or 'he's Army, *stage* Army.' Mrs Hamnett was hardly 'stage Army' but she was a fish out of water in Fitzroy Street. Once her shyness had worn off, she was easy to talk to in spite of her air of dumb protest. If she had a failing, it was over-modesty; she seemed grateful that any remark should be addressed to her and the only subject to avoid was her brilliant daughter.

Nina could hardly be accused of self-effacement but neither was she assertive; she had the good manners that spring from utter unself-consciousness, boyish, direct, and not without dignity. She had decided views on the consideration that members of a polite society owed each other and she deferred charmingly to opinions and ideas that were not her own; for her part, she welcomed the newest theories about everything but you were not expected to do the same and she chose her friends from different cliques, stipulating as it were that they should be good of their kind rather than that they should be of her kind. Like Sickert, she was anxious to show them in the best light and bring them out as much as possible; acting as a sort of liaison officer was perhaps her chief delight. She was never so happy as when she was the leader of a large gathering, squandering her vitality and fascination on a parcel of people that she might never see again. She had a passion for parties; all the meditation and silence enjoined by Sickert were beyond her comprehension; she hated to be alone. I do not think he ever realized this. He had a high opinion of her talent; he foresaw a future for her in the art world. But the luxury of solitude was not for Nina and this basic difference between them was, I think, the reason why her visit to Bath under his auspices was not a success. Sickert was very anxious that she should join him during his last summer there, taking much trouble to find lodgings that would please her; he met her at the station and looked after her when she arrived, but he suffered from the delusion that she wanted to work as much as he did and although Nina was ready to work, she needed the stimulus of other workers around her to do her best. The visit to which they had looked forward was a disappointment to them both.

After the first few days, she was suddenly confronted with a completely detached Sickert; the muse had seized him and as always at these times, it was as if a veil was interposed between him and the outer world. She had expected parties, outings, and that he would introduce her to all Bath. He was surprised that she was not as excited by the superb old city as he was himself. But for once, his perceptions were at fault. She had nothing to do with its tremendous past, she produced nothing because she was bored and lonely; she counted the hours until her return to London and was hurt that for the time being she meant no more to Sickert than any stranger.

Shortly before her death Nina showed me the letters Sickert had written to her, although he usually disliked writing. I quote some of them here. Like most of Sickert's letters the majority are undated.

10 Bladud Buildings,
Bath.

'Dear Nina,

'Enclosed drawing from balcony of little house kept by ideal policeman's wife with a son who is a Lieutenant.

'It is halfway down Beechen Cliff, 2 minutes from station and five from pump room . . . The place is divine. It is on our way down to town. I found my Christine burnt brick red, so that her eyes looked very blue. Our house is tiny, but solid and well kept. Marie mutters because there is no work to do. I advised Christine to tell her to scrub the hearthstone at Beechen Cliff. I said after all Ulysses kept Penelope waiting for more than ten days, and he had no chests of drawers to move across the road. But she explained that Ulysses didn't send her wires to say he was coming in a day or two. The beauty of the place is incredible. My walk down after breakfasting à l'Anglaise in the kitchen at about 6 is like a German woodcut of the views down through beech trees on the elaborate town. It only wants a young poet in the foreground with long hair, a wandering stick and his goods tied up in a cotton handkerchief.

'You could walk in these gardens and orchards in perfect peace. Such roofs, such roses, such contorted walls . . . such bracing air . . .'

(no signature)

'My dear Nina,

'I have naturally been thinking about you, so that I will trouble you with a censored selection of my thoughts. Most of which you have heard before.

'I am anxious you should put your efficiency to work to eliminate as far as possible boredom in gangs from your existence. My experience is exactly the same as yours. I only smoke too much or drink too much when I have to traverse the efforts and fatigues of useless company, or unrefreshing company. We who like to work best, and work for all our strength is worth, can only do with company which is nourishing either to body or soul or both. Two things in company are good, friendly assemblies (luncheon parties, dinner parties, tea parties, supper parties, concerts, music halls, theatres, breakfast parties, etc.) these we can enter and leave when we like, so we are the master of what the French call le dosage . . .

'Secondly tête-à-tête. . . . Tête-à-têtes with someone who is a comrade is probably best and the most refreshing recreation in the world. Use your masterful ability in quite cutting off any drifting in droves that you don't expressly and exactly intend or desire . . . Don't be a tin kettle to any dog's tail, however long.

'Here endeth the first lesson from,

'Your devotissimo
'Walter Sickert.'

'No, not a sermon exactly. But as I said, if so be it you can work some part of every year in England, your work on the French market will have an English savour, and French connoisseurs will be interested in it. It will be in Paris, distinctive. Whereas will you be able to whip Marchand, say on his own ground? I don't say you won't, only you would be throwing away a unique weapon for the Paris market if you despised English subjects. Make these as canaille as you like. God, aren't we canaille enough for you? Didn't Doré and Géricault find English life sordid enough? Madame est bien difficile! . . .

'I have a spiffing stunt for small studies out of doors needing rapidity. A pochade box with a screw through it standing solid on a photographic tripod. I give the two wooden panels a wash of violet in watercolour i.e. stain them. Then trace my drawings on to them with commercial blue paper. Then I give the panel a coat of white hard varnish (what actors put their moustaches on with) et allez!

'Yours
'Walter Sickert.'

Telegram from Bath: 3rd July 1918.
    'Found divine lodgings free next Friday letter follows Sickert.'

'I have taken a room for the 20th. Write too if you like. Your bedroom is amazing. From the bed it looks as if someone had chucked the roofs of the whole town in at the two windows with the Abbey in the middle and the tower of your old school on the horizon.

'I have spent the day in the usual blasted lugging of easels and glass, palettes and canvases upstairs and installed an excellent studio in the heart of the town . . .

'Walter Sickert.'

'My Nina,
    'Thank you for your enchanting letter. There is certainly one of your more or less ex-male friends by whom you will be surrounded when you are 40, if he is still alive, which alas he won't be.

'I will meet the 5 o'clock from Paddington on Monday. Don't tell anyone, especially not Christine, but I am not very well and if I have to "lay up" and rest she will meet you. I write this provisionally in case of that alternative occurring. I am not surprised or injured that 2 years off sixty I may be having to take in sail. My father died when he was two years younger than I am, and I have had a wonderful look in already. Perhaps the Bath water and swimming is too fatiguing . . .

'A bientôt dear and delightful garçon

'Your
'Walter Sickert.'

'Don't destroy the Bath picture. Wait, you may come again. Never destroy the idea sketch for a possible work.'

'I have certainly solved the question of technique, and if you would all listen it would save you twelve years muddling.

'The difficulty in oils is we don't like it clumsy with thickness, but if we thin it with medium it gets nasty and poor.

It is extraordinary how agreeably undiluted paint *scrubbed hard* over a coarse bone-dry camaïeu (in quite light tones, practically all white, only just enough coloured to distinguish light from shade, by making all lights one colour and all darks another, say white-indian red for shadow and white and cobalt for light) becomes. It tells semi-transparent like a powder or a wash, and this with no dilutent. Of course, this is for the earlier coats of the true colour, as one finishes one can't scrub and, in consequence, the touches become fatter. Then in the end nothing is prettier than the non-coloured spaces semitransparent and the laboured ones fatter and more opaque. I believe technically that is the ideal use of oil paint at its best. Courbet's knife business necessarily lacked form and couldn't be gone on with because the knife left no tooth. In Ingres painting is a little poor.

[last sentence queried in margin.]

'All this of course is for painting from drawings. Painting from life prima over and over again can only be done in the one way. But that is one of the chief of the 1,000 arguments against it. You couldn't, for instance, do a certain view of Bath I am doing from where I sat for the studies in the street, and the wind and the dust and the changing light. Besides carts and horses don't stand still while you execute them in oil—

'Yours

'Walter Sickert.'

'My blessed Nina,

'Of course I am dying to know how things are going at Vincent Square.

'I am absolutely convinced that once the students have had [a] fortnight's experience of you, you will create an enthusiastic following, because firstly you have been through so much and secondly because you have so much intellectual vitality, and students feel that quickly.

'Be pliable and conciliatory and amiable with the authorities. Don't let any trifling stones in the way, if there are any, wreck the important car you are setting out to drive. You are cut out for a teacher. There will be time to consider how not to allow your teaching to interefere with your own work when you have consolidated your authority as a teacher.

'I am very glad Meninsky is able to take one night. It is very good of him. Give him my love and tell him I would rather see him teaching drawing than put out of drawing by shrapnel. If you have friends who want to draw from the model try to get them to come to Westminster to help swell the initial numbers. Once

87

you have been given a chance you will fill the classes fuller, perhaps, than is comfortable . . .

> 'Your devotissimo,
> 'Walter Sickert.'

'2nd July 1918

' . . . If you use a colourman's or any canvas prepared with oil paint always always always wash it with soap with soap and sponge till the surface grease is attacked.

'The sharpness of your first, fresh drawing may be blunted by the grease and the necessity of making a stroke several times before it takes; il faut que la peinture s'accroche tout de suite.'

'July 17th 1918.

'I am glad you are drawing. You must have one more or less conventional den and more or less reposeful studio to receive non-hogwash in as a matter of business and a pigstye as much as you like for private use. I haven't read Lytton Strachey's book. It must be most amusing. I imagine it is what most people of our period see when we read biographies of our grandparents' time. I am glancing at an idiotic book by Frith on Leech. Leech wisely said—"When you have given the idea of that you have to express why do more to it?"

'Of course he is right; when Leech draws a man putting on his coat, he *is* putting on his coat. When most painters paint one, he isn't.

> 'Goodnight, dearest Nina
> 'Yours
> 'Walter Sickert.'

'Tu me manques, mon petit chat . . .

'I am working myself silly to get the work done. I am shocked and upset by poor Miss Cutter's accident.[1] It is quite possible at the present moment she is no longer alive.

'Blessings on you, chère enfant, and for God's sake take care of yourself,

> 'Yours
> 'Walter Sickert.'

(From France)
My Nina,

' . . . If you go to Barnstaple have a look at Mortehoe, which I think adorable, probably because I used to make love to the milkmaids there when I was 14.

'More power to your fist, My Nina, and best love. I miss our family breakfast.

'I love the sea bathing, but there is something melancholy about Dieppe. Perhaps it brings back the shock of 1914 rather acutely.

> 'Ever yours,
> 'Walter Sickert.'

[1] My friend Chris had had a railway accident.

After Sickert left for Dieppe towards the end of 1918, there was no one to hold together the diverse elements of Fitzroy Street; everyone drifted in different directions. It was left to Nina to say something about the *quartier* in her strange, vivid, tangled book, *Laughing Torso*, named after the statue by Henri Gaudier-Brzeska. She had every reason to be proud of her book, as exchanging her brush for the pen must have been a tremendous effort; painters seldom write, and I do not remember anyone else who tried to capture the atmosphere of those years when Sickert was presiding over his large, restless family of followers, her experiences with him at Bath and her own subsequent adventures in Paris.

Today, Nina is chiefly remembered for her line drawings, in the manner of Gaudier. But some years ago, Mr Oliver Brown was showing me pictures in the basement of the Leicester Galleries and we came across a sparkling portrait of the artist Horace Brodsky which struck us both with its intensity. Another Nina that impressed me when I was young was an orchard with trees in bloom. I have always wanted to possess that picture; I think her early work has never had its due.

She had an attractive little laughing face with an impertinent nose and a coltish yet graceful figure. She posed for Roger Fry as well as Gaudier and she was one of the models in Sickert's 'The Little Tea Party' (plate 13) now in the Tate Gallery.

Soon after the last war, I was looking after an exhibition of local art in Paddington, when Nina called on me. It was a joy to see her again, but I was distressed to find that she was very poor indeed. I do not think her health was equal to a steady output of work, although she still made pathetic efforts to paint every day, and concentration was now lacking. She had never seen her way to following the advice of Sickert, leading a quieter life and spending more time in contemplation; she could not do without her parties and now that the war had deprived her of her social life, she was lost. Possibly she had never had the necessary stamina to forge ahead; at all events she had never quite managed to develop the talent that Sickert had perceived in her youth. A new generation of influential men had arisen who were not interested in Nina; without private means or steady backing, the struggle to keep any footing in the world of art had been too much for her and the privations of the war years had proved the last straw.

We had luncheon together to talk over old times and she told me that a cousin allowed her two pounds a week; she could count on a starvation diet from this and her own uncertain earnings. When he left London, Sickert had made over to her his evening classes at the Westminster Institute, but although she had been a lively teacher, this source of income had petered out long since and now she was not equal to the strain of lecturing or conducting large classes. But there were still her social gifts and laughter, echoes of the old gay Nina; she exerted herself to entertain me with anecdotes and gossip and chattered away in her clear low voice, precise but rapid, although I noticed when we reached the coffee that she was getting exhausted. I mentioned the charm of her voice once to Sickert, who looked thoughtful; I do not think he noticed voices much, at least he never remarked upon them.

Among other people who came on Wednesdays to the Frith was Enid Bagnold, now Lady Roderick Jones, famous for her novel *National Velvet* and her play, *The Chalk Garden*. She was a tall, golden haired girl, perfectly tailored and groomed, who was not in the least like the popular conception of an artist; but she had studied etching seriously with Sickert and had already published a short account of her nursing experiences in the war, called *Diary without Dates*. The Sitwells—Osbert, Edith and Sacheverell—came nearly every week. They usually arrived together but if they came singly, each would enquire anxiously for the others and once united, the family would settle down side by side, blissfully content.

W. H. Davies, the poet-tramp, was a great friend of the Sitwells, who treated him with exquisite solicitude. Everyone was sorry for him, as he had lost a leg in an accident, but he would have firmly repudiated any expressions of sympathy. He preferred to breakfast with Sickert rather than to join us on Wednesdays, when the Frith became too crowded for him. I think Davies got rather lost in London; he was essentially a countryman. His tweed coat, scrupulously neat, had a pleasantly peaty smell, his eyes seemed to be looking towards distant horizons, his speech was mournful and deliberate with a soft Welsh inflection, and he took his time about everything.

Epstein would look in sometimes on Wednesdays; he drifted in and out of our world as the spirit moved him. He was a great friend of Walter Taylor's and enjoyed tea parties in Oxford Square. I think it was while contemplating Taylor's water colours that he began to experiment in the medium for himself. Whatever the cause, it irritated him, fascinated him and haunted him with persistence. 'Water colour!' he exclaimed one day as we all left Taylor's house and proceeded to the bus stop. 'Water colour is a kid's game,' he declared, rapping his stick on the pavement. But when he came to tackle the despised medium himself he found it madly elusive and although it must have been a refreshing distraction from his other problems I always rather wonder why he persevered with it.

Epstein was by temperament a happy man, but he was also sensitive and he had a persecution complex, which was hardly surprising when one remembers the abuse that was showered on him when he was poor and struggling for recognition. Still smarting from the sense of injustice which the barbs of the critics had implanted, he was now hostile to all their tribe; when he was famous, and one of these gentlemen was complimenting him on a recent work, he retorted:

'Yesterday I sat on a bus and the conductor said—"You're Epstein aren't you?" "How do you know?" I asked. "I've seen your photo in the newspaper, you did that statue for the convent in Cavendish Square, didn't you? Well, I like it," replied the conductor.

'*That* pleased me,' added Epstein.

The reader will be relieved to know that there was a sprinkling of freaks, idlers, vagrants and humble people among these glittering constellations. Dear Mr Woad was not exactly a freak nor idler; we were a little vague about his activities, he might have been an undertaker or a tax collector or something of that sort but these occupations sound rather too strenuous for him; he seemed to have a good deal of free time in the afternoons. He wore a collar so extremely high that it appeared to choke him, and he always brought a large posy of flowers on Wednesdays for Christine, whom he revered above all women. Having presented his offering, he would sit down beaming with goodwill, prepared to enjoy himself, a hand on each knee. Mr Woad came from Holloway and was blessed with seven sisters, so Sickert promptly christened him 'Seven Sisters Woad'.[1] But at that time, from 1917 to 1918, he was living opposite, at Number 8. We were very glad to have him there; when we were occupying the Whistler, in 1918, I was terrified of the basement and the rats that I saw scurrying about at the foot of the long, dark, winding stairs, their eyes shining like red lamps in the dusk. Always the gallant, Mr Woad would brave the horrors below and empty my litter for me into the dustbin. My gratitude to him was boundless; unless he had rescued me I doubt if I should ever have found the courage to face the trip across the area to that dustbin and the return journey among the rodents.

But Mr Woad was rather a handful for the other inhabitants of Number 8. He persisted in smoking cigarettes in his large four-poster bed as he read himself to sleep, so that oft in the stilly night the whole house was awakened by roars from his room when he had set himself alight again. The other occupants, resigned but resourceful, took the emergency in their stride. Methodically, they advanced in mass formation from their various chambers with pitchers of water which they poured over Mr Woad, his bed and anything else that they could find, sousing him accordingly, and leaving him to dry off as best he could. Curiously enough Mr Woad bore them no ill will for saving his life once more; he was actually grateful for their ministrations. He still continued, however, to smoke in bed.

There was one intense female, whose surname I have forgotten; I only remember her as 'Helen', an ex-pupil from Rowlandson House days. For some reason Sickert considered it his duty to see her at intervals, as prolonged as he could contrive, but he made shameless use of us or anyone else who could be pressed into his service to help him to entertain her. One morning we lunched at Shoolbred's, when she was in a particularly exalted mood.

'You and I are so much in sympathy,' she assured him, 'that I feel we must have met in some former life.'

'Tiens,' said Sickert, immediately bored. 'Isn't it enough that we know each other *now*?'

During luncheon, his manner varied as it always did when he was bored, from

[1] For those who are not familiar with London, Seven Sisters Road is a very long road running north-east from Holloway Road to Stamford Hill High Road.

sudden exaggerated politeness to complete abstraction and the air hung heavy with silence. I thought, however, we might come through without disaster but before we left, Helen raised her lorgnette and swept the restaurant and its occupants in one encompassing glance.

'I suppose,' she asked him, 'that all these people are bourgeois?'

'And what the hell,' said Sickert, 'do you suppose *we* are?'

Sickert had tried to join up with the French Army in 1914 and was mortified to find himself rejected on account of his age, but by this time he was resigned to watch and wait and had completed his series of war pictures, beginning with 'Tipperary'. Sickert did more for the war effort than expressing it in paint. He was deeply interested in the younger generation; his efforts on behalf of the East London Group and art schools all over the country are well known. During the war years his studios in Fitzroy Street were swarming with khaki. Sickert gave these boys not only his models, paints and brushes without thought of payment, but his time, brains and energy in unstinting measure. They might receive drastic criticism and robust reproof but they also received encouragement and support, and they never hesitated to approach him.

A special protégé of Sickert's was a boy called Joe; I never knew his surname or whether he possessed any talent for painting. An ex-pupil from the Westminster, he was now a soldier, waiting to be sent to France. There was something very moving about Joe with his round, candid face, his shock of fair hair and his shy friendly smile; he had such a great capacity for happiness. Whenever he could get leave he would be present on Wednesdays with his girl; sitting side by side, they seldom spoke, and he had no eyes for anyone but the Master. He worshipped Sickert. I suppose no distinguished man had ever taken such an interest in him before. It was enough for him just to be there, listening and watching, in an ecstasy of wonder. His little companion would chatter away to Christine, telling her all they were going to do after the war; get married, of course, and then! It could not be much longer now.

But Joe was sent to France and in a few weeks he was lying dead with a bullet through his brain.

Christine wrote to his girl and asked her to come and see us on Wednesdays, just as before. The girl answered by thanking Christine for her invitation but she was sure she would understand, she didn't want to see Fitzroy Street or any of us, ever again.

After Sickert heard of the death of Joe he shut himself up for three days and would not open his door. When he emerged, he never spoke of Joe and no one dared to mention his name.

Sickert had four brothers, of whom he was the eldest. Walter Taylor used to say that he had stolen all the looks and energy that should have been shared out among them. But although it was true that the others were for the most part only echoes of Walter, they would have received more consideration had they not always suffered by comparison with him. Oswald, if not creative, had a keen critical intelligence; he travelled all over the world for an advertising agency connected with *The Times*, and made friends everywhere. Bernard took to the brush, after several false starts in life, aided and abetted by Walter. He was a 'prima' painter, quick to seize his first sensation before nature but unable to improve it by successive study, and it seemed that he had nothing much to say. He wrote, however, a good short account of Whistler, and Mrs Swanwick, the only sister of the family, also wrote; she published her memoirs in 1935 under the title *I Have Been Young*. Mrs Swanwick was a great suffragette and able committee woman, altogether too strong-minded for Sickert, with whom she had little in common; in fact, she rather alarmed him. He used to pretend, when he was talking about his childhood, that he would climb out of his cot in the nursery to pull her hair, but otherwise he never spoke of her and she did not visit him in Fitzroy Street.

Sometimes, Robert and Leonard Sickert joined us on Wednesdays. Robert Sickert was frail and gentle, with a faint ghostly resemblance to Walter; extremely thoughtful and intelligent but far too sensitive to face the battle of life. Fortunately, he was appreciated in his own quiet circle, being lavishly endowed with the family charm. Leonard Sickert, on the other hand, was sturdy enough but otherwise unlike his eldest brother. His head was bullet shaped, his hair cropped, his eyes a shade paler than Walter's, his whole colouring washed out, his figure rather short but stocky. Walter always referred to him as 'the independent dependant', remarking that 'it was no use being a professor of singing if you told your pupils that they hadn't got a voice when they hadn't got a voice' although this was precisely the sort of thing that he did himself whenever he had a mind to. He said once to a student after her second lesson at the Westminster, 'I shouldn't waste any more time here trying to paint if I were you.'

After the visitors left on Wednesdays, Robert and Leonard would linger round the fire and we all had another brew of tea. Sickert, unless he had relapsed into one of his silent moods, still led the conversation with his usual quips and jokes; he might, on rare occasions, start mimicking a guest who had just departed with such fiendish accuracy that Leonard once remarked:

'Oh Walter, how *glad* I am that I am not one of your friends!'

We, on the other hand, fairly revelled in his impersonations. It was not often that we got the chance to see them but these performances were so precise, so finished, that it seemed as if he must have been practising them all day, and when he was really in the vein, we might be able to coax him to take off one person after another. It was of course even more entertaining if we happened to know the victims. Roger Fry was one of his best turns but Fry, perhaps, was easy game, being a very mannered man. Sickert could give us all sorts of people from his vast circle, more difficult to impersonate than Fry because more stereotyped, from cabinet ministers and dowagers to chorus girls.

Leonard Sickert was not easy to know; one could guess nothing of his inner life, his friends, his interests, his opinions, as he never gave himself away. We were left with the impression that he did not find it worth while to reveal his true feelings about anything; the family secretiveness had taken a cynical turn with him. I cannot say how far he had succeeded with his profession; according to all reports, he had given many successful concerts but at this time he seemed to be drifting along without much purpose. A shining instance of his almost inhuman detachment occurred many years later, just before the Hitler war, when he and I were both present at a lecture on Sickert, sponsored by the L.C.C. No one knew that he was among the audience until afterwards and he never challenged any of the assertions about his famous brother, sometimes very wide of the mark, that ensued in question time. But although he might disagree entirely with the views that were being so freely canvassed by various speakers, he would not take the trouble to say so or to give us the benefit of his own information. As he was not in the least shy or tongue-tied, this attitude of the onlooker, not especially concerned with the game, seemed due to indolence, or perhaps, secret amusement that the audience could be so mistaken.

Chapter 7

Number 8

The shades of Whistler, Sickert, Augustus John and Duncan Grant haunt Number 8 Fitzroy Street; all of them worked here, although none of these painters had such constant associations with the place as Sickert. A plaque on the front of the old building, before it was demolished to make way for a block of offices, marked the passing of Octavia Hill but no mention was made of the painters it had harboured, or of their work. And since the demolition of the house in Granby Street where 'Ennui' was composed, there is no sign of the presence of Sickert anywhere in Fitzroy Street or Camden Town. Nor of Whistler either, so far as I am aware.

Number 8 was a very tall house and I do not remember who lived on the top floor, except Fred Porter, a painter who was a protégé of Roger Fry and a member of the London Group. Dora Sly rented a room on the next storey down. She was a young woman with an attractive Danish accent, and a part-time husband who lived at the Piccadilly Hotel and appeared occasionally in Fitzroy Street. Sickert used to call her 'the Fairy Queen on the top of the Christmas tree'; she was something of a mystery but as so many of the inhabitants of Number 8 were mysterious, we took her for granted with the rest. It was whispered that she was retrenching from luxurious interludes at the Piccadilly Hotel; there were dramatic suggestions that she was a decoy for Dr Sly, who was suspected of being involved in a gambling club in the West End. There was no proof whatever of all this gossip; all we really knew was that Dora would disappear to the Piccadilly for weeks on end and suddenly return to her bedsitter in her own good time.

She belonged to the Edwardian era of hourglass figures, flowers, lace, furbelows, curled fringes, long chains and plumed black hats. Even until the Hitler war, the Burlington Arcade was peopled by these sirens from a more voluptuous past, all waists and hips and bosoms, Parma violets pinned to their blouses, teetering along on tiny feet, their pekes tucked under their arms. Dora was the opposite of the pattern that was already emerging in the war, a pattern of flat chests, short skirts, spindly legs and tight helmets crammed down on cropped heads tricked out with perhaps one diamond arrow as a concession to ornament. And she was prettier than most of these new rivals with her pale yellow hair, grey eyes, clear as water, and rosy Dresden-shepherdess complexion.

But the chief thing that one remembers about Dora was her pluck. When Sly disappeared, as he was wont to do at intervals, it seemed that she was left to fend for herself; this she did to admiration until one bitter winter's day arrived, when she contracted pleurisy. The third floor back at Number 8 must then have seemed a very grim place indeed. Everyone did what he could. Walter Taylor brought fruit and flowers, Ginner produced bottles of stout, Chris cooked little dishes to tempt her feeble appetite, James Manson brought books, Sickert hauled buckets of coal up the winding stairs, leaving a black trail behind him on each step, while Dora languished in bed in her lace cap trimmed with cherry ribbons, looking absurdly pretty and plaintive.

After the sudden death of Sly, Dora fell on hard times. She left Fitzroy Street and re-married, to live comfortably if not happily for ever after. Soon, she wrote to us, inviting us to meet the new husband, who doted on Dora and could hardly bear her out of his sight. He did not need visitors or any other distractions; his idea of Paradise was to sit on one side of the chimney piece, indefinitely, with Dora at the other. But Dora had been used to a life of freedom for too long. Rigorous domesticity was not for her; she wilted rapidly under all this cherishing. The past became enveloped in a rosy mist, she forgot the hardships and the money worries and thought only of the gay life she had left, the sense of purpose underlying the lightheartedness of Fitzroy Street, her adventures with the brilliant and unreliable Sly.

At least, she could now indulge her taste for pictures. She collected moderns, mostly of the French school; her Sisley was important and she also owned a good Sickert, a crescent in Bath.

I had seen him at work on this picture. With a few full brush strokes, he had painted a taxi in the middle of the crescent because he felt he needed a dark patch of colour in that particular place, then changed his mind and knocked it out, then replaced it again, all in a few minutes. Dining with Dora in her new home, I would remember this as I gazed at the crescent, and the taxi seemed to twinkle in and out of the great yellow sweep of buildings like the beam from a lighthouse, as I had seen it vanish and grow again under his hands.

The new husband did not live long and Dora was alone again, this time in a big house and her second world war. Her pictures were flooded after an air raid and badly damaged, her friends all scattered, and Dora herself was now so frail that she could hardly endure fresh rigours. But with her usual courage she served as an air raid warden or, for her, something equally preposterous; I remember sadly our last meeting when she was all rigged out in uniform, her little face and flaxen hair half hidden under an intimidating crash helmet.

Soon afterwards, she died too. But one could never imagine Dora old.

Sickert complained that Dr Sly's moustache was too black and his collar was too high. He resembled exactly, in fact, the stage villain of Victorian drama or possibly, had one ever been privileged to meet that sinister being, Dr Fell. But Sickert always had a soft spot for him and Ginner had assured us that Sly could be charming.

We found Sickert in the hall at Number 8 one day, looking most elegant in his new navy blue suit. He announced that he was just off to Pentonville.

'Going to see the Guv'nor,' we supposed. We knew that he enjoyed an occasional luncheon with the Governor of the prison.

'No. I'm visiting my old friend Sly who has been detained there,' he explained, polite but preoccupied.

'In quad,' he added briefly, as he disappeared through the front door.

Another old friend of Dora's who frequented Number 8 was James Bolivar Manson, writer, painter, lecturer and Director of the Tate. Dora was always a staunch ally; her advice and sympathy were particularly valuable to Manson. He was a gifted creature with a distinguished presence, gay, witty and charming, the life and soul of the company when he felt at home in it. But he was subject to fits of depression, partly due to weather and partly to a deeper cause, the frustration of the painter with no time to paint. I used to meet him as I met Roger Fry, jogging along in our omnibus to the West End on winter mornings, I to Fitzroy Street from my home in Regent's Park, he to the Tate. He was a very different companion from the suave and equable Fry. A creature of impulse, he needed the sun of southern climes, blue skies, flowers and birdsong, a paintbrush in his hand. Not for him the gloomy splendours of London which inspired Sickert. A bleak mood usually enveloped him on these cold raw mornings and there were days when it was impossible to cheer him.

Once, we argued about his house in Hampstead Garden Suburb. I declared that it was a nice house, airy and sunny.

'No it's not,' he replied crossly, 'it's a nasty little house. I live in it because I can't afford anything better and you know it.'

Sensitive, easily cast down, he took criticism very much to heart. One evening, when he was seeing me home after an evening with Dora and we were musing over the other guests at her party, he remarked suddenly: 'Dr X doesn't like me.' It seemed odd that he should suspect this, as Dr X had always been studiously polite to him and I wondered that he, with his engaging personality, should trouble himself about the hostility of an acquaintance, even if it existed. But hostility, however veiled, was like a hairshirt against his skin to Manson. It brought out a perverse streak in him; he made no effort to adapt himself to uncongenial company or to conceal his boredom. This was unfortunate when he found himself at official functions. As long as he was able to devote a few hours here and there to painting, the exercise of his gifts steadied him; but time went on, his duties at the Tate grew heavier, painting hours grew less and Manson was more and more inclined to flout Mrs Grundy.

Dora was always uneasy when he was due to attend some important function. '*Do* be careful, Jimmy,' she begged him. 'Promise me you'll be careful.' He promised her in all good faith that he would be as good as gold but alas, 'cheerfulness was always breaking in.' When the fateful day came, he might be so oppressed by the solemnity of the meeting that he could contain himself no longer

7—S

and as usual, began to be too much at home. Official occasions were even stiffer in those days than they are now; a super-human gravity masked the proceedings. Any sign of disapproval would only fan the flame of mockery in Manson; he may have brought a breath of fresh air along with him but his colleagues were not always grateful for this; they found his flippancies misplaced. As, no doubt, they were. When he felt especially reckless he would sing about 'A Bird in a Gilded Cage', a Victorian ditty which delighted him, summing up as it did his own predicament; but it was less acceptable to his august confrères. Or he might even execute a little *pas-de-seul* on the parquet floors. But if he did not exhibit a becoming seriousness about public meetings he was always serious about painting. Apart from his passionate interest in French Impressionism, which perhaps became too much of an obsession, he took almost as keen an interest in the younger generation as Sickert did and helped them whenever an opportunity arose. He gave up much of his precious time in the evenings to his disciples and they in their turn were devoted to Manson. He resembled Sickert in some ways; neither of them were at their best if their surroundings were too formal, although Sickert could keep up an air of intense solemnity longer than Manson; neither of them had any flair whatever for advertising themselves or their contributions to the common weal. Manson especially was lacking in the gentle art of getting on. He did not seize his opportunity to recommend himself when he was at the Tate; he made no use of the publicity that the post conferred upon him, although before the days of television that publicity was much less than it is now. Of his administrative capacity I am not qualified to speak but as painter, teacher and writer he has received scant recognition, has in fact been almost ignored. He was a classic instance of the square peg in the round hole, the failure of a certain kind of artist to adjust himself to bureaucracy.

To return to Number 8; the Whistler, which Sickert lent Chris and me for the afternoons in 1918, was a huge room at the back of the first floor of that vast rambling rookery of a house; one reached it by winding passages and steps turning odd corners that seemed to double on themselves; strangers seldom managed to find their way through the labyrinth without assistance. But when one did finally arrive, the picture was unexpected. One was transplanted suddenly from the mundane present to the heart of the eighteenth century. Number 8 had been of no account for years; it was not worth anyone's while to interfere with the character of the place, so that its atmosphere was unchanged. I doubt if there was another room with more echoes of the Georgian era in all London. Spacious, beautifully proportioned, rather dark, with long windows looming through the dusk and misty looking-glasses on the high walls, it held secrets that were all its own. We greatly preferred it to Number 15, the great barn of a room on the opposite side of the street which seemed remarkable for little but its size and association with Frith, although Sickert clung to it longer than to any of his fastnesses. The Frith seemed bald and empty in the morning light, whereas the Whistler never lost its air of mystery and grace and here, with great banked fires leaping in the cavernous grates and candles shedding soft beams over floors and ceiling, the setting was perfect for parties. Against the sombre background, the heads of the women and the colours of their gowns stood out more clearly than they ever did in bright ballrooms; as the evening wore on, the filmy blue haze of candlelight, firelight and cigarette smoke softened their features and lent romance to the most prosaic faces. The Whistler then seemed to be floating in a golden dream, like Hogarth's 'Ball at Wanstead Assembly', surely the most poetic rendering of a party ever painted . . .

But at four o'clock on a winter's afternoon the darkness of the great studio might seem overpowering, almost sinister. Some of my friends who did manage to grope their way through the maze of passages at teatime would exclaim: 'How can you bear to be here so late, all alone?' They looked mystified when I declared that I would rather work there than anywhere else. Many people were attached to the Whistler; as for me, I loved it with passion.

For music at parties, we were beholden to Ethelbert White and Claud Marx, with their songs and guitars. Ethelbert White is a well known landscape painter; as a young man he was a follower of the hedgerow school and he has left for posterity many touching reminders, in water colour, woodcut and oils, of the loveliness of the vanished English countryside. He has given us joyous interpretations of Surrey; he has a caravan at Shere, where his output has been considerable; for my part I hanker after his limpid studies of Suffolk, all tumbling skies, water and trees, painted directly and simply with a full fluent brush. Roaming over farms and woodlands, hills and byways, living with his subjects, he knows England in her most capricious moods and has a depth of country lore which marks the born *paysagiste*. Sir Charles Wheeler has described him as our first lyrical water colourist and although he is now an elderly man he is still young in spirit, painting with the same eagerness.

But it is not so generally known that he has a musical turn as well; accompanying himself on the guitar, he still sings very sweetly, dramatically when the fancy takes him. His good nature at parties was inexhaustible; he was in demand everywhere, but he treated each party as if it were the gayest he had ever attended; he and Marx would carry on hour after hour with ditties, dances and *flamenco*, which his wife danced for us as well. Betty White, like her husband, has defied the years; she has always identified herself with his interests, sharing the caravan at Shere in all weathers, reading aloud to him when he wanted to rest his eyes, sitting by his side all through the night at parties, prompting him if he had by chance forgotten some word or other in his song. Of late years she has begun to paint and has shown a number of her flower pieces in various exhibitions.

The Whites had collected all kinds of songs, from Irish ballads to sea shanties; their repertoire seemed endless. Having travelled all over Europe, they had opportunities of hearing strange old tunes and melodies which were gradually being forgotten and they memorized them on the spot, Betty taking care of the words and Ethelbert taking care of the music. But it was not always necessary to go far afield for this purpose; sometimes an ancient song from our own country would be rescued from oblivion. In a little pub on one of the old quays of Bristol, Augustus John heard a sailor singing a ditty which he had never heard before. It had been handed down by word of mouth for so long that its origin was forgotten, but John preserved it on the spot and presented it afterwards to Ethelbert. He and Claud Marx rendered it with just the right touch of melancholy.

'In Newry Town I was bred and born
In Newgate Jail I'll die with scorn
I served my time at the saddler's trade
But I always was a roving blade.

'At seventeen, I took a wife
And loved her as I loved my life
And for to keep her bright and gay
A'roving I went on the King's Highway.

'I robbed Lord Golding I do declare
And Lady Mansfield of Grosvenor Square
I shut up the shutters and bid 'em good night
And I carried home gold to my heart's delight.

'Now when I am dead and gone to my grave
A decent funeral let me have
With six highwaymen to carry me
Give them broadswords and sweet liberty . . .'

No one sang *Frankie and Johnnie* better than Ethelbert White, or that nostalgic refrain:

'A Rovin', a rovin',
Since rovin's been my ru-i-in,
I'll go no more a rovin'
With you fair maid—'

No Fitzroy Street party, however, would have been complete without 'She was poor but she was honest'. Foreigners complain that England has no folklore but we can always confound them with this immortal ditty:

'She was poor, but she was honest
Victim of the Squire's crime

For he wooed and he betrayed her
And she lost her honest nime.'

When it came to the chorus

'It's the same the whole world over
It's the same thing every time
It's the rich wot gits the pleasure
It's the poor wot gits the blime.'

Ethelbert and Mark intoned it in the true cockney whine, Ethelbert's forelock
leaping about and his eyes flashing with righteous wrath as he related the wrongs
of the rural maid, deserted by her lover and cast upon the town.

But old Taylor preferred the third verse

'See him riding in his kerridge
In the Park and all so gay
With the swells and nobby persons
For to pass the time of day.'

'What *is* a nobby person?' he asked.

'You are,' I explained.

'Oh,' said Taylor.

This ditty amused Robert Bevan immensely. He was one of the more important members of the Camden Town Group, a small band of rebels who had
decided to break with the New English Art Club. If I have had little to say about
the Camden Towners it is because they have been so efficiently dealt with
elsewhere and Sickert's interest in the group was not exclusive, as in the case of so
many members; Gilman for instance, thought that no one counted outside it. In
fact, they were greatly neglected in their own day; they merged later with the
larger London Group, which brought in such forceful personalities as Epstein and
David Bomberg. But there was a great deal of talent in the original Camden
Town Group and they are slowly but surely gaining ground today, when it is
increasingly difficult to buy the work of Innes or Gore or Gilman or, for that
matter, most of the members of the group. Greatly influenced as some of them
were in their earlier work by Sickert, they launched out for themselves and
became individual painters; it would be difficult to imagine two more different
points of view than those of, say, Gilman and Wyndham Lewis.

Robert Bevan had wider interests than the average British artist of his time. He
had studied abroad and known Gauguin, and he was greatly helped by his wife,
Stasia Karlowska, a Polish girl whom he met in Paris and pursued to Poland to
her country house, determined to marry her. She told me that she was combing her
hair when she heard the clatter of hoofs in the courtyard and looked through the

window to see the rider and dropped the comb in surprise, saying 'Why, that's my Englishman!' This pursuit must have been most flattering; Bevan had travelled many versts across Poland to find her, but her father was not so impressed, he wanted to know more about this young Lochinvar before he gave his consent to the marriage. But of course they married eventually and Stasia Karlowska traversed Europe to lead her new life in a strange country and battle with an alien tongue; she always found English difficult to pronounce, like Joseph Conrad. But she was the greatest asset to Bevan; a painter herself, she could sympathize with his work and they liked the same friends, entertaining all kinds of artists at their house in London and helping the other members of the group. But Bevan did not give his friendship readily. He took his time about it, and was careful not to commit himself until he had made up his mind. Once he had decided to go ahead, he was a friend for life and would take endless trouble to prove it.

He used to take up his stance at our parties by the chimney piece, having arranged his glass of beer and smoking apparatus on the shelf with deliberation. From this advantageous position he could observe in the looking glass before him every newcomer who entered the door. Bevan was no equalitarian, and Fitzroy Street at this time was full of gate crashers who descended like locusts on neighbouring parties, to consume as much as possible of the food and drink before the invited guests arrived. He felt it was his duty to see that Chris and I were not exploited by these people and he subjected each guest to a prolonged glare, to assure himself that they were presentable. Sometimes, when he was doubtful of their respectability, he would question us loudly about them in his own particular brand of Anglo-French, much to their joy if they happened to understand him.

He was a versatile painter, concerned chiefly when young with horses (see plate 20), but his landscapes, especially of Poland, were far more colourful than those of most English painters of his time and today he is also much appreciated as a draughtsman and for his lithographs. He and his wife are both represented at the Tate and in spite of a long marriage, Stasia Karlowska's work always kept its charming Polish flavour.

Valérie Cooper lived on the ground floor at Number 8. Everyone knew Valérie; she belonged to no clique. She was a teacher at the Jacques Dalcroze School of Eurhythmics and worked hard at her profession, taking long journeys every week into the provinces. But in spite of this arduous toil and the fact that she had no private means, she managed to keep open house for her large circle of friends and even for acquaintances who descended upon her at all hours and often kept her up half the night. Nobody ever considered whether she might be tired, nor did she remind them of the possibility. Coming of sturdy East Anglian stock, she enjoyed burning the candle at both ends; into the wasted air of London she brought a breath of the country with her rosy, choirboy face, steady blue eyes and thatch of goldish-brown hair, cut in a thick fringe across her forehead. She must have been uncommonly strong to survive the social clatter that followed her wherever she went but she always seemed as fresh at the end of her parties as at the beginning. She was one of those rare souls who are blessed with radiant health and can take liberties with it, when and where they will. In any case, she had little time to think about herself, as there was always some lame duck or other waiting to be propped up and fortified. Sometimes these people took her kindness as a right and forgot it as soon as possible but occasionally, when she cast her bread upon the waters, the gesture was truly appreciated. I suppose no more unsuitable epithet than lame duck could be devised to fit Matthew Smith, brilliant and established painter as he was at this time, somewhere in 1923; but even prominent painters are not always very good at taking care of themselves. It was a bitterly cold morning when Valérie first met him, drifting towards her from his studio in Charlotte Street. He was so white and shaken that she stopped him to enquire how he did, with her usual solicitude.

'You look ill,' she said. 'I feel like death,' he confessed, shivering in the wind. 'I've just had flu.' 'Have you eaten any breakfast?' No, he hadn't felt like breakfast. Knowing that he would probably recoil from bacon and eggs, Valérie took him back with her to her studio, planted him by the red-hot stove and gave him tea, toast and plenty of porridge. When he took his grateful leave some hours later she forgot all about the matter, but next day he called on her with one of his pictures under his arm, which he presented to her in return for her thoughtfulness. Matthew Smith was noted for his generosity and Valérie treasured this instance of it. It was a fruit piece of a large green melon, now owned by the Renaissance Society at Richmond.

After this, Matthew Smith came often to her parties. Her studio was at the back of the ground floor, deliciously warm in winter with the huge stove jutting out into the room but not so far that it interfered with our dancing. Matthew took his pleasure seriously; between us, we taught him the two-step but although Valérie was a professional dancer and would have been only too happy to instruct him, he would not commit himself to the intricacies of the waltz. We must have looked comic, prancing solemnly round to the strains of the two-step, but we were not considered funny then. Two-stepping was still the thing.

On a short acquaintance, no one would have suspected, from his mild and friendly exterior, the hidden fires within. Matthew Smith saw and heard all kinds of outrageous things without turning a hair but once, when he was confronted by a flashy and pretentious painting upon which he was called to pronounce a blessing, a sort of electric shock ran through him, his eyes blazed, the very hairs of his skin seemed to rise in protest, although the effect only lasted a few moments; he soon regained control of himself, turning his back on the offending object with a shudder. I realized then the connection which had often puzzled me before between this diffident, gentle man and his fiery, bold, colourful painting, and how much painting meant to him.

His life, on the whole, was tragic in spite of fame and recognition, although he mastered the tragedy almost to the end. His childhood was unhappy, partly owing, I think, to his introspective nature. He was a fish out of water in his native Halifax, his father was not in sympathy with him, he longed to paint but received no encouragement. Later, when he had fought his way to the Slade, Tonks was unkind and refused to see any promise in his work.

'What in the world made *you* think of taking up painting? I give you six months to see what you can do.'

Tonks must have been in one of his worst tempers when he said this and it was hardly one of his more intelligent remarks, as six months is an absurdly short time for anyone to make good in painting. But the snub had a parlous effect on Smith and I think might have seriously retarded his progress, but that he went off to Brittany, settled in Pont Aven, and as he said to us and to Sir John Rothenstein later, 'here, my life began.'

We always felt that Matthew was a family man *manqué*. Whatever had gone wrong with his marriage to Gwen Salmon, a gifted Slade student, no one would ever know; but he needed a home and seemed helpless at supplying himself with one on his wanderings. His two boys were his last link with domesticity. I remember a private view of his pictures which I attended, I think it must have been about 1927; the little boys were rolling about the floor of the gallery like puppies. They were both killed flying in the Battle of Britain, before they were twenty, within a fortnight of each other. When the second son was killed the two shocks rolled into one and Matthew collapsed. Some friends took him down to the Gower coast in South Wales, then mercifully quiet and lonely, and used to plant him in the mornings in a deck chair by the sea. When they went back to collect him in the afternoons they would find him as they left him, slumped in his chair in the same position. I do not think his painting was ever the same after this.

A word about the landlord. Always in the background, quiet but indispensable, Hubert moved among us. I would look up from my work at Number 8 to see him outside our window, a quaint little barrel of a man, crawling perilously across his steep ancient roofs to see that they were watertight, deedy with hammer and nails on the stairs or in the passages, or receiving our tardy rent in his sitting-room on the ground floor.

A school of thought has obstinately persisted which maintains that although the butcher, the baker, the grocer, the undertaker should be recompensed for services rendered, the wicked landlord should house his tenants free or so nearly free that the so-called rent is an affront to his intelligence. This delusion was never more clearly shown than in the case of our landlord, Mr Hubert. Chris and I paid him an absurdly small rent; we occupied a light, largish room at Number 8 for years, for the ridiculous sum of seven and sixpence a week, which, I blush to record, was often in arrears, although we always paid up in the end. We took him for granted, like the rest of the *quartier*. Very often his tenants flitted without warning; his bad debts must have been terrific. Or they would sub-let their rooms

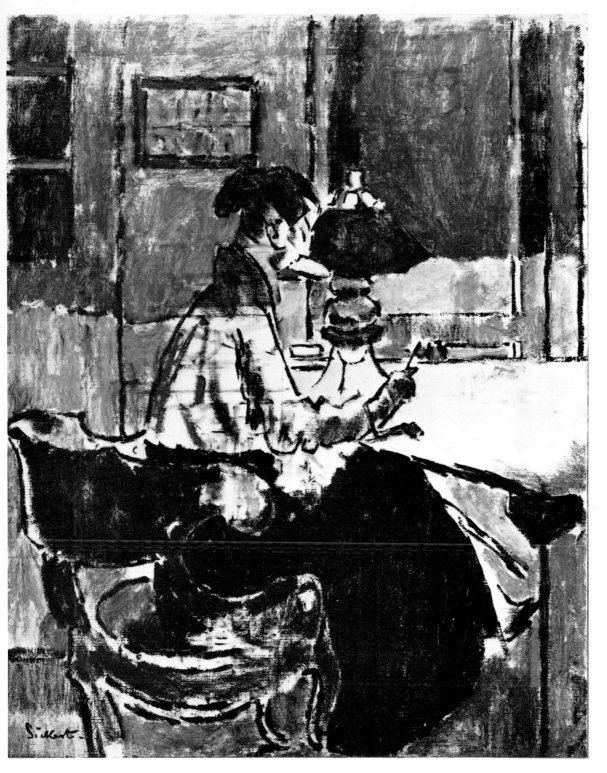

19. Walter Richard Sickert (1860–1942).
CHRISTINE BUYS A GENDARMERIE, 1919. Oil.

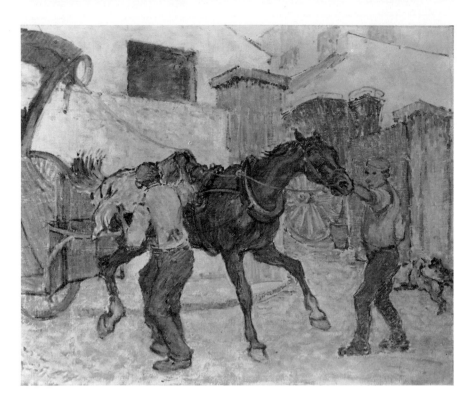

20. Robert Bevan (1865–1925). THE CAB HORSE, exh. 1910. Oil. 25 × 30 ins.
Tate Gallery, London

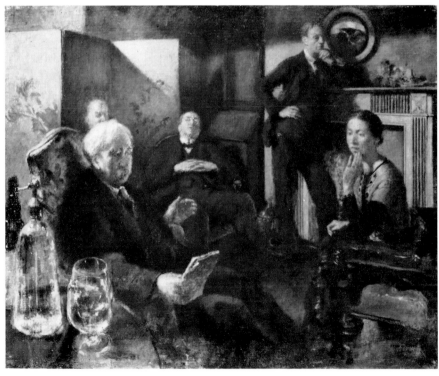

21. Henry Tonks (1862–1937). SATURDAY NIGHT IN THE VALE, 1928–9. Oil. 20¼ × 24 ins.
Tate Gallery, London

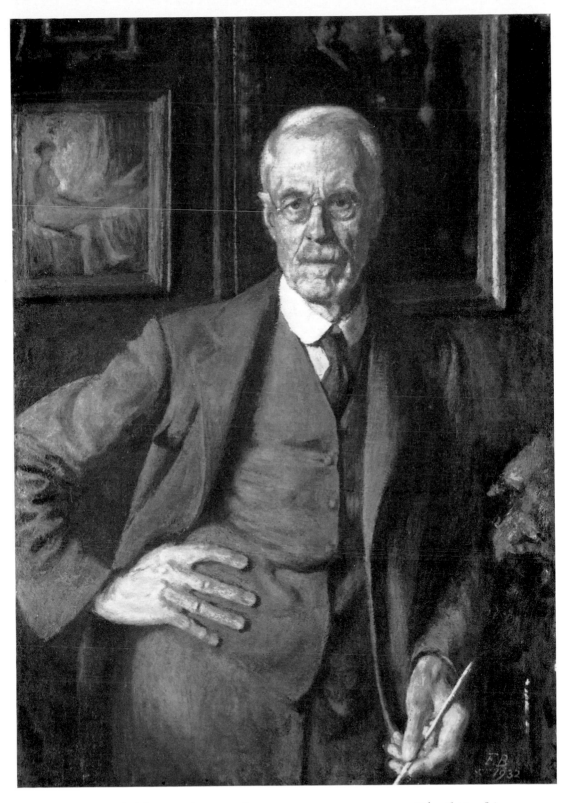

22. Frederick Brown (1851–1941). PORTRAIT OF THE PAINTER, 1932. Oil. 36¼ × 25¾ ins.
Tate Gallery, London

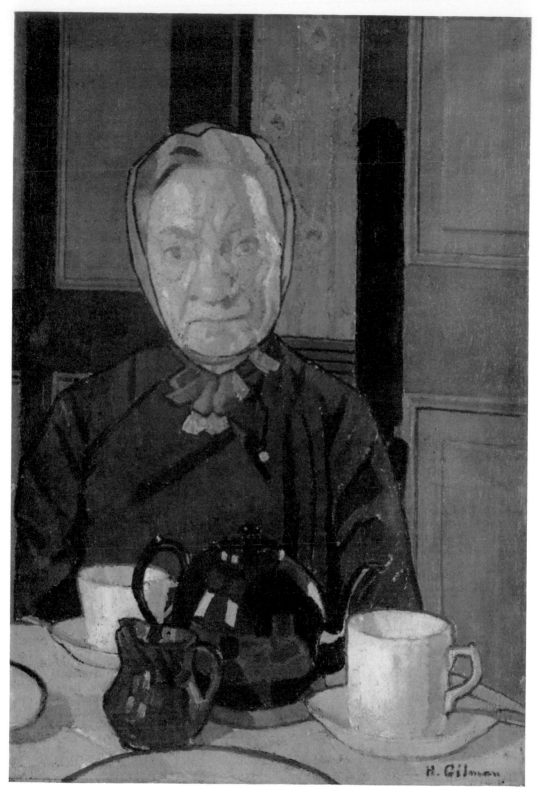

23. Harold Gilman (1876-1919)
MRS MOUNTER AT THE BREAKFAST TABLE, exh. 1917. Oil. 24 × 16 ins.
Tate Gallery, London

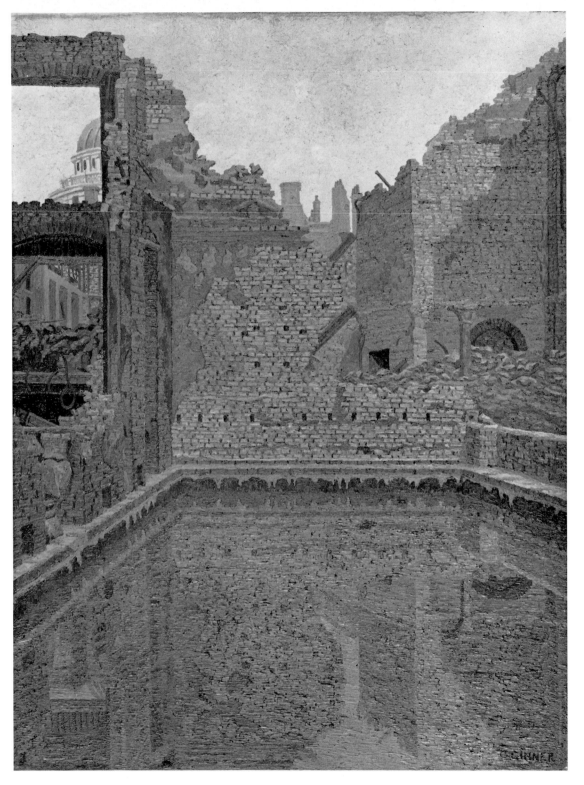

24. Charles Ginner (1878-1952).
EMERGENCY WATER STORAGE TANK, 1941-2. Oil. 27 × 20 ins.
Tate Gallery, London

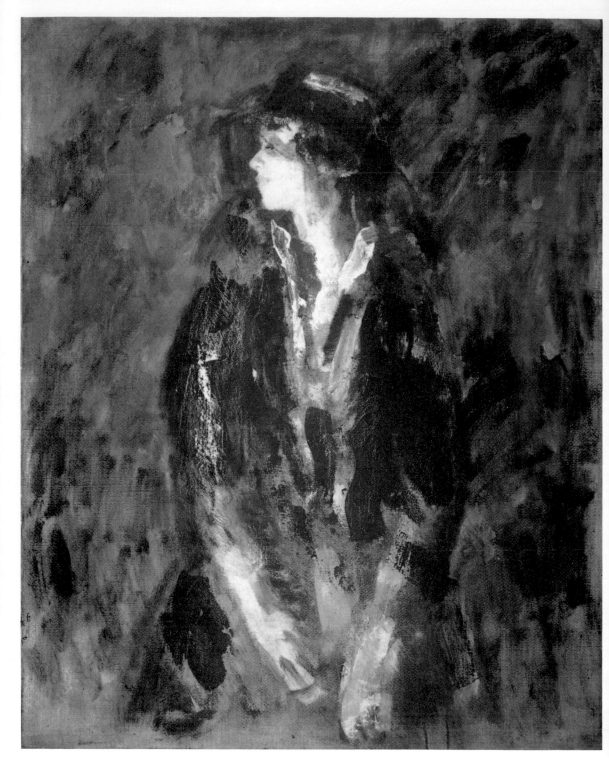

25. Ambrose McEvoy (1878-1927).
THE HON. MRS CECIL BARING, *c.* 1917. Oil. 50 × 40½ ins.
Tate Gallery, London

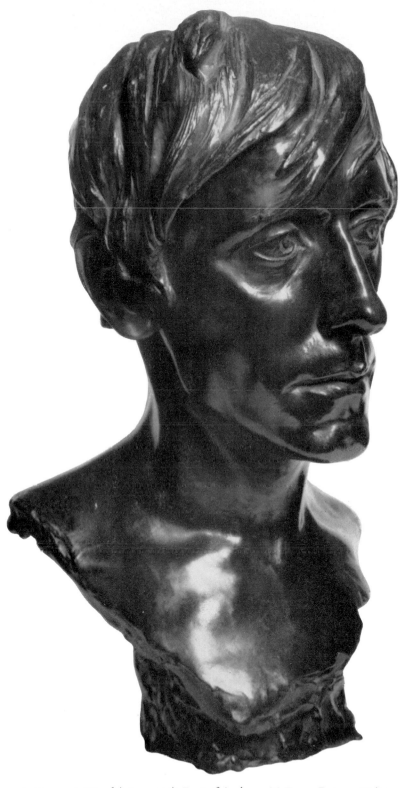

26. Derwent Wood (1871-1926). Bust of Ambrose McEvoy. Bronze. 17 ins.
Royal Academy of Arts, London

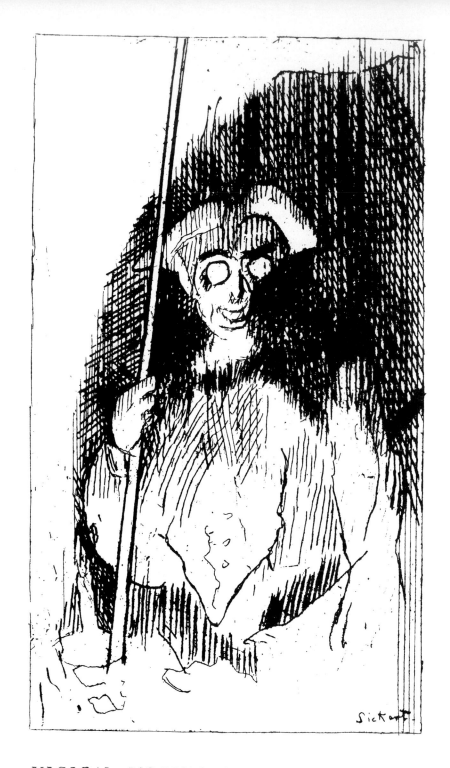

VISION VOLUMES AND RECESSION

27. Walter Richard Sickert (1860–1942).
VISION, VOLUMES AND RECESSION, *c.* 1911. Etching. $7\frac{3}{4} \times 4\frac{1}{4}$ ins.
A caricature of Roger Fry, making fun of his lectures on Cézanne
and the abstract qualities of painting. *Islington Public Libraries*

to all and sundry without having the courtesy to let him know about the matter. I never heard him grumble and he never once reminded me when my miserable contribution was grossly overdue. In fact, the only approach to firm action that I ever knew him to take was once when I told him we were giving a party, and asked his permission. It was granted, but with conditions. 'No orgies, mind!' said Hubert severely, shaking a fat minatory finger at me. Here, he did not display his usual acumen. He had had, no doubt, some wild spirits to cope with in his time but orgies presupposed a lavish flow of alcohol and our modest assortment of beer, cider, and perhaps a bottle or two of whisky was hardly on such a scale that any of our guests could indulge in Bacchanalian excesses.

I liked going round to Number 6 to pay up because the Hubert parlour was a fascinating place and I enjoyed my chats with his wife, a little blue-eyed creature as paper-thin as Hubert was plump. Situated at the back of the house on the ground floor overlooking his decrepit chimney-pots, it was crammed from floor to ceiling with everything you would expect; a Victorian sideboard complete with biscuit barrel and cakestand, crochet mats, an aspidistra in the window, oleographs on the walls which were so darkened with soot that the original pattern of the wall was obscured; gas brackets and an enormous contrivance with a deep red shade hanging over the round table in the middle of the room; a yawning fireplace where a coal fire blazed away in the winter and a shaggy black rug on the hearth with—yes, with the fat black cat that one would expect to round off the picture curled up across it, which always seemed asleep. All this and more too, pervaded with a general odour of dog, cat, biscuits, food, dust, fog and the unmistakable, overall, unique smell of Fitzroy Street. One remembers Hubert's parlour so clearly because one often had to wait some time while Mrs Hubert searched for the scratchy pen and the clogged inkwell to sign the rent book; time enough to absorb the surroundings.

Hubert was very proud of his oleographs, but it is a sobering thought that if he had not been so faithful to them he might have assembled a collection of modern pictures in no time which would have secured him a cosy old age, independent of tiresome tenants, delayed rents, decaying roofs, burst pipes and all the other thousand and one irritants by which the landlord is singled out for affliction. He need not have taken the trouble to hang his bargains either; he could have nursed them in a cupboard until he decided to sell them. I never heard him on the work of the *quartier;* I am sure he held it very cheap. He might have landed a Matthew Smith or two, had he possessed even the ordinary amount of guile; he could certainly have acquired important Sickerts in lieu of rent, and canvases by many other less august but promising performers.

Chapter 8

Wives

Ellen Cobden Sickert, the daughter of the politician, Richard Cobden, is a remote figure. She married Sickert in 1885 and they were divorced in 1899. Any further information about her that I have been able to collect is a little vague, rather perhaps a little dead; those who might have brought her to life by recounting their memories of her have also died and I have only hearsay to help me to describe her. There seem to be scarcely any records of her appearance; it is odd that Sickert did not draw and paint his wives more frequently. He was as vague about the look of Ellen as he was about everything else concerning her on the few occasions when he would begin, suddenly, to speak of his first marriage; rarely did he rouse himself to be more explicit. But he referred more than once to her hair. 'That was *hair*,' he would murmur, more to himself than to us.

'What colour was it?' Chris asked him.

'What colour?' He waved his hands as if to explain the colour. Then he added slowly, 'It had lights, it had lights.'

Once he went further. 'She used to scold me sometimes. And she went very pink when she was angry . . . a sort of carnation . . . charming. I had to fetch my palette and state the tone . . .'

Miss Madeleine Whyte, a cousin of Lady Churchill, was not more forthcoming. She had once lived with Ellen Sickert for six months and when I visited her at St Andrews I found an interesting reminder of the Sickerts—a wedding present to them from Whistler. It was a luxurious wardrobe, designed and painted in green and white by the Butterfly himself; it seemed to bring the Sickerts nearer to see this speaking relic of their marriage. But although Miss Whyte was very patient with my questioning, she had little to say about the first Mrs Walter. She did not find her brilliant or handsome or interesting. She did not remember much of her conversation, her opinions, her prejudices, she was just Nellie. Arthur Clifton, one of the few others who might have enlightened us on the subject, was equally detached; she had made, it seemed, no particular impression on him. And yet she must have been a woman of character to have risked marriage with a man so much younger than herself and to have encouraged his work for so many years before their way of life became incompatible. She was a fashionable hostess and a personality in her own right when he met her, with a large circle of friends, although her taste in people was less catholic than his, and she had a literary streak.

As usual, proud and delighted when anyone connected with him did or said anything at all worth mentioning, he brought the novel that she had written for us to read. The hero, of course, was Sickert himself. I remember one outstanding fact in the story; that he would disappear at intervals, perhaps for weeks, and turn up again suddenly as if he had never been away. (This tendency to vanish seems to have lapsed while he was married to his second wife, Christine, but it reappeared in his old age, after he became the husband of Thérèse Lessore. When the Sickerts were living at Brighton, Thérèse came to his friend, Mrs Wylde, to ask her if she knew where Walter was as she had not seen or heard from him for a week.) It is probable that this urge for privacy widened the breach between him and Ellen. She may have been more exacting than the self-effacing Christine or Thérèse, the only wife who was herself a painter and could appreciate his reasons for seeking solitude. But Ellen was fully aware of the importance of his gifts, and heart and soul for his career; she did not try to keep him dancing attendance on her and her friends when he should have been working, indeed when they were first married she was disturbed by his nonchalant attitude, fearing that society might prove too much for him and ruin his painting. For this reason, she did not want him to have much money to spend. 'Walter works better when he is hard up,' she remarked. There seems to have been a doubt at the time among fellow artists as to whether he would do justice to his gifts and work as hard as he ought to. But Sickert in his youth did not really need the spur of poverty to goad him to further endeavour; the inner urge, if pent up for long, would always drive him back to the easel. He knew that much was expected of him by Degas, who was impressed by his power, and that when he was about twenty-five, Whistler had said at a party, pointing to him, 'There is the young man of the future.' Although he played hard, he worked harder; as he would paint through the night or put in several hours before breakfast on the actual execution of the idea, once it had matured, the work always got done. People had not yet perceived that he was often working while he was amusing himself and that neither women nor song—wine may be discounted as a minor temptation—could deflect him for long from his chosen course.

He told us that divorce from Ellen was the last thing he wanted. It distressed him so much that he left the country.

Ellen was fragile; she spent much time on sofas. At the end of the famous sofa epoch so triumphantly sponsored by Charlotte M. Yonge and Elizabeth Barrett Browning, delicacy was still in vogue. One received, propped with pillows, in a hushed interior with shaded lights; attendant swains hovered, solicitous, with nosegays. It all seemed very far removed indeed from world war number one. We wondered how it would be to recline in state, showered with floral tributes; it sounded a little dull but it might do for a change from serving meals in an open hut in Regent's Park at four o'clock in the morning. It was fascinating to find, when Sickert described the proceedings to us, that he took it all for granted as the order of the day, but imagination failed us when we tried to picture him as part of that twilight atmosphere. It seemed, however, that it did really happen; young, glittering, vital, he did really burst into that silent sea.

During my last visit to him at Bath I gained a clearer impression of Ellen than I had done before. A sketch of her that he had drawn at the time of his marriage hung above his bed, which I could study at my leisure. He had once referred to her as 'pretty, absurdly pretty' and this careful little head bore him out. It revealed a conventional yet poetic prettiness, a heart-shaped face with small childish features, with the expression one sees on the faces of Botticelli's women, sweet yet complaining, framed in the famous hair.

Of his three wives, it is Christine Drummond Angus, whom Sickert married in 1911, who begins to emerge now most clearly from the shades; her brave figure, undermined but undefeated by physical weakness, is a shining instance of time's revenges. Odd that we have no important portrait of her from his hand. There is 'Christine Buys a Gendarmerie', (plate 19) which brings out her exotic quality but is more picture than portrait; it conveys to admiration her erect poise, her deliberation, the way she handled things, but there is, to my knowledge, no painting of her by her husband commensurate with the fine record he has left of his third wife, Thérèse Lessore.

When we met Christine, in 1917, she had been married for six years. Always reserved, she was now retreating into a sombre world of her own, from which she emerged at intervals to endure as best she could the frightening demands of London in wartime. No one, least of all her husband, realized quite how ill she was becoming. The relentless consumption that killed her had already sapped her energies; strangers, sitting through her long silences, thought her moody when she was merely too exhausted for speech. During their engagement, her family had warned Sickert of the weakness that threatened her, but his only answer was: 'All the more reason that I should look after her.' With his persistent fancy for delicate women he meant every word of it, although it was not always possible for him to carry out his intentions. He did his best to meet her faltering pace but when I first knew her she was already coming to the stage when she would need incessant care and Sickert had to earn his living; her tiny income would not stretch far enough to cover him. War or no war, however, she managed somehow to provide a home for them both where he would find the comfort that was lacking in Fitzroy Street.

They were both eager to return to France. The longer they stayed in London, the more involved they became with persons and things, and it was easier for her to rest in the country. Although, for his sake, she struggled to preside over the Wednesday gatherings, Fitzroy Street, with its clutter of rookeries that served for studios, was not her setting. I do not think she liked even the Whistler, that paradise of painters; it certainly required seven maids with seven mops to keep it clean and she shared Sickert's passion for cleanliness. 'One must always observe the daily routine of the bath.' But his business, obviously, could not be carried on in the sort of surroundings that were necessary for her. 'You must have one presentable room and a pigsty.' It was unthinkable that Christine should suffer the pigsty or the sinister garrets that were the source of some of his finest work. Yet she was in sympathy with his aims and her taste was sure. Her embroidery was good by professional standards, her drawing sensitive; one year, she designed a Christmas card, the subject of which was children singing carols, in the manner of Walter Crane. Sickert was so proud of this feat that he delivered the cards himself on Christmas Eve at the front doors of her friends.

When she was well enough, she enjoyed formal dinner parties where she could display her flair for dress. She told us one day about a chalk-white brocade gown, looped with cherry ribbons, that she intended to wear for an especial occasion and, as she described it, we looked bemused; accustomed as we were to years of wartime winters, this sounded a thought daring. But as she always looked right, whatever she wore, we concluded that it would probably suit her to admiration. Unfortunately, she did not have enough high life to refresh her. Even after four years of war there were still some lavish entertainments being held in London, but Sickert was apt to dodge large parties; he preferred meeting a few intimates in a smaller setting, where he could be silent or chatty as the fancy took him. Sometimes, he would refuse invitations that she would have liked to accept because he forgot how much she would have enjoyed them; but he did go to great houses now and then, to please her, and the ease, the glitter, the colour, did her good; it was a blessed interlude from the rigours of war.

She was unlike anyone else I have known. One man told me that she was the most distinguished woman he had ever met. It was a distinction that depended as much on manner and bearing as on appearance. She called up images of far off things; she was excessively thin through the hips and shoulders and her waist was childishly small; her poise, stiff, angular, immobile, was Egyptian; her slanting eyes and fixed smile were early Greek. She never fidgeted or fussed; she never lounged, sat or stood carelessly; her collected gestures revealed a curious, jerky grace, her arms moved forwards and backwards but never sideways, like a Dutch doll. She used no make-up even when her face was colourless from fatigue; she discarded ornaments but she would sometimes wear a huge Victorian brooch, a present from her mother-in-law. However weary she might be, she was always perfectly arranged, not a fold of her dress out of place; very upright, hands locked across her knee, turning her head with its burden of abundant plaits slowly to the last speaker, she presided over the teacups in Fitzroy Street. Sickert was enchanted with her appearance, especially her blue eyes. They were the true dark Scottish blue and when she was tanned by the sun they glowed deeper than ever, to his great satisfaction. Christine, for her part, lamented the fact that he was always trying to spoil his good looks with some fresh disguise. 'Walter is in full beard *again*!' she sighed one day, 'Isn't it sickening?'

Illness had taught her an iron self-control. Imposed on a nature already too suppressed for happiness, she found it almost impossible to show her feelings. Lack of control in others made her uneasy; viewing with distaste the wild mirth that Nina Hamnett and others would display at studio sprees, her thoughts might escape her with the nearest approach to asperity that she permitted herself to show. 'How I wish that Nina wouldn't get so excited at parties!'

In one respect only, she had a masculine trait. She indulged in no small talk whatever and only spoke, in a precise, rather grating drawl when she had something to say. Her criticisms of people were usually gracious, if non-committal, but she could be disconcerting. Speaking of a mutual acquaintance one day, she said, 'I rather like her, you know; she's so silly.'

On the face of it, this seemed to be an unlikely marriage. His friends shook their heads at the time, prophesying disaster, pointing out that they had little in common; her friends feared that she was not strong enough to share his austerities. There seemed to be every reason why they should drift apart. She was forced more and more to observe an invalidish way of life and rest constantly; he only seemed to relax in odd snatches of sleep during the day and was seldom in bed until after midnight, when he might get up again to wander about the streets until dawn. She joined him when she could at the music halls, but a long day was too much for her and he had to curb his fancy for wandering through the back streets of Islington after the performance. She liked polite society, he took his society as he found it, asking only that 'the fizz' should not have gone out of it, that his companions should provide the spark of life that was vital, although with one important reservation; when he dined out, he preferred, like Christine, to meet polite society. She dreamed of having a family, which, in her state of health, was out of the question; he seldom gave the matter a thought, collecting a mixed bunch of young people for his amusement in Fitzroy Street which completely satisfied his patriarchal instincts; although I have heard him airing his pet theory occasionally, half in fun, half seriously: 'You can't have four generations of painters, it wouldn't work . . . a son of mine would probably be an imbecile.'

They both liked living in France, which for her part, seems odd, as the hardships of Envermeu, the village where they lived, some ten miles from Dieppe, must have been greater than in her own country, but his London was not her London; the stern quality of Islington that inspired him oppressed her and she was not really at home in the milder region of the Camden Road. Bath was more to her taste and they spent happy summers in that lovely city. It was such a favourite haunt of his that when he was once installed there it was difficult to dislodge him. Christine and Marie would come back to London in September to open up the house in Camden Road, expecting him to follow shortly, but for days on end Christine would receive telegrams from Bath instead, repeating the same refrain:

'A thousand apologies . . . to-morrow . . . Walter.'

When they went househunting, he was concerned merely with the look of the thing; charming chimney pieces, doors, ceilings, windows, all adding up to style; it was Christine who examined the sink in the kitchen and the damp courses and enquired about the roof and the drains. If these were unsatisfactory but the house was pretty, she had to cajole Sickert to look for another home elsewhere; not an easy task if he had taken a fancy to the proportions of the rooms.

It distressed her to find him ordering collars and ties in profusion when she considered that half the quantity would have sufficed, or to suffer his habit of keeping taxis waiting all over the place, regardless of time or expense; it was all the more bewildering because, in theory, he strongly disapproved of extravagance. She did not think it funny when she reminded him of a small sum he owed her and he laughed at her as he fished out the money.

'What a little Scot you are!' he mocked.

'I can't think why you married me,' she retorted.

'I married you, my dear,' replied Sickert promptly, 'because you are so like a pelican.'

There was a faint resemblance to a pelican. All Sickert's associates had some likeness, for him, to something or other. Thus, one of his friends was like a rook, another like Pope Pius the tenth; Chris was 'early Empire', Nina Hamnett 'a monkey' and that sultry beauty, Barbara Boreel, 'a morsel for a Sultan'.

Some well-meaning people, baffled by her languor and unaware that Christine was ill, decided that she was too withdrawn to identify herself with Sickert's interests. In their anxiety for his welfare they built castles in the air, probing the might-have-beens, arguing about the kind of woman he should have married; most of the malcontents held the view that the ideal wife for him was one who would revel in the lively atmosphere of Fitzroy Street and that Christine would have been happier in her own more conventional setting of Kensington. The only drawback to these theories was the fact that Sickert was blissfully content with things as they were. Those who knew him intimately could see why. His Scottish wife summed up for him all that he most admired in his favourite race; humour, intellect, sanity, independence. Of the humour that he saw in her, we found little; illness had quenched that spark for ever; but we could appreciate the steadfastness that was her chief hold over him. She saved him from reckless actions that would have complicated still further his already tangled life; she watched over his health and sorted out his muddles; she curtailed useless expenditure without his knowing it; she was kind to his friends and models. Above all, she gave him peace of mind. When everything proved 'a little much' for him, there was always Christine to return to, and the home she had made for him in the Camden Road. Although the house was never built that could contain him for long, she provided the background that was more precious to him than he knew until he had lost it—his fortress and his ease.

Curious that, in spite of all the shocks she had sustained on his behalf, one aspect of his nature seems to have been a closed book to her. Years of experience had never quite taught her that he could not take care of himself. At her death in 1920, she left him all her little capital instead of tying it up to him because, as she explained, she would not like to hurt him.

He never quite got over her death. For a time, he seemed to forget her, although he remarked that the mainspring was broken. He began to work steadily again, made another successful marriage; went to live in Brighton and St Peter's where there was nothing to remind him of the past; took up his old friends; did all those things which, we are assured, will prove a cure for hurt minds. But the bond that had persisted between them hardened to adamant through the years. In his old age he began to speak of her constantly, as if incredulous that she had left him.

> 'A self-contented wren
> Not shunning man's abode, though shy
> Almost as thought itself, of human ken.'

These words might have been written for the third Mrs Sickert.

One day, early in 1918, Sickert came to the Frith bubbling over with enthusiasm; he had just returned from Holly Place, Hampstead, where he had been visiting Thérèse Lessore, wife of the painter Bernard Adeney, herself an ardent painter. He described her studio, her painting, the house tucked away up on its little ledge overlooking the High Street, her appearance. 'She's like a Persian miniature,' he declared. He admired her pictures, finding in them movement and a fascinating economy of style; he decided to do something of the same sort himself and the result, which he began immediately after he left her, was one of his larger canvases, 'The Objection' (plate 32). Painted in a light key, depicting a woman leaning against a high backed chair, her arms resting casually on it, the whole pose conveyed what Sickert sought in his own work and admired in hers, 'the echo of movement passed and the promise of movement to come'. The spirit of Thérèse certainly hovered over this picture, although Sickert soon reverted to his old ways.

From that time onwards, the Adeneys were frequent visitors in Fitzroy Street. When they left Hampstead to join the *quartier*, they gave evening parties at Number 20, their new home across the road. Thérèse saw the possibilities of her long front room flanked by three tall windows, overlooking what was then a quiet street; she kept it bare and spacious, relying on its beautiful proportions for interest, and lighted it with candles. Dingy but dignified, the old room lived again; one might have stepped back a hundred years. Sickert attended her parties whenever he could; I remember him running down the street in his eagerness to be there, dragging Christine and myself in his wake. Like a tiny bird fluttering just out of reach, apprehensive lest we should come too close, Thérèse would dart her bright eyes from one to the other, quick, wary, intent. She spoke seldom and when she did it was to talk of painting, to challenge some headlong remark with her precise, faint mockery or to ruffle her feathers with distaste or to supply a missing name that Sickert had forgotten, as once when he enquired, 'Who was that chap who followed Ingres, you know, beginning with F, no not

Fantin,'—and inevitably, it was Thérèse who whispered the correct answer, 'Flandrin.'

But if she seldom spoke, she held strong views about people and things. She would sum up a situation with severe little comments which amused Sickert vastly; he liked a touch of asperity in women; once, when I complained that a mutual friend had a sharp tongue, he exclaimed, 'For me, that's just her quality.' But he found Thérèse soothing in spite of her decided opinions. 'She's so gentle,' he would repeat when we were talking about her.

Considering how little she contributed to the conversation in words and how silent she could be, it seems odd to say that she was easy to get on with. But she possessed the rare and mysterious gift of drawing people out and everyone was conscious of her bright intelligence playing over the scene. The perfect listener, her interest in people was intense but she only talked freely to her intimates; she did not perform to strangers. Years later, after her marriage to Sickert, she became even more reticent. Once, after they had been lunching with Frank Schuster, the musician, whom she had not previously met, he remarked, 'But Mrs Sickert was dumb.' I was so used to her shyness that I remember feeling disconcerted with this criticism.

She was small, frail and foreign looking; not entirely French as her name would suggest but with something more alien, more remote about the moulding of her little face; Sickert had defined it when he called her Persian. Her eyes were light gold in a smooth olive face, her teeth very white, her hair black and massy; when she was amused she would shake her curls over her forehead in a characteristic gesture, laughing silently. She wore Libertyish clothes, made by herself in a straight pinafore style which clung to her childish figure, white stockings and prim little black dancing sandals. For the street, she was wrapped in a long black cloak; I have no recollection whatsoever of her hats but she must have worn one, at any rate after she married Sickert, as he was horrified at the growing tendency for women to appear hatless in the street. But Thérèse was not in the least an out of doors person. One saw her rather as part of the great gaunt interiors of Fitzroy Street where she was generally to be found painting, flitting softly in her tiny sandals across the old bare floors like a small dark ghost. Sometimes, I would look up from the street at twilight, on my way home, to see her pale face against the gathering dusk, close pressed to the window, motionless yet intent, lost in one of her brooding fits, when one might smile and wave to her in vain. To this day, whenever I pass Number 20 Fitzroy Street I think I see her at the tall window, looking through me rather than at me, nursing her thoughts.

After a few years, she and Bernard Adeney drifted apart. He married again and Thérèse buried herself in her work. She painted incessantly through a difficult period, which was when I really got to know her, if anyone could be said to know such an elusive personality. When Sickert returned from Dieppe in 1922 she went with him, night after night, to music halls, where they both drew. She was a godsend to him in his loneliness, she identified herself completely with his interests and eventually, in 1926, they married.

His previous marriages with Ellen Cobden and Christine Angus had been very different affairs. Sickert was now in his mid-sixties, his restlessness curbed by bodily fatigue, his painting erratic. He was far more dependent on Thérèse than on his first wives and during the days when he was obliged to take it easy he could always discuss his work with her, confident of her quick response; he respected her opinions and she had a formidable fund of information about painters and their procedures, worthy of an art historian. Their minds were in close contact with each other, although she was more solemn about painting than Sickert could ever be. How amused he was one day when he found the colour terre verte on her palette!

'Why terre verte?' he asked.

'Because Michelangelo used it,' replied Thérèse loftily.

'You would,' laughed Sickert.

She often helped us with our work and was always ready to lend an ear when we complained of our difficulties. Once I announced, to her great amusement, that I intended to use a preparation of size and gesso for the underpainting of a canvas; she suggested, tactfully, that it might be rather an elaborate cookery and next morning she came to Number 15, heated the concoction in the correct quantities herself and spread it afterwards over several canvases for me. She had certainly achieved just the right consistency for the mixture and it proved to be the most agreeable surface I have ever worked on.

I think her pictures lost their special flavour when she was so much with Sickert. She withstood his influence at first but gradually it gained on her; by degrees, her fey quality disappeared and like so many others who came under the Sickert spell, she began to turn out echoes of him rather than her own strange little interiors. Music halls were too vast, too overpowering a field for her; they used up her energies. She was, as it were, to borrow a rather far-fetched literary association, the Charlotte Mew of English painting; she had her own secret fleeting charm, her small but acute sensation which was swamped by his personality. She began to be exclusively interested in him; she loved talking about him and his ways, infinitely amused by his whimsies; when he became ill and old she was devotion itself. It could not have happened at a worse time for her; the Hitler war was raging several years before he died and few people could spare a thought for this frail little creature, alone with her august charge at Bath, cut off from most of her friends and desperately short of money. But she was fortunate in being able to count on a loyal few; Clifford Ellis, art master at Corsham, was a staunch supporter and Sir Alec Martin and Sylvia Gosse did all they could; she was supplied with a nurse who helped to shoulder some of the responsibility for Sickert, now becoming more and more helpless. In fact, her last period at Bath was perhaps easier for her than her time in London with him, before she had persuaded him to seek a simpler life in the country.

The best record that Sickert has left of his three wives was the portrait of Thérèse, formerly in the possession of the Leicester Galleries. No other portrait of any of them that I have seen is so carried through; so far as I know, we have only sketches of Ellen, and 'Christine Buys a Gendarmerie', a speaking likeness up to a point, is not a straight forward portrait. But although we have more information about Thérèse than about the others, Sickert certainly portrayed her as a sombre rather than as a cheerful personality. This must, I think, have been subconscious on his part; I do not remember her always like this; as she grew older she was less shy, less remote, often gay.

Chapter 9

Colleagues

'I have enjoyed much of life but if it were not for painting, life would be unbearable, that makes part of it divine, but you must get beyond the stage of seeking for public recognition.'

Thus spoke Henry Tonks, the most famous art master of his day. He taught at the Slade for almost forty years and his astonishing hold over the school never slackened; to the end, students sought his approval. Not deluding them with easy words or lies, he ruled the Slade with an iron hand, but although exceedingly formidable, he was never indifferent or remote; underlying the fierceness there was keen response to their difficulties and the desire of the born teacher to infuse them with his own enthusiasm. He had all the qualities of a leader; an imposing figure, a musical voice curiously at variance with his severity, a biting wit and an eye like Mars, to threaten and command. With his aquiline nose and falcon stare he was like Julius Caesar and the Iron Duke rolled into one but he could never have been mistaken for a soldier; he looked what he was, every inch a surgeon. He was dedicated to his easel as a saint to the Cross. At the age of thirty he had finally deserted medicine for art, sacrificing an assured future to a pittance of £150 a year at the Slade, which was increased later. But time was what he needed most, time to make up for the years when he had been, perforce, a Sunday painter. He never regretted those years. When it was suggested to him that he should call his autobiographical essay 'Lost Years', he replied: 'No, because I would not like to say that'. Medicine always attracted him; he thought it was probably the most interesting profession in the world. But the advantage of his Slade post was that it afforded him enough leisure to develop his own talent; he attended about three times a week. He was seldom without buyers, although the sums for which he sold his early work would be called negligible today. A poorer man than was generally thought, but his wants were few; some good wine in the cellar, the models he preferred, little dinners for his friends, a country pub in the summer from which he could sally forth to paint, made up almost the sum total of his needs. There seemed to be complete unity between him and the Slade Professor, Frederick Brown, whom Tonks succeeded in the Chair of Fine Arts at the end of 1917; their aims were identical and all honour was due to the Professor for having chosen as his assistant one who might so easily have eclipsed him. But the association worked. The Slade was Tonks, and Tonks was the Slade, yet the

Professor was still valued and his influence felt. Peace in the staff room was reflected throughout the school. And without the aid of Tonks, it is doubtful if its standard could have been maintained or if the Professor, single-handed, could have stemmed the tide of dilettantes with which it was threatened. These people followed the classic pattern of dilettantes the world over; some had talent, many were eager and friendly, with a warmth and frankness of manner that were engaging, but on the whole they proved a disturbing element. Restless and preoccupied, they were always coming and going, their presence was always being demanded elsewhere; dragonflies, flashing their wings across those sober walls, gay, colourful, daring, they streamed into the void as swiftly as they came. And none more colourful than Lady Oxford, who was constantly darting to and fro during the term she was 'doing' the Slade, returning at tea-time to hold her little court in the hall. The students found her very good company as she waved her mug of tea and her doughnut in the air, pronouncing upon art to an admiring audience.

'Always remember, darlings, that the Slade is the place for form but not for colour, no *not* for colour, darlings.'

She was right about the colour; there seemed to be no settled policy about the approach to painting. Steer was only at home with advanced students who were already finding their own palettes, McEvoy was only present for a few terms and the other masters were chiefly concerned with the main preoccupation of the Slade—drawing. But Tonks and the Professor were disturbed lest the working atmosphere of the school might suffer through these social incursions. They were determined that it should live up to its high reputation; those who did not work seriously must be discouraged. However, these people soon solved the problem themselves, by flitting off elsewhere.

I remember one occasion only when the native sagacity of Tonks deserted him. Blinded, presumably, by talent and charm, he actually reposed his trust in the most glittering dragonfly of all, a student named Phyllis Boyd. Tonks was impressed by her marked ability and when he was choosing a few students to paint some panels under his supervision at a girls' club in Fulham, he promptly included Phyllis Boyd in his team.

For a time, all went well. Tonks was enjoying himself, painting two panels of his own while he was looking after his students and making friends with the Bishop (Dr Ingram, I presume). Work in the club was proceeding steadily when Phyllis vanished on a jaunt to New York and was invisible for months. The panels were completed in her absence but on her return to London she went alone to Fulham and painted a green tree in the middle of the floor. The Bishop was aghast. He took violent exception to the tree, demanding redress from Tonks, whom he held responsible for the disaster.

This was the gist of the situation as related to us by Phyllis when she wandered into the hall of the Slade one evening to see her friends. We could offer no consolation for her plight; the situation was grave. All we could suggest was that she should depart instantly, as Tonks was still in the building. But it was too late, he heard her voice, the door of the staff room flew open and he came down on us like a wolf on the fold. Phyllis retreated behind the table but her pluck was admirable; she stood up to him as best she could, although she had no case to defend. Convulsed with rage, his hands clenched on his chest, Tonks recounted his wrongs. It had been necessary to try to scrub out the offending tree as soon as possible in order to placate the Bishop; this had involved much time and labour; no chemical, so far, could be found to efface it. There had been embarrassing interviews, explanations, apologies, debates. With horror, Tonks realized that he was now regarded at Fulham as a man of straw. The Bishop had been let down, and said so. Faced by that steadfast, dispassionate, ecclesiastical displeasure which is so telling, Tonks was forced on the defensive—the last attitude in the world that became him. Nothing was wanting to complete his discomfiture.

All this and more he explained, with mounting fury, to the delinquent. If she tried to move or speak, he thundered louder; pinned between the table, the wall and his accusing form, she was unable to escape. Finally, she did break away and fled through the main door, whisked to safety by the kindly old porter, Campion. 'And I let her go!' cried Tonks. 'To think that I let her go!'

Next day, he was still cursing himself for his clemency. 'Fool that I was, to let her off so easily. I hadn't half said my say. Oh, that I had only said more!'

But he could console himself with the reflection that they would surely meet again before long, when he would be able to redeem himself for this unaccountable weakness and really tell her what he thought.

To models, he was more considerate than any of the professors. When he saw that they were tired, he would order them to rest and he would even lower his voice if he was discussing them, although this was partly due to his stern theory that people must not be encouraged to feel too pleased with themselves. 'This chap has a cynical twist to his mouth,' he said to me about a model whom he was carefully drawing. 'But I shan't let him hear me say that. Everyone likes to be thought cynical.'

He praised nobody until he had satisfied himself that they had staying power, when he would take infinite pains to help them. Some students, however, found him so overpowering that they bolted forthwith, before giving him a fair trial; to whit, a young Belgian with whom I shared my first day in the Antique. He sustained a bombardment from Tonks during the morning session which shattered him, little as he understood of it, and his confidence was not heightened when Tonks launched his next offensive. After attacking the Belgian, he found another newcomer cowering behind her donkey (drawing stool) whose general inefficiency increased his ire. 'Your paper is crooked, your pencil is blunt, your donkey wobbles, you are sitting in your own light, your drawing is atrocious. And now,' fixing her with his piercing eye, 'you are crying and you haven't got a handkerchief.'

After luncheon, the Belgian enquired anxiously:

'Zis man, he come back zis afternoon?'

'Yes,' I replied.

'I go,' said the Belgian, gathering up his gear and making for the door. We never saw him again.

Invitations from Tonks were hardly effusive, in spite of his interest in his flock. I once heard him inviting two young men to his studio, a great concession on his part, as he feared that visitors might see some of his unfinished work, which he disliked showing to anyone. 'Come at five o'clock,' he commanded. 'Don't be later than five but on *no* account come before.'

It should be added that if his guests were not put off by this sort of thing, they could be sure of a royal welcome if they took care to comply exactly with his instructions.

Beginners were confined to the Antique and not allowed to draw from the Life until they had made some headway with casts. This precaution was necessary for another reason; the Life Room was always full. Although most of us floundered dismally when confronted with the subtleties of the Antique, it did succeed in sorting out the sheep from the goats. The idlers found the Antique tedious beyond words and soon melted away; the serious students met it as a challenge and became absorbed in the problems that it posed. As Tonks had no notion of keeping up the numbers of the school but was concerned only with maintaining the highest possible standard, this procedure worked. His severity with drifters had its advantages; one soon discovered that there was method in his rudeness. After a time, those who wished to work were conscious of support; as Joseph Hone puts it, of being under a wing. Obstacles were quietly removed from their path and an atmosphere of calm imposed upon the classrooms in which they could wrestle with their difficulties in peace, safe from intolerable interruption. Above all, the student felt that his struggles, if not praised, were being observed. The Puritan streak in Tonks approved the tortoise even if he was sometimes dazzled by the hare; if the tortoise happened, with the advent of time and his own efforts, to become worthwhile, no one was more grimly delighted than he.

He was generally considered to be the best teacher of figure drawing in England. So potent was his sway that too many of his followers mistook his meaning and concentrated entirely on drawing the isolated figure against what Sickert called 'a buff vacancy' as an end in itself, forgetting the importance of relating one object to another, and thus remaining professional art students for the rest of their lives. As time went on they became more rather than less dependent on the school and were all at sea when they left the Slade to paint in attics of their own. One sympathizes with those who disliked leaving the incubator if they could contrive to prolong their stay beyond reasonable limits. What with the really amazing inspiration afforded by Tonks himself, exchanges of opinion with foreigners, mutual comparisons of work with other students, exciting productions from star pupils that were constantly appearing at the Sketch Club, lectures in University College by Roger Fry and Tancred Borenius, the general ferment of bubbling ideas, drive and enthusiasm, it was bliss in that dawn to be alive. And all very dull when students began to fend for themselves afterwards in the solitude of hired rooms, unless they had already begun to compose and make their own pictures while they were still at the Slade.

Carping critics complained that the school was a forcing house for overstrained talents which collapsed when its backing was withdrawn, that the swans cherished by Tonks were sometimes geese and his geese the true swans. It may seem strange today that he can have failed to see the possibilities of Matthew Smith, admittedly a late developer; but in spite of blind spots, Tonks did discover many talents; the training of a whole galaxy of stars can be laid to his door. A more serious indictment against him would be that his strictures, if taken to heart, might lead to that lack of self confidence which is fatal for any beginner. Once, he asked a friend of mine why he never sent anything to the Sketch Club. 'Because I can't stand being flayed alive in front of everyone,' was the answer. Tonks pondered this, looking very surprised indeed.

What exasperated the victims was not so much his abuse of their work as the peels of sycophantic laughter from other students which greeted every broadside that was hurled at their hapless productions. Sometimes one resented his harshness deeply, feeling that it may have extinguished many a sensitive talent. But Tonks had a robust belief in his mission. Sensibility, he agreed, was a rare and precious quality, an essential ingredient in the make-up of any budding performer; but too seldom, alas, could the over-sensitive plants branch out and toughen; he had seen so many of them wilt away after the first flowering. If they could not stand up to the east winds of criticism which would assuredly blow upon them, they should give up this most rigorous and exacting of professions. There was so much else to do.

All this he explained at the Sketch Club, and more besides. He would improvise about his own work, taking us into his confidence, relating his own mistakes and muddles and how he fought his way out of them; we ranged wide, from painting to ballet, from Shakespeare to Greek drama, returning to our muttons by way, perhaps, of sculpture or architecture or anything else which would help him to prove the point he wanted to make. He discussed that elusive quality, originality; as a conscientious teacher he did his utmost to make his position clear. I recollect especially one occasion when he was criticizing a pen and ink illustration of a Blake poem by Paul Nash, then a struggling student. I think we had all rather missed its quality because the drawing was still tentative but Tonks saw its promise at once and praised it warmly. He reminded us that an individual outlook was very rare, getting rarer every day with the advent of photography and the cinema but unmistakable when it did appear. He quoted Aubrey Beardsley as a precocious original, one who found himself at an unusually early age. Tonks and he had worked together when they were students and Tonks described to us how Beardsley drew at night between tall candles in a closed chamber, his pen travelling over the paper at precise speed without second thought or corrections.

But it was useless for the student to strive for originality by short cuts, selecting eccentric combinations of objects, painting huge canvases whether they were the right size for the idea or not, being blinded by the glare of fashion to follow the latest 'isms' even when they cut across the grain of his own temperament, going one better than the latest 'shock' painter, shouting generally at the top of his voice. All this would lead nowhere. Not that Tonks condemned serious experiment. No one was more interested in it than he. But the experiment should be sincere, expressed with all the technique the student could muster. He did not profess to supply his pupils with imagination but he could, he thought, put them in the way of becoming good draughtsmen and provide them with what has been the basis throughout the ages of pictorial art. Even if they could not aspire to marked originality they might become good painters and achieve something personal. He agreed with Sickert that where there is a real urge to paint there is talent, if only a spark, somewhere.

Therefore, he did not disparage the small talent. He had seen it grow sometimes to unexpected proportions and he held that it is the amateur rather than the professional who is apt to deprecate those minor achievements which have their place in the hierarchy of painting. He would have said with Chardin that far from condemning a picture for being second rate it is well to remember that very few people succeed in even being third rate painters.

The Slade was in a strong position when it recommended the importance of academic training. It had fostered the talents of artists such as Matthew Smith, Wyndham Lewis, Augustus John in the golden age before his work was sometimes marred by sweetness, Ambrose McEvoy and hosts of others (Sickert was there hardly long enough to be counted as a Slade production). There were other stars to come: Paul Nash, the Spencers, William Roberts, Mark Gertler and many lesser lights. Tonks could claim that none of these artists was crushed by tradition and that their powers had been developed by academic discipline.

He differed greatly from Fry about the guidance of the younger generation. Although his talks at the Sketch Club were not only brilliant but sound, he complained that he could not always write exactly what he intended and 'got muddled up with syntax'. It seems a pity that he mistrusted his literary powers so deeply, his letters are precise and vivid; but I think having heard him discuss the matter, that the real reason why he did not assail Fry in print was that he knew only too well that there are truths about painting which cannot be put into words because there are no words to express them. Had he conquered this reluctance to write rather than speak, we might have had an entertaining correspondence between the two men. Fry was eloquence itself, in speech or on paper, but Tonks had the advantage of great personal experience of students and what was more, of their subsequent careers. He had, therefore, an accumulated fund of practical wisdom and it filled him with fury to find that he could not always annihilate the adventurous theories of the canny Quaker.

Drawing was not a complete obsession with Tonks; it was his flock, *plus royaliste que le roi*, who made a fetish of it until they could hardly see beyond it. He might repeat that it was the trump card of the professional, necessary if one wanted to keep visually fit, but we were not regimented to death in the cause of line. I remember a hard-working student who was once in despair when he was giving him a lesson. 'I shall never draw,' he sighed. Tonks looked thoughtful. The student had immense application, but had not yet found himself. 'I have known good artists who were not first-class draughtsmen,' Tonks assured him. He went on to prescribe a more balanced diet, a fresh approach to his difficulties; more brushwork, a course of water colour. He had a knack of offering comfort when it was needed.

He gave us charming water colours and pastel portraits but I think his most interesting work was his series of little genre pictures, 'Saturday Night in the Vale'.

Here, he recounts intimate occasions between his cronies; the best is probably that of George Moore reading to his friends with Tonks himself, an excellent portrait, leaning against the chimney piece (plate 21). 'Sodales', with Steer dozing and Sickert sprawling opposite in the very loudest of check suits is a good likeness of Steer but Sickert is curiously unlike; the face bears not the slightest resemblance to him, whether in full beard or not, although Tonks has caught his pose. Anyone who has attempted these small genre pictures where so much is said in so small a space will admire the virtuosity of Tonks in keeping the portraits alive, broad yet detailed; these small heads are especially difficult if painted in such a cumbrous medium as oil paint. Their importance as social documents is obvious.[1]

On balance, the effect of his fervour outweighed by far the effect of his severity. Praise was especially valued when it was so seldom bestowed and students knew in their hearts that he passionately wanted them to succeed. He was no soured schoolmaster who had fallen back on teaching as a livelihood but a man who had succeeded in three professions and was teaching not only because it provided him with a small income but because, up to a point, he liked it immensely. Being human, he might take umbrage at some unfortunate student now and then but these lapses were rare. His burning faith in his calling swept like a tempest through the Slade; his flaming beliefs and certainties, his integrity, even his prejudices, gave them something to hold on to in face of the shifting values of the modern world. His prejudices, perhaps, endeared him to us most of all. He hated what he called 'soppy' thinking and the ever-growing sentimentality that Sickert also deplored; we could not but be reassured by his warning to the Vicar of Northbourne, who was preaching universal tolerance: 'You must be careful not to be too broad-minded or you will have nothing left.'

His views about women seemed illogical. He took great interest in their work and encouraged them with all his might, while realizing that their interest in art would probably peter out in their twenties if they were considering marriage or

[1] Whenever I see the small head by Constable of his wife in the National Gallery I am overawed again by the great power of this painter, saying so much on a small scale.

that if it persisted, the cares of a family threatened to smother it for good. Unlike Sickert, who held that women had neither the necessary concentration nor stamina for painting and that the few exceptions merely proved the rule, Tonks thought that they might do interesting work if they had the chance; he took their talent more seriously than Sickert. Both believed in marriage, but whereas Sickert prescribed it for everyone, Tonks gave the impression that it counted only for women. One never heard him recommend the state for men. The reader may wonder, in a world of dedicated bachelors, how Tonks proposed to equate the problem. I can only retort, as the Doctor retorted to Boswell: 'Sir, you *may* wonder.' He had long since decided that marriage would not suit him and would most certainly not suit his wife; as the leading spirit of a little band of confirmed bachelors he was the most confirmed of all.

In spite of his many interests, he could hardly be described as a happy man. He could not share the high spirits that attended Sickert or Matthew Smith or any other instinctive painter when they were winning a victory over the canvas. Tonks was never satisfied with his work. As Joseph Hone says: 'There was one thought, his dearest, which he kept alone locked up in the darkness crying for the moon. The pictures which he painted were in truth his life, his soul and very self.' That one thought tormented him; painting was anguish but he was bound to it, body and soul. One day perhaps, if he willed it enough, the Fates might for once be kind and he would surely paint something that did not displease him.

I understand that in his last years, Tonks mellowed. Worse, I have heard from those whom he favoured that he was often enhaloed with an aura of benevolence and inclined to mete out praise on the smallest provocation. In fact, as one student put it to me, 'Tonks treated me almost as an equal.' Better that he should be remembered in his heyday, untamed, still defiant of life and its setbacks, admitting no compromise, fearing neither God nor man. Those who knew him then will always recall his reign with gratitude and affection.

An affection he inspired in his own generation as well. Many have written of Tonks with insight and sympathy but the last word of all is with his old friend Henry James.

'*Dear* Henry! So joyous in his gloom! So *gloomy* in his joy!'

The Slade Professor, overshadowed by the mighty Tonks, has never had his due. His shy manner masked a furious application to painting, equal to that of Tonks, but Tonks had wider interests than the Professor, who was quite happy to return to Richmond after the daily round and sit among his household gods with his sisters and his friends. His chief hobby was buying pictures from his contemporaries or some promising juniors to add to an already interesting collection; he also liked fishing, and he was a tremendous walker. It is difficult to imagine him consorting with those who did not care for painting, however intelligent they might be; he had his own set, mostly bachelors like himself, and sought no others; throughout a long life, few fresh people were admitted to his inner circle.

Richmond had been his home for years when I knew him; it was blessedly quiet in those days with plenty of fine houses still left, and lovely walks for the taking. There was nothing the Professor liked better than to potter along his favourite beat, past the mysterious old Queensberry estate, now a block of flats, past the bridge and Cholmondeley Walk, watching cloud effects and reflections on the water. He would speak sometimes of that especial lassitude that one feels after a long day at the easel when, keyed up and restless but physically spent, a stroll in the open air seems the only remedy that one can bear. It was then that he found how much he owed to his beloved river; mooching along beside it, he was soon restored again.

There is a powerful portrait of a red-haired girl at the Slade, broadly treated in the manner of Sir Joshua Reynolds, which shows what he might have achieved as a painter, had his energies not been drained by teaching. When I first knew him he was already elderly, his lessons becoming stereotyped, too obsessed with detail, but there was enough left to indicate what he must have been capable of imparting in his prime. Some professors chose their pupils quite openly, for which one really could not blame them; the Professor, however, worked his way steadily and impartially down the line, taking the rough with the smooth, the bad student with the good, in strict rotation. Often, he was faced with some frighteningly dull performance which would have evoked an explosion of wrath from Tonks, but he stood up to these pathetic scrawls with his usual composure and merely relieved the tedium by scribbling all over them. If he seemed less violent about poor work than Tonks, he did not show the same enthusiasm for promise. A perfectionist, he thought nothing of altering a painting which was nearly complete for the sake of a trifling adjustment, which caused many students to dodge his lessons if they were preparing studies for the summer competition. He might pass his brush across a portrait that was almost finished because some passage seemed a thought out of drawing, or he might change his mind again and restore the original statement, moving on serenely, careless of the havoc he had wrought and leaving the student to wonder if he could possibly repair the damage in the time left at his disposal before sending-in day.

When he addressed the Sketch Club he was equally difficult. A grain of humour might have sweetened the dose but it would never have occurred to the Professor to be flippant about such a tremendous affair as painting or to soften the effect of the wounds he inflicted. On one occasion, he dismissed a still life of some fish by Mark Gertler, as too realistic, 'I can almost smell them—faugh!' he exclaimed. A criticism which surprised us all, as we had been impressed by Gertler's herrings. No doubt the Professor had his reasons for disliking them, but poor Gertler took his rebuffs very much to heart; he was desperately poor and to win a prize in the summer competition meant a great deal to him. I can see him now as he stood by the door in anguish, hearing his still life condemned.

I do not remember that any of our other teachers came to the Slade picnic, which was held every year at Burnham Beeches, but the Professor always appeared. Many old students turned up too; the Spencer brothers came over from Cookham. It was cool and shady under the great trees and the atmosphere was delightfully informal. The Professor was a different man on these occasions, shedding his responsibilities, prepared to enjoy himself like a schoolboy, taking his pleasures as thoroughly as he took his work, playing cricket and rounders and jumping about like a man half his age, the noblest reveller of us all. In fact, so difficult are people to please, that we could have wished him to be a little less hearty sometimes; we deplored his passion for riding in boatswings and the old stagers were always missing when he was looking round for a partner with whom to indulge in this excruciating pastime. As a new student at my first Slade picnic I was wandering about innocently while the initiated had made themselves scarce and were lurking behind trees until the coast was clear; they had seen the Professor on the warpath, and knew that he meant to find a partner for the boatswings. I was of course promptly swept up by him as the nearest available victim, whisked into one of these infernal contrivances and hurled into space. Time seemed endless as I sat cowering opposite him, clinging to the ropes and praying desperately that I might not be sick while he hoisted me to the heavens and dropped me again, with giddy swoops, to the reeling earth.

Next day, the Professor would be back on his pedestal, severe and glacial, as if these goings on had never been.

Friendships between the sexes were not encouraged. On hot days, the Professor would let the women students out on the grass lawns in front of the Slade at stated intervals, but he was on the alert, watch in hand, to shoo us all in again before the men were released in their turn. This pantomime was replayed regularly throughout the summers and had the desired effect; romance was nipped in the bud. He need not have been so afraid. The girls were curiously apathetic about the men students, taking them for granted as part of the furniture of the place, and friendships with them were few. But there was a sad occasion when a pathetic little couple met in the Antique and wandered about hand in hand, lost to everyone but themselves. Their idyll did not last long, they were soon brought to book and haled into the staff room. From the very tattered hearthrug the Professor reminded them that the Slade was not a matrimonial agency; it seems he waxed quite eloquent, and the poor little girl dissolved in tears.

We could hardly credit this, as he was usually laconic. But Sickert used to chuckle about 'Fred's speeches', declaring that the Professor was one of those speakers who are too embarrassed to sit down again once they are on their feet. 'I had to pull Fred's coat at an Academy dinner when he was thoroughly wound up and couldn't stop.' He insisted, which we rather doubted, that the Professor was grateful for this intervention.

Years later, I found myself standing next to the Professor at the New English Art Club, studying the same picture. He was now very frail indeed but the flame burned as brightly as ever; he led me firmly round the Exhibition, examining each canvas minutely, concerned lest he was not giving each painter his due and delighted when he saw progress in the work of an ex-student. Gravely he sought my opinion; gravely he considered it when replying. This was promotion indeed, I thought, from the rigours of the Life Class. Could this gentle, almost diffident man be the austere Slade Professor?

But I had already learned at Slade picnics that he could be Dr Jekyll and Mr Hyde; it was not really strange that now, having put off his official mantle, he should prove himself such a charming companion. When closing time came, I was surprised to find that we had been wandering about for so long; I was tired but he looked game for another exhibition, in fact stimulated by his arduous afternoon. I parted from him sadly, feeling that although he had still so much to live for his days were numbered, and that I was seeing him for the last time.

But we met once more. My final glimpse of him was on the towpath at Richmond, where I was teaching two pupils one summer morning. He came slowly past us, a ghost of a Professor now. For a moment he did not recognize me, then he smiled and passed on. But he was thinking us over; when he was some distance away he turned back with a searching gaze at the pupils and hesitated, irresolute. I knew then that he was longing to come back, see what they were doing and give us all a lesson.

Philip Wilson Steer did not seem at all puffed up by the importance of being Steer, although he lived in an atmosphere of perpetual fond reverence. Few men can have sailed through life as he did, moving placidly from strength to strength, ending up with an O.M. and his work sought after from far and near. I do not suppose that he had an enemy in the world in spite of his handsome presence, his health, his success, his gifts, his charms, his riches. Everyone combined to make life as easy as possible for him; his home life was cushioned by devoted servants, his friends shielded him from daily frets, his painting hours were sacred; Tonks acted as a watchdog to keep away boring or difficult people. Even Sickert, who had roughed it all his life and was still living hard, seemed to think that Steer must be protected from discomfort at all costs; his other friends were equally concerned that their studios should be comfortable enough to receive him, above all that he should never be exposed to the slightest suspicion of a draught. But every heart knoweth its own bitterness. In spite of his blessings, I have sometimes wondered what could have been the bitterness of Steer's.

It says much for the sweetness of his disposition that he should feel in any way responsible for the younger generation and turn up once a week to teach us painting. This must have often interfered with the train of his thought when he was in the throes of one of his own pictures. But he had promised Tonks to stay with him until Tonks retired, and he kept his word.

On Wednesdays, he presided over a small class as Professor of Painting. Before he sat down on the proffered stool he would take a good look, with his searching kindly eye, at the pupil; then he lowered his bulk on the stool with a sigh and held out his hand for the brushes. So far, the silence was unbroken. He might get up again after a prolonged stare at the canvas before him, saying, 'Well, get on with that' or, more gently, 'Well, I don't know, I'm afraid you won't pull it round.' Or worse, he might say nothing at all and pass on with a sigh—sometimes he went off into a profound meditation, almost a doze; sometimes he would suddenly begin to paint, precisely and deliberately, partly for his own amusement: the time he gave to this varied according to the interest that the subject afforded him; he would leave off as suddenly as he began and one was left staring at the passage he had painted on one's canvas, trying to follow his mental processes after he had wandered away without giving any further instruction. We were amused that such a lazy man should undertake such an exacting task as painting; his natural indolence must have been constantly at war with his urge to create. But there was no indolence about him when he was actually at work. Every stroke he applied to the canvas was calculated, powerful, decisive.

However bored he felt with our efforts, and he did get dreadfully bored with us sometimes, he was never cross or disturbed; he merely looked plaintive and said less than ever. For many years he supported Tonks and attended the Slade regularly, although he admitted that the guineas he was paid for teaching were the hardest he had ever earned. Somehow, he taught us a good deal, as one always learns from the expert in action, and if he did give one of his rare criticisms one did not forget what he said; it was always to the point. A detailed analysis was not to be expected from him and little in the way of future direction, but rather suggestions and interventions. He was of infinite value to the Professor and Tonks when they were judging entries for the summer competitions, as Steer detected promise or performance at a glance; he had the final word on the award of prizes, indeed the Slade owed him more than we knew for his wisdom behind the scenes.

I can recall only one instance of Steer losing his temper and that is hearsay, although I have the story direct from the painter concerned, Mr Geoffrey Hamlyn. He was in his last year at the Slade and Steer was examining one of his drawings. Steer had always taken an interest in this student's work but something about the drawing exasperated him beyond endurance; suddenly, he tore it in half and handed the pieces back to Mr Hamlyn. This procedure was so unlike Steer that Mr Hamlyn could hardly believe it had happened. Next day, Steer sent for him and apologized for his unkindness. The incident is odd, unpredictable, out of character.

His appearance is familiar from the caricatures of Max Beerbohm; a big heavy man with sloping shoulders, a head rather small for the torso, and large hands. But the caricatures do not suggest his distinction; the fine brow, the level deep-set eyes with their measured glance, the general air of knowing exactly where he was going and why.

Students sometimes described Steer and Tonks as 'Mr Bingley and Mr Darcy'. It served, although to be more precise, Steer was too intellectual for Bingley and Tonks was too impulsive for Darcy. But if the likeness between the two professors and these famous characters was superficial, the likeness of their situations was amusing. Steer did allow his social life to be organized by Tonks, who took the lead with Steer following patiently behind because it would save him a lot of trouble if Tonks did the talking, and he didn't really mind. Tonks was devoted to Steer, and Steer let him be devoted. He had no intention whatever of allowing anyone to interfere with his inner life in the slightest degree, but he managed Tonks as he did most people, by his famous combination of humour, tact and charm.

When he was threatened with blindness, he said: 'If I had another eighty years I would start where I left off. I should not have to make all my mistakes again. In fact, when my eyes failed, I had only just got going. It seems as though one has only begun to feel the way when one has to stop.'

He did not miss anyone much in his old age. When his friends had left him, one by one, he liked to sit and meditate in peace; he insisted, when condoled with about his blindness, that he still had his secret garden, his mind.

'I sit now and put two and two together', he said to his friend Ronald Grey.

Harold Gilman, second son of the Rector of Snargate, was one of a family of eleven children. When he was twelve years old he suffered an injury to his foot, which had to be put in plaster, and he lay in bed for months. During this period, he started to draw and paint, although he had never done so before. So far as is known, none of the rest of the family took to the brush nor had any of his forebears shown aesthetic leanings.

He spent four years at the Slade School; his masters were Brown, Tonks and Steer. Then he worked for a year in Spain, copying Velasquez at the Prado. He was at first entirely occupied with tone values, painting in a low key; even the lights were subdued. These quiet harmonies in greys and browns have been criticized as weak echoes of Whistler but there are some beautiful examples of this early work in the Tate Gallery and they proved a valuable training in tone relations, paving the way to more daring colour later on, when he came under the spell of Van Gogh.

Already he struck a personal note; perhaps it was just this hint of individuality which enraged the Mayor of Lewes when Gilman held an exhibition in this little Sussex town. The Mayor was so incensed by Gilman's pictures that he beat his stick on the ground in fury when he inspected them. Gilman was completely mystified by this outburst. After all, as he pointed out, his painting was in the accepted tradition.

Fortified by his study of Velasquez, Gilman went on to building up his picture in separate touches but observing each touch in relation to its neighbour. He never blended the tones at their intersecting points, the gradations between them being obtained by close research; research was a word that cropped up frequently among Gilman and his friends.

This passion for research became almost a vice at times, when Gilman was inclined to overload the subject. As Steer once remarked to Tonks, who was tearing his hair about the additions he should make to his picture in order to finish it, 'perhaps, Tonks, it *is* finished.'

Gilman worked slowly, putting deep thought into each stroke of the brush. Like Sickert, he felt that he could paint the same subject several times if it still excited him; when he discarded a canvas it was usually only for the time being, not because he had exhausted all its possibilities. He would revert to it over and over again or he might start a fresh study of the same subject, intending to carry it further. At first, he painted from nature but when he came under the influence of Sickert he worked from drawings. He used no medium with his oils; when I knew him there might be five coats of paint on his canvas and when he was finishing the picture I have seen him pause for several minutes between each stroke, giving the utmost care to every touch to ensure that it was a necessary contribution to the whole.

Sickert deplored this heavy impasto and would grumble, 'I can't think how you can work over all that rough stuff, Harold. Must be like trying to walk across a ploughed field in pumps!'

It was Sickert who showed him the poetry that lies hidden in unlikely places; iron bedsteads, Camden Town coster girls, public houses, sombre alleys, North London interiors. Responding ardently to these tales of mean streets, Gilman travelled on through canvases of brighter and ever brighter colour; he was now discovering Gauguin and Van Gogh and Toulouse Lautrec. He thought he preferred Gauguin; then he found him too classical in spirit, and Van Gogh became the inspiration of his life. One of his greatest ambitions was to create a character in painting; in his portrait of 'Mrs Mounter at the Breakfast Table' (plate 23) he has surely attained it. Gilman was sincerely attracted to his charlady but we do not feel here that he is deliberately recording pathos. The battered spirit of poor Mrs Mounter emerges almost subconsciously on the canvas; she speaks for all the chars in Christendom.

If the colour of this picture is as straightforward as a stained glass window, in his paintings of woodland interiors Gilman has caught another aspect of nature; the diffused, faint, infinitely subtle gradations of light to be observed in those green dusky caverns of foliage. He found this subject entrancing and he came back from Gloucestershire in 1916 with nothing but trees. Of all his works, I would prefer to own one of these woodland scenes.

Someone has said of him, 'If you mix the Signac palette, Van Gogh's strips and Sickert's spots, Charles Ginner's careful formularization of modern buildings, all their bricks painted in, a little Vuillard and a little Vlaminck, you get the material of his talent. His sanguine and sensitive personality worked on that to individual ends.'

One important ingredient of the recipe has been omitted; there is no mention here of Toulouse Lautrec and the profound effect of his morbid and intense art on Gilman.

We met Gilman in one of those rambling old rookeries which once abounded in the heart of London. In Pulteney Street, near Piccadilly Circus, he and Ginner formed a little club where friends could meet and paint during the winter evenings of 1916. Everyone enjoyed it and we all attended regularly until we were driven away by bombs. I fear it was not a lucrative venture; fees I think were paid up but expenses were heavy. I am not sure whether Gilman and Ginner even 'got home'; they must have been out of pocket in spite of all their trouble. While the club lasted, however, it was a blessed escape from the pressures of war.

On one side of the room was a reproduction of Toulouse Lautrec's picture 'A la Mie' and on the other wall a print of the famous Van Gogh self portrait with pipe in mouth and bandaged ear. Before he began to paint, Gilman would wave his brush in the air and bow towards the portrait, crying, 'A toi, Van Gogh!'

Van Gogh was his idol. He adored the vehemence of the master's colour, built up in the rugged strips of paint that so offended Sickert's sensibilities. Van Gogh's *Letters* lay on his table, reproductions of his work were pasted on the walls at Pulteney Street, he took pilgrimages to distant and difficult places if there was a chance of seeing one of his pictures there that he did not already know.

Much as I enjoyed Pulteney Street, I rather wonder what I was doing there or why or by whom I had been invited to join the club. The standard of painting was too advanced for me. Everyone followed in the steps of the master and I found this orgy of rainbow hues confusing; I was battling with combinations of new colours before I was at home with the old ones. As for spreading the thick paint, of the consistency of clay, on the canvas, I soon decided that Sickert was right; it *was* like walking across a ploughed field in pumps. Although we were not encouraged to use any medium I longed to smuggle in a little turpentine when no one was looking to thin this stiff mixture, but that would soon have been found out and my unworthiness proclaimed to this select company. Gilman was very patient but he was used to practised painters and he would stare helplessly at the mess on my canvas, wondering what to say. Fortunately for me, Ginner came to the rescue. If Gilman supplied the enthusiasm, Ginner supplied the know-how. He understood my limitations at a glance and carefully set up a more restricted palette for me.

But although I was unable to follow Gilman's instructions about technique, I found his conversation about painters, his wholehearted enthusiasm for his chosen masters, most exciting. One criticism of Van Gogh interested me especially. He pointed out, while discussing many other beauties of the master, the wonderful 'placing', how each stroke of paint was dead on the target, which lent his brushwork its uncanny force.

When Sickert returned from Dieppe in 1916 he resumed his old post at the Westminster Technical Institute as if he had never been away, thus supplanting Gilman. This caused bitterness between them. Gilman had been drifting away from Sickert's precepts for some time, drawing closer to Ginner as he heightened his palette, and Sickert had little love for Van Gogh; he always declared that 'those strips set my teeth on edge,' adding that 'Gilman and Ginner were the thickest painters in London'. And now they clashed over Gilman's innovations at the Westminster evening classes. They were agreed about the right methods of teaching students to draw but they did not see eye to eye about teaching them to paint. No wonder that their pupils were disturbed. Gilman had been tempting them with every bright colour under the sun; Sickert held that they should master a few colours before they indulged in orgies of crimson and emerald green. Now they found themselves put right back to the beginning, reduced to a palette so restricted that it was almost monochrome. All over lighting, too, was suppressed. There was widespread indignation and one student, describing the arrival of Sickert, recited his woes to me.

'You can't imagine how furious we were to find the place all dark except for one strong light and to be allowed only three or four colours at most. After all, Gilman uses plenty of colours so why shouldn't we?'

He forgot that Gilman, the colour rebel, had disciplined himself severely when young with just that restricted palette which he deplored.

Coolness with the Sickerts continued. Gilman had a habit of taking his friends to the Sickert's house in Camden Road on Sunday evenings and leaving them there, like parcels, to be called for later while he went on elsewhere. Sickert laughed at this but Christine found it embarrassing to have total strangers on her hands all the evening, especially as Sickert himself might also disappear for a little nap if the intruders did not take his fancy. But, in any case, the friendship was waning. The bond between Sickert and the Camden Towners was Spencer Gore; if anyone could have kept Sickert constant to any society, it would have been Gore; but after Gore's death he was almost bound to stray from the fold. Groups, circles, coteries meant little to Sickert; once a society that he had helped to create had found its feet, his instinct was always to move on to pastures new.

Gilman's life was one severe battle against poverty. As I have shown, he was a most extravagant painter; his paint bill today would be astronomical and he bought new brushes incessantly, holding that every painter should buy brushes whenever he had a few shillings in hand. The trouble he took over each picture used up so much of his time that he was hardly prolific enough to be a money-making proposition for the dealers and in any case his work did not sell. At the age of forty-two he fell a victim to the Spanish influenza which was ravaging the country; half starved, he could not resist the disease.

One morning in 1919 Bernadette Murphy, a great friend of the Camden Towners, came to Number 15, looking exhausted. She had been nursing Gilman and Ginner in Maple Street and she told us that Gilman's temperature was now sub-normal, which made us uneasy. But little did we realize that in a few days he would be dead.

No one could have looked less arty than Charles Ginner. Most people would have taken him for a bank manager, an engineer, an accountant, but never for a painter. Nor would his manners have provided a clue to his calling. He was quiet, composed and non-committal. Only once did I see him throw off his armour of reserve completely and that was at a party, when he pushed aside a sofa to clear more floor space and executed a neat little French song and dance with complete abandon. His French was perfect; he had been born and brought up at Cannes.

He was a thick-set, sturdy, short-necked man with a round, bald head and a bun-shaped face; disarmingly modest, and like all the Camden Towners, a glutton for work. When I first met him as a teacher in Pulteney Street he was very poor but he never descended to pot-boilers and like Gilman, he persisted in an extravagant use of oil paint. It always seemed to me that Sickert did not give him his due; he seldom referred to Ginner's work except to exclaim at the thickness of his paint. Probably the 'strips' that he objected to in Van Gogh's brushwork afflicted him also in Ginner's handling of the medium. Yet Ginner had a marked individual style. The Group prided itself on the fact that although they were so intimate with each other, meeting constantly, working in unison and often taking their pleasures together, each member had a personality which could not be confused with his neighbour's. Early Gores and Gilman might resemble each other to some extent but no one could mistake a Ginner for anything but a Ginner when he got into his stride. His world is a curiously airless world, completely lacking in atmosphere; everything is as set and precise as a Henri Rousseau but lingered over with affection; at his best, there is a blunt sincerity and the very slowness of his technique, his plodding tenacity conveys to the spectator if not excitement, at any rate a queer, solid satisfaction.

He held that true originality cannot be forced; the only way for most people to acquire a personal approach to their subject was to work steadily on and hope that with experience and research and the constant handling of their tools, they might evolve a handwriting of their own. This sounds dull but Ginner would retort that there were worse things than dullness. In any case, originality was not so blindly sought after then as now. He did not object to borrowing, provided the student borrowed intelligently and chose the best models; he would quote Turner, the arch-borrower, who knew instinctively what to absorb from the work of others. In his early days, he himself borrowed much from Van Gogh but he had many masters. He was a great admirer of Fragonard and liked to take a friend with him to the National Gallery to see 'Fête Champêtre' in the Gulbenkian collection, so that he could praise that wonderful symphony of cyclamen pinks and olive greens to a sympathetic listener. In some ways, more latent than apparent, his work has a literary, pre-Raphaelitish flavour but latterly he became a student of Wordsworth and when I visited him in Claviton Street, Westminster, shortly before his death, he was doing a series of pictures in what he called his 'Wordsworth mood'.

His drawings, whether objects in their own right or working notes, were highly elaborate; when finished, he would square them up, scoring them heavily and sometimes carelessly with heavy red ink lines. His friends deplored this ruthless treatment, which was accorded to the best as to the worst drawings; they presented him with architect's paper, already squared, to pin over the next drawing. Ginner thanked them politely but never used it. He would find his own way about the drawing under the red scaffolding and he did not seem to mind whether he had ruined it or not; once he had composed a picture from it he lost all interest in it.

During his later years he had one unswerving method of technique. He drew in his picture, faintly but carefully, then applied a thin colour wash of approximately the right colours, using turpentine so that it dried quickly. Then he started his real painting with a quantity of rather small, flat brushes and in his methodical way working from left to right across the canvas, finishing the picture in one very thick coat of paint. His aim was to complete this second coat without any corrections.

If ever a painter died of overwork, it was Ambrose McEvoy.

When he was in his teens, Whistler took him to Hampton Court to see the pictures. Stopping before a Tintoretto, Whistler said 'Drink it in, my boy! drink it in!' McEvoy did drink it in and when Whistler advised his father to send him to the Slade he spent a long apprenticeship there working slowly and laboriously, studying the old masters, and their methods, from Titian to Hogarth. On leaving the Slade he continued his researches at the National Gallery, producing little himself, but if he had not yet found his personal style he knew very well what he wanted to do. Always a tonal painter, in spite of his linear training at the Slade, he worked on with slow deliberation until suddenly his technique became more effortless, his outlook more assured. Some of his early things remind us of Sickert but he was soon striking a note of his own; his dreamy landscapes and pensive interiors have the tonal unity that he sought; they are romantic in feeling, classical in calculation and control.

It is generally supposed that his interest in landscape waned when he was caught up in the treadmill of portrait painting, but Slade legend had it that he was heard to declare that he would drop portrait commissions and paint where inspiration led him when he could afford to do so. This story may be only hearsay but it is true that his desire was to put aside enough capital to ensure his independence.

He inherited the poetry of Gainsborough, and to enhance the flowerlike quality of his women sitters he adopted a sort of double lighting which made them seem as if they had been blown on the canvas. As he became more overworked, this device hardened into a formula; he seemed at the last to be relying on charm and facility rather than on research into character. The simple integrity of the earlier portraits, lingered over with such close affection, gave place to more sketchy conceptions of his subject; the later work tends to become strained, a little scattered; there is a spasmodic flicker over the canvas like the last streaming flare of the candle before it gutters into night.

He was leading a strenuous social life during the few terms that he taught at the Slade and he would arrive there exhausted, his face drawn, his eyes bloodshot with late hours and excessive painting. This fatigue did not deter him from giving us all the help he could; we learned more about the technique of portrait painting from him than from anyone else. His methods of teaching differed from those of the other professors; he treated us as colleagues rather than as students, making suggestions rather than laying down the law, discussing our difficulties as if we too were professional painters. After long discipline with the pencil, Slade painting was inclined to tightness; McEvoy found this tendency displeasing, especially in the case of women sitters, but he had his own way of trying to counteract it. He would shake his head sadly as he inspected our over modelled, maplike studies, sighing, 'It's as hard as a board.' Then he would take a large brush filled with white paint, turpentine and a dash of umber which he scumbled lightly over the painting, in order to break down the stiffness of the contours. This veil dried quickly, so that he could soon proceed to refind the features of the face, still showing faintly through it. According to Epstein, every face has its key feature and McEvoy knew at a glance what this feature would be. With women, it was often the eyes; he would retrieve them with a few touches and re-state the whole head slightly but surely, marking the accents intuitively, the strokes of his brush fluttering down like snowflakes, leaving the foundation underneath to play its part in providing mass and substance. Gradually, the head emerged through its transparent covering of white and umber; vivid, soft yet precise, a shaft of light emerging from a cloud.

Most of us could produce a head of sorts at this stage of our training; we could enjoy masking it afterwards with a thin wash of paint to blur the edginess; but when it came to re-stating the features through the haze and accenting them just enough to sharpen the effect and pull the drawing together again, our efforts did not look in the least like a shaft of light emerging from a cloud. After frantic attempts to follow him we were reduced to despair, but always hoped that he might take pity on us again and infuse our daubs with a spark of life.

Teaching of this kind is arduous; looking back on the time and energy he might devote to some favoured student, one is surprised that he cared to repeat such an exacting demonstration. I fear that he took more trouble over us than his ebbing strength could afford; we must have proved as exhausting as his portrait commissions. But I think he enjoyed his visits to the Slade. He could take what liberties he pleased with the model, he could experiment without causing offence and he could drop the subject whenever he had solved the problem without bothering to finish it, as bridge players throw in their hands without playing out their cards. But McEvoy could not help giving himself up to whatever he was doing at the moment; he had no notion of husbanding his forces and he threw himself into his teaching with the same intensity that he displayed in his own painting. It is not to be expected that all his sitters should have realized the strain he was undergoing or have proved sympathetic enough to put aside their own concerns or give themselves up for the time being to the exigencies of the portrait. Not for him the endless sittings exacted from their victims by Whistler and

Rembrandt; times had changed since then and McEvoy was too easy-going to enforce his will upon his clients. There was also the financial aspect to be considered. When he had struck out a likeness, enhanced by his own inimitable blend of charm and elegance, he could seldom afford to go further and carry the painting through; other sitters were waiting to claim him. In the end he was working in a feverish state of tension. Sitters might default at the last moment when he was all keyed up and ready for action, his palette set, awaiting their arrival; they might leave early or come late or bring friends who filled the place with their clamour; his telephone, his front door bell were constantly ringing. Impossible to imagine the Professor, Tonks or Steer submitting to these conditions! And McEvoy had not half their physical stamina. He was already tired out, tired and defenceless when he was finally engulfed in sitters, but to give them their due, some of them must have been sympathetic or interesting personalities and the sheer springtime loveliness of girls like Daphne Baring (plate 25) would lift the heart of less susceptible painters than McEvoy.

But he was always rushed for time. One wonders whether he could have been saved if he had taken a long rest from London and moneymaking before it was too late; if he could have painted as the muse moved him, in some sweet Auburn, loveliest village of the plain . . . But it is idle lamenting the might have beens. He has left us many sensitive portraits, achieved before he was driven beyond his strength, and a few elegiac landscapes, which I do not think are so well known.

The successful portrait painter needs the constitution of a camel and a rudimentary nervous organization. McEvoy had neither, only his poetic talent and his sensibility. So that all these exactions cut short his life and his career and he died at forty-nine.

Alas, poor McEvoy.

Chapter 10

The Bloomsberries

Bloomsbury and Fitzrovia, geographically speaking, were only a short distance apart, separated from each other by Gower Street and Tottenham Court Road. But they are generally thought of as states of mind rather than as geographical concepts. From this point of view they were widely separated in spite of their mutual interest in ideas.

In 1917, Bloomsbury was a right little, tight little island peopled by intimate friends and presided over, more or less, by the great economist, Maynard Keynes. Bloomsbury met in Gordon Square, waving aloft the banners of liberalism and adventurous thought with some philosophy for full measure. Many of the Bloomsberries were friends from Cambridge days; they were immensely loyal to each other, presenting an unbroken front to the outside world. Travelled, well-read, creative, they spoke as well as they wrote, Roger Fry and Maynard Keynes especially being fascinating talkers. Most of them were of the same generation, some had private means.

Fitzrovia, on the other hand, was a large, shifting, classless society of oddly assorted persons linked together by a common interest in painting and sculpture, a rough and ready camaraderie which would have jarred the heightened susceptibilities of Bloomsbury, and generally speaking, no private means at all. I do not think that women counted for much in this varied company, except behind the scenes; Fitzrovia had no well known hostesses who entertained lavishly and frequently, such as Lady Ottoline Morell and Mrs Clive Bell. Sickert was a born host, but he lacked the means to entertain as he would have wished; Epstein who did not, strictly speaking, belong to Fitzrovia, was chiefly interested in artists and the same applied to Old Taylor, who preferred his fellow workers and had almost turned his back on the outside world when I knew him.

But the important difference between the two groups was that Bloomsbury was composed of writers, not painters. E. M. Forster, Lytton Strachey, Virginia Woolf, David Garnett, these are household words, and a glittering array of other literary stars surrounded them. Needless to add, the pen is more easily circulated than the brush and has a wider following, especially when wielded by such brilliant performers. Bloomsbury was ninety per cent literary; there must have been more but I cannot call to mind any painters of note save Vanessa Bell (Mrs Clive Bell), Roger Fry and Duncan Grant. And Fry, I would suggest, will be remembered

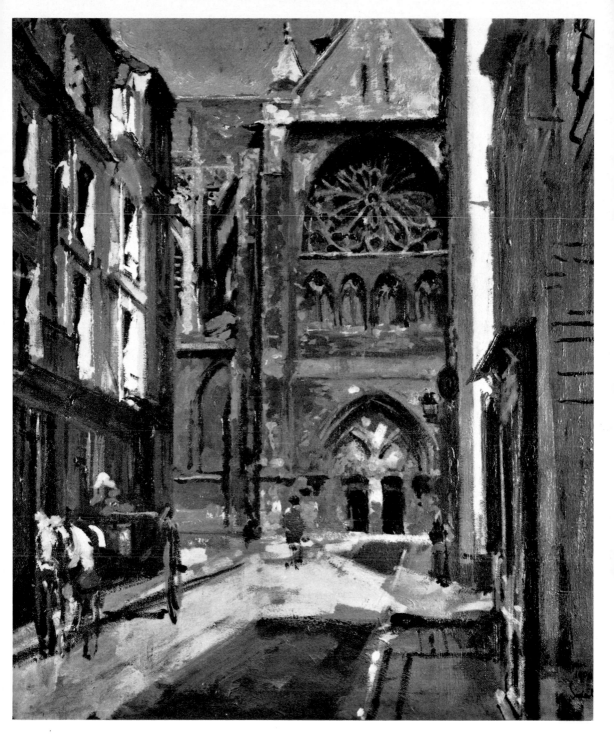

28. Walter Richard Sickert (1860-1942).
LA RUE PECQUET, DIEPPE, *c.* 1900. Oil. 21½ × 18 ins.
City Museum and Art Gallery, Birmingham

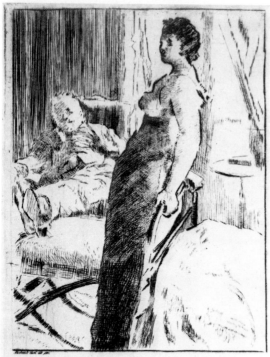

Et delator es, et calumniator;
Et fraudator es, et negotiator,
Et fellator es, et lanista: miror
Quare non habeas, Vacerra, nummos.
Martial Epigr. XI. 66
Published by Carfax & Co. 24 Bury Street, S.t James's

29. Walter Richard Sickert (1860–1942).
ET DELATOR ES, *c.* 1913. Etching. 5½ × 3¾ ins.
The lines from Martial contain various epithets
appropriate to a quarrel between a man and a woman.
Islington Public Libraries

30. Walter Richard Sickert (1860–1942).
SALLY, *c.* 1915. Etching. 6¼ × 3¾ ins.
Islington Public Libraries

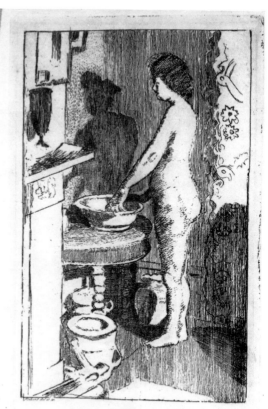

SALLY.
Published by Carfax & Co 24 Bury Street S.t James's

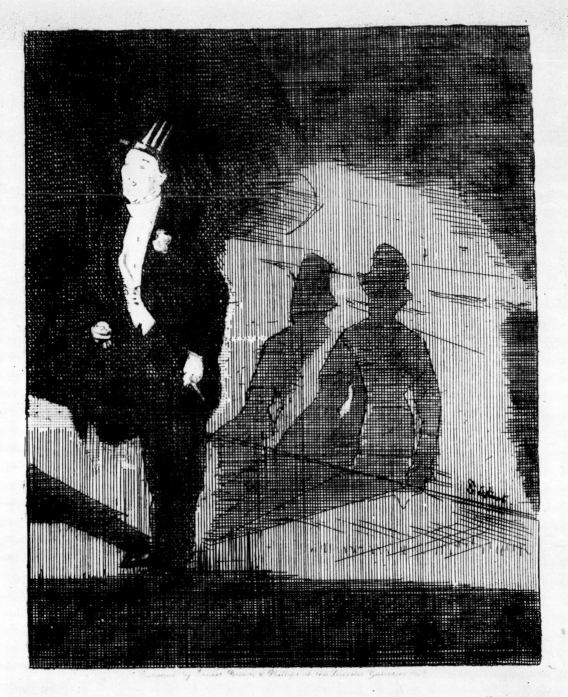

"THAT OLD-FASHIONED MOTHER OF MINE"

31. Walter Richard Sickert (1860–1942).
THAT OLD FASHIONED MOTHER OF MINE, 1928. Etching. $7\frac{3}{4} \times 5\frac{3}{4}$ ins.
The song which inspired the etching was popularized by the singer Talbot O'Farrell.
Islington Public Libraries

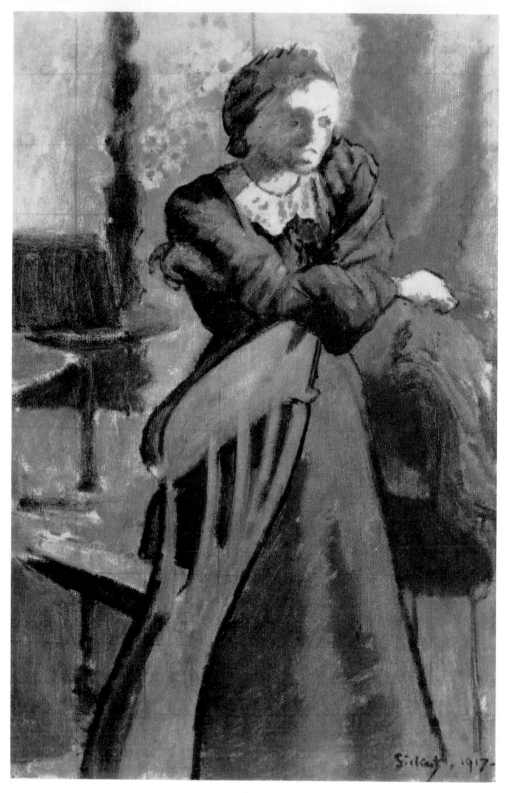

32. Walter Richard Sickert (1860-1942).
THE OBJECTION, 1917. Oil. 33 × 21 ins.
Collection J. O. Stanley-Clark

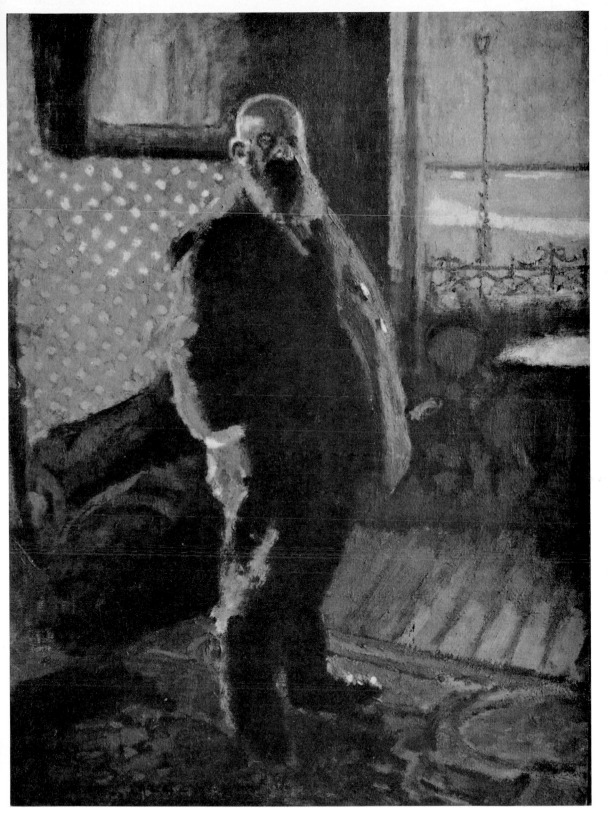

33. Walter Richard Sickert (1860–1942). VICTOR LECOUR, 1922–4. Oil. 32 × 23¾ ins.
Manchester City Art Gallery

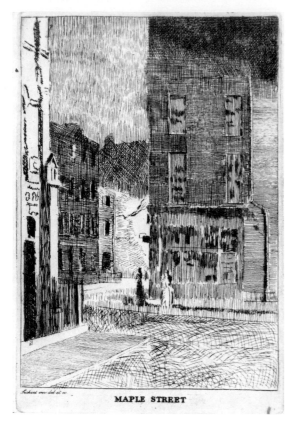

MAPLE STREET

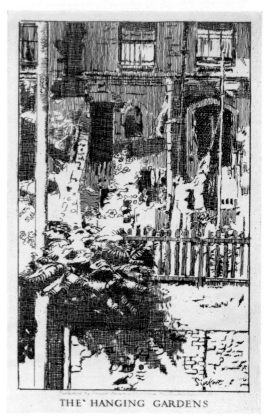

THE HANGING GARDENS

34. Walter Richard Sickert (1860-1942).
MAPLE STREET, *c.* 1920. Etching. $7\frac{3}{4} \times 5$ ins.
Maple Street was near Sickert's studio in Fitzroy Street.
Islington Public Libraries

35. Walter Richard Sickert (1860-1942).
THE HANGING GARDENS, 1929. Engraving. $7 \times 4\frac{1}{2}$ ins.
The house is 56 Noel Street, now Noel Road, where
Sickert lived for some time. *Islington Public Libraries*

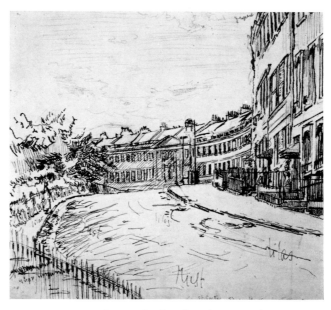

36. Walter Richard Sickert (1860-1942).
LANSDOWN CRESCENT, FROM LANSDOWN PLACE EAST, BATH, *c.* 1916-18.
Pencil overdrawn with heavy ink. $9\frac{1}{4} \times 10$ ins. *Collection John Perry*

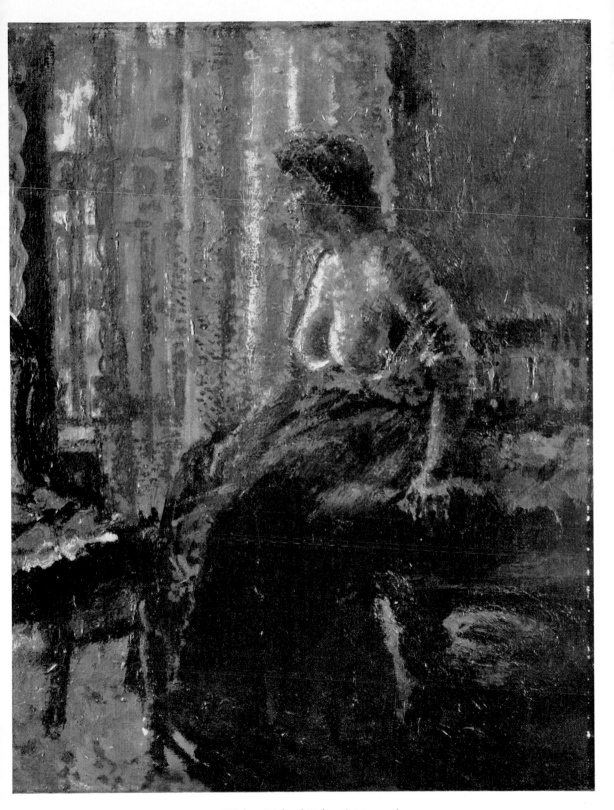

37. Walter Richard Sickert (1860-1942).
SEATED WOMAN, GRANBY STREET, 1900. Oil. 20½ × 16 ins.
Collection E. M. Behrens

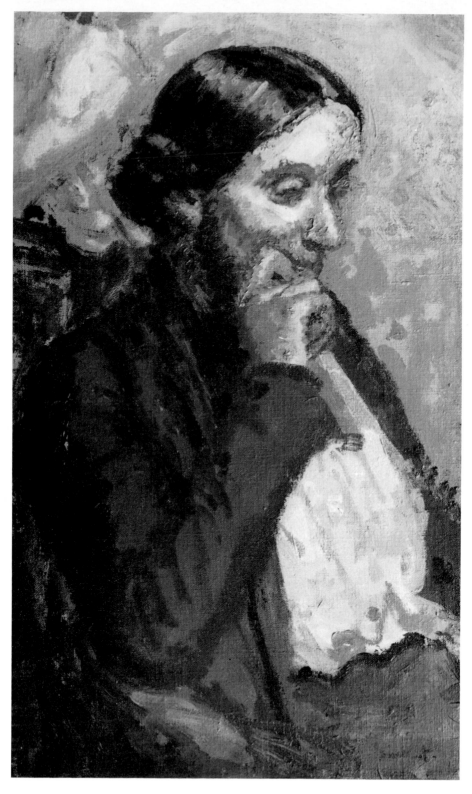

38. Walter Richard Sickert (1860–1942).
PORTRAIT OF A WOMAN, believed to be Virginia Woolf. Oil.
St Felix School, Southwold

chiefly for his lecturing and his writings, although painting was dearer to him than any of his other activities.

With the exception of Sickert, Fitzrovia was almost inarticulate. And generally speaking, it did not deplore the deficiency; the visual arts were all that mattered here, considered as more important than literature or any other civilized achievement. But as a group, Fitzrovia suffered severely from a lack of publicity agents. Not so the Bloomsberries. More practical than Fitzrovia, they wrote each other up and have continued to do so till the present time, thus keeping their memories green with the public. During the twenties and thirties they led the literary and art worlds of London through their pens; passionately Francophile, especially Clive Bell and Roger Fry, they worshipped Paris as opposed to London. Even the French themselves could hardly find their Gallic fervour wanting and Fry enlarged the emotions of many art lovers in this country with his Post Impressionist Exhibition of 1910, his lectures and his classic work, *Vision and Design*.

Clive Bell, however, art critic of the *New Statesman* from 1933 to 1943, did praise a few English cronies besides Duncan Grant and his own wife, Vanessa Bell, and had a lasting influence in America. To this day, his criticisms are quoted by critics in New York. He had a charming, easy style, discussed problems of painting more from the point of view of the painter than the literary critic, and his enthusiasm was catching. In 1919, he wrote an appreciative preface to a Sickert exhibition at the Eldar Gallery, where he says, 'Sickert is always making something; what he is making however is not the familiar picture of commerce but an expressive form, a form that has an independent existence and significance, something, we feel, that could not have been other than it is. That is where his conviction and artistic common sense come in; and from this innate conviction—this bent, gift, talent, genius, call it what you will—comes that personal quality, that style, that distinction, which makes a Sickert a Sickert, and, incidentally, a work of art.'

But Mr Bell was moody. Years later he wrote a rather petulant article about Sickert in the Cornhill Magazine, which he repeated afterwards in his book *Old Friends*, and reproduced a rather dull drawing of Bath, from Sickert's later period, when the master's eye was losing its hawk-like precision. No doubt this drawing was chosen because a more exciting one was difficult to find; Sickert's work had nearly all disappeared by now in museums and private collections. But when he wrote this later article, Mr Bell seems to have decided that he did not like his old friend Sickert after all. It is idle to speculate on what had passed between the two men to estrange them, but Mr Bell was no longer the ardent crusader of his youth; Bloomsbury was breaking up, his health was impaired and he had lost a son in the Spanish war. It was a far cry from the old days in Fitzroy Street when, gay and impetuous, with a ringing laugh that echoed through the old barn of a studio, he would pop into the Frith on Sickert's Wednesdays. I remember especially one afternoon in 1918 when he bought a charming Sickert oil of a woman with an armful of flowers, which entranced him. He went off as delighted with his purchase as a schoolboy with a new bicycle.

It seems ironic that Professor Quentin Bell, son of Clive Bell, should have written one of the most profound and sensitive criticisms of Sickert's work at his centenary in 1960. Professor Bell is a painter himself and writes, as his father did, from the painter's point of view, which restores the confidence of the bewildered layman who has been so knocked about since the last war by endless gimmicks and violent changes and theories. He also gives him useful information about the different periods of the master, pointing out what so sadly needs stressing, that the golden period of Sickert is, roughly speaking, between 1900 and 1925 with occasional late flashes of magic in his old age.

I did not see Clive Bell again until after the Second World War, when we met at an exhibition of paintings in Sussex. The old fiery spirit was still there but the eager clutch on life was gone; it seemed to have no more to offer him. His companion was Duncan Grant, as serene as Bell was peppery; he was, I think, by common consent their most gifted painter, gifted by any standards. But although Duncan Grant lived at the Whistler studio for a time, he was seldom there in spirit and if some rather pushing acquaintance tried to buttonhole him at a Fitzroy Street party he would listen politely for a few moments, then explain, 'excuse me, but I really must find Mrs Bell . . .' while he drifted away to his own more congenial atmosphere. As he always seemed to be discovering Mrs Bell, people soon learned to leave him alone. He never did really associate himself with Fitzroy Street, even when he came to rent the Whistler after Sickert had departed to Dieppe in 1918. Gordon Square was always his spiritual home.

Roger Fry came to the Frith as late as possible on At Home days, so that he could get Sickert to himself after the other guests had gone and talk his fill about painting.

Fry had discovered modern art rather late in life and was enthusiastic about it as only converts can be. His scholarship was impressive. He had studied painting with the thoroughness he brought to all his undertakings, he was at home in galleries all over Europe, he was a formidable art historian; but when he began to paint, he was Mr Facing Both-Ways; a thousand theories assailed him, paralysing every stroke of the brush. The connection between him and his work was elusive, the eloquence of his speech missing as he approached the canvas. Being a rapid and restless painter, he produced quantities of pictures; when he let the subject move him, they could be charming; all too often they were a little dry, a little anxious, a little tame. It might have been more exciting if he had struck out some path for himself but he preferred to follow, awestruck, in the footsteps of Cézanne, whom he regarded as the noblest work of God. I do not think Fitzroy Street gave him enough credit for his courage and perseverance as he pursued his arduous journey to Aix. But people rather dreaded his prodigious output. They respected his general powers but they did not know what to say about his painting. Having lured his friends to his house in Dalmeny Avenue, he would spread his pictures on the floor, inviting comment on each one in turn. The visitors had to maintain a constant polite response to his work and they longed sometimes not to have to think up any more adequate replies, to see him remove the canvases and resume his usual enchanting conversation. In many ways the most tactful of men, his passion for painting got the better of him when he was showing his things and he exhausted his audience without suspecting it.

'What can one do about all those acres of canvas?' sighed Fred Porter, after an extra long session of private viewing at Dalmeny Avenue. 'I'd said all I'd got to say in the first half hour.'

Sickert and Fry had known each other all their lives; Fry had lived for a time with old Mrs Sickert and her sons. The relationship between them was a curious one. Sickert had been a steady support when Fry was passing through a tragic phase; they always rallied to each other in moments of crisis but they could hardly be described as intimates. If they had been constantly together they would not have hit it off. Sickert could not refrain from teasing Fry, as he teased all his friends, and this Fry enjoyed, being very well able to hold his own; but the common interest, painting, which should have forged a link between them, did nothing of the sort; it merely drove them apart. Sickert mistrusted Fry's views on painting and he could be ruthless when his idols were attacked, as on the famous occasion when Fry, all unwittingly, probed him in a tender spot, his affection for Degas.

Fry: 'It took Degas forty years to get rid of his cleverness.'

Sickert: 'And it will take you eighty years to get it.'

This well-known retort may seem unduly harsh; I have resurrected it to remind the reader how quickly Sickert resented any criticism of his friends. And Degas was more than a friend; he was the revered master, the father figure; as Sickert himself put it, 'the lighthouse of my existence.' A blander example of his wit occurred when he and Fry were looking at an exhibition of the Allied Artists.

Fry: 'There's something to be said for this picture.'

Sickert: 'Say it, Roger, say it!'

Reacting violently against his Puritan background, Fry worshipped France and all her works; he seemed to feel for England a sort of nervous distaste and he deplored the cooking, the climate, the hearties and the whole establishment of his native land. But Sickert was attached to England as well as France. And there was a deeper cause of estrangement than this. Sickert valued Fry for his intellect, his scholarship, his industry; he attended Fry's lectures and sat applauding vigorously in the front row of the audience; but he was not interested in Fry's painting. Sooner or later, in their conversations together, they struck, inevitably, the final, the inescapable rock.

Nor did he particularly wish to discuss art with Fry. But Fry came to the Frith to do just that. Unmindful of the gods who had showered so many blessings on him, he did not want praise for the qualities that Sickert was the first to recognize;

he longed only to be accepted as a painter. One word of praise for his pictures meant more to him than oceans of appreciation for all his other gifts and that word Sickert withheld, not from churlishness but from conviction. It is indeed possible that he underrated Fry's talent, that everyone did and that posterity will be fairer to him than Fitzroy Street; but painters thought of Fry almost exclusively as writer and lecturer. Sickert led the conversation away from painting when they were together but Fry, gently determined, pinned him down to it again and again. Sometimes, Sickert took refuge in silence. Only once, years afterwards, did I hear him refer to Fry's work. He was inspecting one of his canvases, shaking his head sadly and murmuring, half aloud, half to himself, *'poor Roger!'*

And on the subject of literature they got no further. One was serious when the other was flippant; their differences could not be reconciled. With his usual disregard for labels, Sickert found talent sometimes in obscure places and might interest himself in various humble literary aspirants; Fry may have taken up humble persons in his maturity but I cannot think that he had ever consorted with them in his exquisitely lettered youth. One afternoon, Sickert praised a little book called *Down Our Street*, the author, I think, was a Mrs Buckrose. The title, naturally, would appeal to Sickert and the story was a plain chronicle of everyday people on the fringe of want, redeemed from drabness by humour and sympathy. Fry had never heard of Mrs Buckrose and was bewildered by Sickert's interest in this obscure writer. He agreed with his usual courtesy that there must, no doubt, be something in the book if it had detained Sickert, even for a moment; but it sounded sentimental and how prone the English were to the vice of sentimentality! He went on to deplore the drivel that appealed to the troops. One song especially had offended his reluctant ear when visiting wounded soldiers in hospital. He quoted it as an instance of the depths to which bathos could sink.

> 'Dear face that holds
> so sweet a smile for me
> Were you not mine
> how dark the world would be!'

There was a pause.

'Well, what more do you want?' said Sickert.

'Really, Walter! you can't—' then Fry smiled. 'Of course, you're joking.'

But he was mistaken. Sickert did like 'The Sunshine of Your Smile.'

The afternoon usually ended with Sickert pottering round his pictures, busying himself with little jobs and putting in a word here and there while Fry talked to Christine. Christine had a fancy for Fry; she found that he had a beautiful head and she could enjoy his charming manners. But he could never be quite himself with Sickert. The slack thread of conversation might suddenly tauten, the easy banter turn to sword play when Sickert would glide into another mood and become, as his critics have complained, the serpent in a basket of figs. In this frame of mind, how he enjoyed pricking Roger's balloons!

One afternoon, Fry got quite wound up as he mounted his favourite hobby horse, England. He was declaiming with his usual eloquence about the English, deploring our insularity, our lack of emotion, our Puritan uneasiness about sex and our worship of Mrs Grundy, to Christine, who had nothing much to say to all this, when a voice came from the corner where Sickert was buffeting his canvases.

'When we were boys together, Roger, I thought that you had decided to be a prig, but now I see that you have decided to be a *viveur*.'

We had attended Fry's lectures at University College when we were students at the Slade. I fear he was too advanced for most of us but he gave us our first taste of the Italians; I remember a superb lecture on Donatello for which I am still grateful. I enjoyed meeting him in our common omnibus, on the way from Regent's Park to Fitzroy Street; he was infinitely kind to young people, leading us on to talk about ourselves when we should have been more profitably employed listening to him, pretending that we were enlarging his mental horizon and expressing ideas that had never previously crossed his mind. 'Do you know, that had never occurred to me.' Differences of age, of standing all dropped away; his patience was colossal and unlike Dr Johnson he never administered a check. Beguiled by this duplicity, this heady mixture of interest and deference to our views, we chattered away confidently, holding forth at length about Art and the Universe, Fry gravely nodding his head at intervals as much as to say, 'You have got something there.' No wonder that he had a host of young friends who were anxious for his company. He even attended our parties sometimes, where he conducted himself with his usual blend of tolerance and sympathy.

It was with his usual wit that Fry summed up his enigmatic relationship with Sickert.

'You and I,' he declared, 'both live in the firm belief that one or other of us is destined to do one of us in, and, that being the only thing that keeps us both alive, we should not do it as we should both have lost our motive for living.'

It must be conceded that Fry had the last word, but Sickert was not the man to grudge him his advantage. He always maintained, moreover, that Fry should be knighted immediately. He could hardly contain his impatience while awaiting the day when he should be able to address him as 'Sir Fry'.

PART THREE

Chapter 11

Dieppe

The Sickerts had only been waiting for the end of the war to hurry back to France. Christine, who was increasingly frail, longed for the quiet she hoped to find there and Sickert desperately needed to free himself from the complications of life in London. First, they took the Villa D'Aumale at Envermeu, a village some ten miles from Dieppe, then they bought the Maison Mouton, on the outskirts of the village, which had once been an inn. They were now more or less buried alive and it would only be a question of time before Sickert needed more scope, but for the moment he was highly entertained with inspecting the alterations that the old villa needed, re-moulding it nearer to his fancy and making friends with the villagers. Happy and busy, he was painting hard, ignoring the bitter winter of 1919-20, out of doors in all weathers; but the cruel cold, the chilly house, and probably her exertions during the move, proved fatal for Christine. During the summer she failed rapidly; in October she died.

Fitzroy Street was shocked to hear the news. She was only forty-four.

No sign from Sickert. We did not expect to hear from him, as we knew he would be shattered and that he had always disliked writing letters. But months went by and the silence was profound. We began to feel uneasy. It was useless applying to Marie for information, she could not read or write, and we knew no one else in Dieppe. It seemed that we had reached deadlock but suddenly, a collector of contemporary pictures appeared on the scene who wanted me to choose a Sickert for him from the studio. This was Frank Pickett, the engineer, inventor and financier, who paid a million pounds after the First World War for half a dozen or so surplus ammunition dumps in France and Flanders, burned the high explosive out of the shell cases and sold the various metals as scrap. My father had retired from business but he consented to be Pickett's financial manager for a year or two, so that he and I were crossing the Channel frequently in 1921; I accompanied him as often as possible, as he disliked travelling alone, especially the prospect of solitary evenings in French hotels. We generally went to Boulogne and so to Amiens, but when we were contemplating our December visit to France, we sent a telegram to Sickert to inform him that this time we proposed coming via Dieppe, and would go on to visit the dumps from there. I was uncertain about our welcome, especially as

I had mentioned that we wanted a picture; Sickert had probably been too depressed to paint during the last year, and might not feel able to see us at all.

The reply to our telegram came back from his flat in rue Desmarets with one word on it—'Surrey'. We wondered what this could mean but proceeded on our way, hoping for the best. It was quite by chance that I happened to ask Sickert afterwards to explain his reply to our telegram, when I discovered that the cryptic word 'Surrey' should have been 'Hooray!' an English greeting which had proved too much for the Dieppe post office.

As we set out for Newhaven, the weather was glorious, one of those blessed days that come so rarely in northern winters to lift the heart and remind us that spring is not so far behind. The sun shone and shone across an untroubled sea, the air was crisp and windless, we were on deck all the time. On our arrival at Dieppe, we had dinner at our hotel and went to bed early, overcome with fresh air and lavish French cooking, but we had reckoned without the prospect of high jinks downstairs; the landlord was throwing a party.

By two o'clock, unable to get a wink of sleep, with a simultaneous gesture we had all left our unquiet beds and met in the *salle* below, wrapped in dressing gowns; a disconsolate little huddle consisting of the English chaplain, my father and myself. The party had now formed a solemn procession which was parading through the ground floor of the hotel, to appropriate music, and seemed likely to continue doing so for some time to come. All we could do was to order coffee and still more coffee.

'What possible gratification can it possibly afford them to make this infernal noise?' groaned the chaplain. But answer came there none. Alas, it afforded the revellers infinite gratification; dawn was breaking before the landlord reluctantly put up the shutters and we crept wearily upstairs again. As a result, it was past eleven o'clock when I woke up with a start next morning, remembering my mission.

Everything seemed to be alive and simmering in Dieppe, so unlike our English Sundays. There was a busy hum in the streets, laughter and voices from open doorways, delicious smells of cooking from kitchen windows, whiffs of coffee, garlic and onions that I absorbed gratefully in my growing hunger. The sun still sparkled over the chattering scene and probed the shadows in those dark, mysterious side alleys, that Sickert had so constantly painted; sometimes it revealed distant glimpses of the cathedral as in those rare canvases that still turn up occasionally at the more distinguished West End galleries. Produced in a vintage period, they give us, as we would say, 'his own particular brand of mud', that mysterious fusion of coffee, sepia chocolate, ochre and ambers with which he created his own particular brand of luminosity.

Dieppe was a delightful town and the natives seemed all busy and gay. I enquired in the market place for Sickert and everyone broke into smiles. 'Ah! Monsieur Seeckairt! Eh bien . . .' and I found myself being hauled along by a stream of boys and girls who sprang up from nowhere, all chattering and cawing and falling over themselves in their anxiety to show me the way. I arrived at rue Desmarets like the Pied Piper with my bodyguard, and looked up at Sickert's windows; he could hardly have failed to remark the visitation. Sure enough, a window shot up and his head appeared.

'Hare for lunch,' he said. And slammed the window down again.

When, after some coaxing and bribing, I had dismissed my retinue, Marie let me in and we exchanged a few words in the hall. She was heart-broken about her mistress and most concerned for Sickert, who had retired into complete seclusion for the past year. Marie said that he never realized that Christine was dying. She had always been fragile, she was seventeen years his junior and she never complained. Whatever the cause of this blindness, he was utterly unprepared for her death, which seemed to have happened rather suddenly. It dealt him a blow from which he never really recovered. Marie was unable to rouse him but she did her best to provide tempting meals, although he was eating little at this time. Physically, he was more comfortable at rue Desmarets than he had been for years; the flat was fairly large but beautifully kept, and Marie understood his ways. The site was charming, tucked away in a sheltered corner overlooking the sea, still in its angelic mood of yesterday; the waves gently lapped the shore and the winter sunshine, pale as primroses, sparkled on the empty promenade. I liked rue Desmarets better than any habitation of Sickert's that I had known, always excepting the Whistler; it was so inviting, almost cosy, that I began to wonder if, after all, he might relax into comfort in his old age like other people.

He was in his most endearing mood that Sunday in spite of the frozen calm that separated us. I wanted to say something about Christine but I did not know how to begin. Helpless before this rooted sorrow, I could only say at last, lamely enough:

'I know how you must miss her.'

'It's not that,' he answered instantly. 'My grief is, that she *no longer exists*.'

There was no reply to such finality, such despair. The unforgiving silence of the dead still hung over us; he had endured it for nearly a year and I wondered what on earth would cheer him. Luncheon was nearly over before I remembered the comment of a visitor to the Frith, which I thought might please him.

'So-and-so once told me that Christine was the most distinguished woman he had ever seen.'

He smiled, for the first time since our meeting. Soon, we were talking about her and her days at Camden Road and Fitzroy Street. 'If I could live through this last year I could live through anything,' he remarked. This was his only reference to his sorrow. And after luncheon he came unexpectedly to my aid about the picture I was seeking and suggested that we should take a turn round the studio.

147

I saw that he had been working harder than I supposed; there were masses of drawings all over the place. He put several canvases on his easel and invited me to choose one of them. Finally, we selected together a girl singing alone on the stage before the curtain, a wistful figure that reminded me of Whistler's women. I felt sure that Frank Pickett could hardly fail to like this and when Sickert said that she was rather a favourite of his, that settled the matter.

But he did not want to talk about painting. After showing me some other things, he locked up the studio and we went away by car to Envermeu.

The afternoon was wearing on, the sun was already waning and the house at Envermeu was cold and hollow as a forsaken nest. But there was still some furniture left about and a few speaking relics of Christine—her workbasket, an embroidered bag, other trifles that I have forgotten. The absence of curtains and carpets spoke of Sickert, but I knew that she would have made it more of a home than this. At first, he started showing me things eagerly, then he fell silent again, his head in his hands, while I mused beside him in the dead room. I wondered afresh about this last retreat to France. It did not seem that he had gained any special advantage by leaving Fitzroy Street to isolate himself in this backwater; he had always maintained that Dieppe was played out and had no more to offer him. Surely, he could have found peace and freedom, so sternly denied him in London, in Bath or Exeter or even his beloved Edinburgh, perhaps his favourite haunt of all. I was forgetting the fascination that this district of Normandy held for him with its memories of Whistler, Degas, Gide, Blanche, Beerbohm and countless other old friends of his youth, whose ghosts met him at every street corner in the neighbourhood. Dieppe and its surroundings had always been his second home and Dieppe itself, grave, sombre, mysterious, had inspired some of his best work. And Christine had always wanted exile.

I did not know then that soon he would be giving us anything so exciting as 'Victor Lecour' (plate 33) which he produced the following year and which alone would have justified a longer stay than he actually made in France. But this afternoon I wondered what mysterious stimulus, what nostalgia for lost youth, could have driven him to settle in this bleak village. Side by side we sat motionless and the room grew colder and colder. He had forgotten all about me and I was struck afresh, as I had often been before, by his capacity for utter stillness. But the winter dusk was gathering round us; I had to remind him that time was marching on and we were due to join Miss Gosse next door for tea.

Sylvia Gosse, well known painter and daughter of the formidable and fiery author and critic, Sir Edmund Gosse, had taken a house at Envermeu to be near Christine. It is no exaggeration to say that had it not been for Miss Gosse, often referred to as Sickert's guardian angel, we might have had no more pictures of importance from Sickert after the Dieppe disaster. He always maintained that 'the mainspring was broken' at Christine's death, but there were still a few bursts of the old magic to come among the indifferent canvases that he painted in the ensuing years; generally, alas, from necessity rather than from inclination, in the forlorn hope of making enough money to live on.

Miss Gosse looked after the Sickerts from their arrival at Envermeu. She had all the strength and vitality that was ebbing from Christine; she and Marie took the reins and managed the daily, endless duties that running a house entails. As time went on, she nursed Christine in her last illness and looked after Sickert, tactfully and almost silently, in the grim months that lay ahead, shouldering many of his burdens until he showed signs of taking up life again. I had not seen her since Fitzroy Street days, when she rented a studio in Charlotte Street. She had never mixed freely with the *quartier;* her sole interest there was the Sickerts, although she had a few other cronies, including Walter Taylor and the Cliftons. She might appear at Number 15 on At Home days, but rarely; being very shy, she always chose the most inconspicuous corner she could find, looking harassed and hunted, and hardly spoke. Indeed, sometimes she seemed so distressed that Ginner once remarked:

'Miss Gosse comes in as if she had just committed a murder.'

Living with her parents in Hanover Terrace, Regents Park, she had met many interesting people from literary and art circles all over Europe. The Gosses entertained frequently, although Gosse was so peppery; gossip had it that a fresh set of people attended his Christmas parties every year because he had fallen out with the old guests in the intervening period. But certain tried cronies, nevertheless, retained his affection; George Moore, Sickert, Henry James and the Chalmers Mitchells were often to be found at his dinner table. Lady Chalmers was always placed next to Gosse, partly because she was his favourite woman and partly because Lady Gosse relied on her to keep him good tempered and if possible, to ward off any sallies of Moore which might offend his ears. Sir Edmund, she told us, suffered the gravest apprehension throughout the meal that Moore would say something improper and sure enough, sooner or later Moore's loud flat penetrating tones would break into a momentary general silence with some inappropriate Rabelaisian jest from which with all her tact and skill, she was unable to distract the attention of her shrinking host. I asked why Moore was invited again and she maintained that this constancy only went to show that he could be loyal to certain old friends. I suspected that Sir Edmund knew only too well that it would be impossible to replace Moore when he wanted to talk about literature. There can be little doubt that as a sensitive and informed critic on his own subject, Moore was the most congenial of companions.

Sylvia Gosse, as she grew up, acted as co-hostess with Lady Gosse on these occasions. But the shyness persisted and Thomas Hardy once complained:

'I've known Sylvia since she was a little girl, when I used to go up to the nursery to say goodnight to her in her cot, but I simply can't get a word out of her these days.'

There seems to be one quality shared by the great, however they may differ otherwise; they seldom suffer from self-consciousness, so it is not surprising if Mr Hardy was mystified by the stiffness that Sylvia displayed towards him. But the diffidence that pursued her all her life, and her brother and sister too, was largely due to their strict upbringing. Edmund Gosse was an eminent Victorian if ever there was one and a Puritan to boot. Sylvia often mentioned the lectures they received as children, warning them not to put themselves forward when their parents were entertaining the great, who would be bored to death with their childish prattle, with the result that they became self-conscious and tongue-tied. At her ease, among a small intimate circle, Sylvia would emerge from her shell and amuse everyone with the famous wit that she had inherited from her father.

Later, after Sickert had left Envermeu, she too gave up her home there and returned to London. For the rest of his life she continued to help him in such an unobtrusive way that half the time he did not even know that the help had been given. Here is an extract from a letter she sent me a few years before her death.

'... But your book. I am so glad you are giving more about Christine, all the others pass her over for Miss Cobden and Thérèse. The former as Cobden's daughter and the latter as an artist, which of course she was.

But Christine is dismissed as the daughter of an industrialist, which she of course was.

But though not a painter she was an accomplished artist too, a fine embroiderer, whether one cares for her particular kind of embroidery or not. And her work is in I forget which churches, cathedrals and abbeys—Westminster Abbey I rather fancy among them.[1] And as we know she was everything to Walter, understanding and supporting—delightful—educated.

Love,
S.'

I cannot imagine how we managed to fit so much in on one Sunday afternoon, but after our return to Dieppe, Sickert and I looked in at the 'fit up', a funny little tent where a much battered travelling company sang songs and danced, the nearest equivalent to his 'Old Bedford' music hall in Camden Town or the 'Collins' at Islington that he could find in Dieppe. It was crammed full of Dieppois when we entered and the fug was asphyxiating, but Sickert of course never noticed extreme atmospheres or uncomfortable seats, in fact the primitive quality of the entertainment appealed to him. He went a good deal to the fit-up at this time, usually accompanied by Marie; I do not

[1] Miss Lillian Browse tells us, in her book, *Sickert*, that Christine's forte was embroidery, a piece of which, a blue damask tunicle, is in Westminster Abbey and was used at the Coronation of 1937.

know whether he used it for his work. It passed the time for him, that was all. As the rather pathetic little singer pranced about the hastily improvised stage, croaking in his worn tenor:

> 'Ma*dame* Canteloup!
> Donnez-moi votre fillette
> J'en suis fou!'

everyone took up the chorus, drumming with hands and feet, except Sickert, who sat wedged in the crowd, smiling benignly but rather absently on the packed audience. He became restless, however, after about an hour of the fit-up and we went back to my hotel to find my father.

Later that evening, Sickert saw us off for Amiens. He promised before we left that he would wind up his affairs as soon as possible, leave this land of heartbreaking memories and return to London.

Chapter 12

London Again

Soon after I left Dieppe, Sickert wrote to me about Thérèse Lessore. He had not mentioned her during my visit, but when I received the following letter I began to think she might become the ultimate solution for his loneliness.

This letter was undated, as was all his correspondence to me.

'. . . Thank you for your letter. You said things about my darling Christine that were very comforting to hear. I remember how touched she was when you left her flowers at Camden Road. I was glad to hear of your last visits to her there in her last summer.

'I don't know what price Thérèse Lessore's plates and other pottery are. I wonder if you would, as opportunity occurs, pick up £10 worth for me. If I say I like things, she gives them to me, and I want so to collect them. I would take anything she does. And when the £10 is gone, probably go on and get more and keep the secret. If you don't mind doing this I will send you a cheque. Thank you for the cheque for £70 for the picture.[1]

'I was so glad to see your father again. I am just off to dine at the sous-prefecture to meet the Abbé Lemire, deputy for Alsace. Other nights the fit-up with Marie who enjoys it. The leading lady you saw in white is such a good comedian.

As much love to Chris as your brother permits—or more.

Yours,
W.S.'

I carried out this commission for him and he wrote again about the pottery:

'. . . Enclosed for crockery, which please if you have room for keep for me for the present until I know where I am going to live. I have bought some of Thérèse direct. Don't let her imagine this lot is for me, but find out what she has chosen for me, and choose something as different as possible. If she has chosen cups for

---

[1] This was for the picture of a music-hall singer that we had chosen at Dieppe for Mr F. N. Pickett's collection. It has since disappeared and I have been unable to trace it.

me, do you choose plates, or vice versa, or if she has chosen lustre, you choose non-lustre or vice versa etc.

Thank you in anticipation and à bientôt.

Yours,
W.S.'

He returned to London in 1922 and put up at Bachelor's Hotel, Covent Garden, after an uneasy interlude at some queer place in Aldersgate. I did not know then that he had given away the Maison Mouton. It was typical, alas, of all his business dealings that he should hand over the house and garden for others to enjoy the fruits of his expense and labour.

From Bachelor's Hotel he went back to his old quarters at Number 15 Fitzroy Street and to a bed-sitting room in front of the studio which he had always retained. Hubert, kindest of landlords, must have been even more than usually accommodating for I suspect that the legacy from Christine was vanishing by this time. I have a vague yet persistent recollection of this bed-sitter; large, high-pitched, faintly sinister with a tall, veiled window facing the street and an iron bedstead furnished with a honeycomb quilt usurping most of the space. That room always reminded me of another Sickert interior not far away in Granby Street; a painting of a young woman looking out of the window as she sits on the side of the sparse bed ('Seated Woman, Granby Street', plate 37). I had always loved this picture, which once belonged to Sylvia Gosse and was painted in 1908 when Sickert was at the height of his powers; the richness and depth of the shadows, the dim light glimmering through the curtains, the beautiful weary head, the grace of the drooping figure are portrayed with the utmost authority and tenderness. It sparks of Whistler yet it is Sickert at his most personal with the inevitable undertone of tragic power.

There was not a comfortable chair or table or strip of carpet anywhere in his bed-sitter; it must have been a cold refuge in the winter for an ageing man. But it was always scrupulously clean and tidy, which was more than could be said for the Frith. Sickert's difficulties had gradually overwhelmed him and he became almost completely unapproachable at this time. There can be little doubt that he was suffering from delayed shock, almost a breakdown, aggravated by lack of recognition, privations, money muddles and the loss of his home. It was almost impossible at this stage of his career to help him. He was not answering letters, even by his favourite method of telegram, he was not opening his door when people called on him and half the time he was not at the Frith at all but hiding himself in some other still more secret abode. He had towering steel gates erected at vast expense across the entrance to the Frith which met with an ominous clash like the lifts in London tube stations, fastened with an enormous padlock, and to crown all he kept a large dog on the premises in case intruders were not already sufficiently discouraged. I was very worried about poor Cerberus, wondering if Sickert would ever remember to exercise and feed him. Roger Fry was also worried for another reason. He told Chris that Sickert, in one of his fits of despair, had been white-washing over some of his music hall canvases. Fry longed to rescue them and stop him destroying any more of his work; judging from Sickert's reckless mood just now, this seemed only too likely to be true. I wish I knew the end of the story; I believe from all accounts that Fry did restore some canvases but I fear we cannot tell today how much damage Sickert actually did and which examples of his work were spoiled beyond repair. As I was living out of London at this time, most of my information about him was second-hand; I had to depend on Sylvia Gosse or Thérèse Lessore or my sister-in-law for news of him. Thérèse found him very changed after his return from Dieppe. She was hurt and bewildered because he began to lock up everything, as if he feared that prying eyes and hands would make free of his possessions; the drawings, of various periods, were especially well guarded. He had never, of course, got on with Mrs Parminter, who still reigned supreme below stairs but it was long since she had been permitted the run of the Frith and it had never occurred to Thérèse that he might become suspicious of old friends. Later, when he was recovering his health and his prospects, he remembered the incident very well and was remorseful about his actions, saying that he did not really mean to be unkind, assuring her: 'I shall never be like that again.'

I seem to have asked Sickert to dinner on one of my visits home, as I found this letter recently among my papers. It is only a note but I think it is worth quoting as it does reveal the hand to mouth conditions in which he was then living.

'15 F.S.

'My dear Marjorie,

'I never thanked you for the hare, which I larded baked and ate with the greatest satisfaction.

'My dear I can't go out at night just now. The cold seizes on my heart, as they say in France, and I get giddy. I am very sorry.

Yours,
W.S.

My best wishes to your father and mother.'

I was rather surprised that he admitted his dependence on the weather but it was now that he began to suffer from heavy colds which had never afflicted him before. He had difficulty in shaking them off; I think that this was due to underfeeding and the discomfort of Number 15. He gave up dining out almost entirely now in the winter; he found that returning on a cold night to damp unheated rooms was too much for him. But he had always been used to regular hot nourishing meals when he lived at Camden Road and now that he ceased to dine out he was, of course, not eating properly at all. He had never been a heavy trencherman and his needs were modest, his favourite dinner being boiled chicken

154

followed by rice pudding. I am afraid he seldom got this now. But it was unwise to commiserate with him; expressions of sympathy, even when his colds were extra heavy and his throat obviously hoarse, were met with a blank stare.

I was only in London for flying visits but I met him by chance sometimes, generally near my home in Regent's Park, when he was kind and affectionate as ever but infinitely remote. He would point to a seat in his taxi, without speaking; I would climb in and we would cruise round the Outer Circle or the Bloomsbury Squares, still saying little to each other. Only once do I remember him discussing his affairs, when he mocked the fashionable world who used art as a party frill, constantly attending private views, pursuing artists and talking pictures to death without ever buying them.

'They've got all the patter,' he commented, 'but nothing will do.'

It was so unlike Sickert to be bitter that I was surprised. He had always known that he was not a popular artist or ever likely to be; but he had never suffered before from the neglect he was enduring at present. In fairness to the discerning public, there was little that they could buy. There was not much selection at the dealers and his best work was nearly all in private collections. I consoled myself reflecting that resentment was preferable to his previous apathy and might spur him on to taking up his brush again.

Many lesser artists have always managed to recommend themselves to buyers, but Sickert was caviare to the multitude and even today when his pictures are fetching big prices he is still the painter's painter. He had no Clive Bell or Roger Fry or John Ruskin or D. S. McColl to trumpet his claims in 1923; in fact, his work was criticized for those very qualities we so cherish today and it is doubtful if even the Bloomsberries knew much of his best period or what heights he had attained. The return from France had not benefited him, he had been away too long; he came back to an England that had forgotten him. A representative collection of his best work was the answer to his problem but his own attitude was daunting; he was not painting at all now and he would hardly know where to look for many of his things. Plenty of people were still aware of his importance, all paid lip service to his genius but no one appeared to have sufficient drive to set about organizing a first-rate Sickert exhibition.

It was at this low ebb of his fortunes that Mr W. H. Stephenson of Southport appeared upon the scene. It would be interesting to know how he side-stepped Cerberus and gained access to the Frith; it must have required much determination for a stranger to get in, with Sickert showing equally marked determination to keep him out. But once in, Mr Stephenson managed Sickert to admiration; he blandly ignored the fact that the master was being difficult and his plan of asking Sickert to lecture at Southport was an inspiration; nothing pleased Sickert more than an invitation to lecture. Mr Stephenson not only had the patience to ferret him out at Number 15 but he gave Sickert sympathy and appreciation when he most needed it, and with his unerring tact helped him more than anybody to take up life again.

Mr Stephenson has given me his permission to quote from his book, *Sickert: Random Reminiscences*, a moving picture of a period in Sickert's life which has been almost ignored; in fact, I remember no other account than this which tells us what was really happening to him in 1923, making this recollection so specially valuable. Mr Stephenson is modest about the part he played in coaxing Sickert back upon the stage but the reader can see for himself how much we owe him.

'The first time I met Sickert was early in 1923, at a critical period of his career. He was apparently living the life of a recluse in London at 15 Fitzroy Street, occupying a bed-sitting room, sleeping on a bare spring mattress, with an old travelling rug for cover. He had practically given up painting, and was receiving but little money for what he did. His studio was situated at the back of Fitzroy Street, a little paved path, passing through a communal passage to a badly lit old barn, giving a romantic atmosphere to the place. Sickert told me that it had been occupied in the past by W. P. Frith, R.A. The interior of this barn-studio was choked up with an immense accumulation of dust and cinders from a large stove, which he used for cooking and heating; cart loads of cinders rose as though from some volcanic eruption towards the roof. Sickert, in apologising for the mess, said that he used the room for his kitchen as well as a workroom. In the midst of this squalor several pieces of antique furniture stood out; a fine painting of Venice which Sickert attributed to Canaletto adorned the studio; an attractive pencil and wash drawing of his recently deceased wife completed the decoration of the otherwise bare walls . . .

'About this time he had, apparently, withdrawn from most of his friends. The loss of his second wife had been a great shock, and he was depressed; his memory of Dieppe, where he had previously been living and working, appeared to be a nightmare to him . . . I asked him why he did not have a woman to come in to clean up and cook his meals? He replied that he was still able to cook a humble sausage and that his wants were few . . .

'After this visit to Fitzroy Street, Sickert was persuaded that there were art collectors in the North of England who would be interested in his work. I had just been responsible for the purchase of an oil painting attributed to him, entitled "The Theatre of the Young Artists, Dieppe", which later became part of the permanent collection at the Southport Art Gallery. Sickert was greatly pleased on hearing this news, for he imagined that he had been forgotten owing to his residence in France . . .

'I had the pleasure of entertaining him in London. I had wired him to join me for lunch with some friends at Simpson's in the Strand. He was fond of a cut off a large joint of roast beef, and a tankard of ale; this was the only occasion I can remember that Sickert really made a hearty meal. He was in good form and greatly amused me with his talk. He said that his one ambition, apart from writing for the Press, was to become a member of that august body, the Royal

Academy, before he died. I thought he was jesting, but, on being assured that it was a serious wish, I suggested that such a master as himself should have no difficulty in securing the necessary votes if his name were put forward when a vacancy occurred.

'Later on the same day, I visited the studio of a member of the Royal Academy, an old acquaintance, and he was informed of what Sickert had intimated regarding his ambition and the Royal Academy. His astonishment was profound. Sickert, he said, was the last man he could have imagined who would wish for such an honour. Being greatly interested and impressed, he agreed that it would be a fitting finish to so great an artist's career, and promised to present the matter in the right quarter. He was duly elected, but he resigned from the Royal Academy in 1935, as a protest against the refusal of the R.A. to support a plea for keeping the Epstein statues on Rhodesia House in London . . .

'When Sickert was well on the way to success I met him very occasionally, and only twice during the period in which he conducted an art class in Manchester. He was then a busy man, an Associate of the R.A., had taken unto himself another wife, a daughter of Jules Lessore, and a painter herself; he was President of the R.B.A. In fact, I never met Richard Sickert, A.R.A., P.R.B.A. and I prefer to remember him in blue melton jacket and bowler hat, as Walter Sickert, of 15 Fitzroy Street.'

Sickert had always enjoyed dining with Taylor, but he avoided the larger parties; he preferred a quiet evening alone with his host or a few other cronies, worldlings and established painters for the most part, not too strenuous or instructive, who knew the people he knew and who would give him the easy casual gossip, spiced with wit, to which he was accustomed. This was the polite society he understood and valued, all the more now that it was disappearing. He could still count on it at the Gosse household in Hanover Terrace, at the Boreels in Eaton Place, at the Sitwells in Chelsea and a few other old haunts; he took it for granted that Taylor would always provide it for him and that after Christine's death, Oxford Square would still be there, a refuge from the brash new world, a reminder of the *douceur de vivre* that he remembered before the war. At large gatherings the lion was expected to roar sometimes or at any rate to make his presence felt, but in Oxford Square Sickert had always done as he wished. He could relax after the day's effort, talk his own brand of witty nonsense, indulge in serious discussion as the fancy took him, or just subside into silence. Taylor, in his unobtrusive fashion, was a splendid host; if Sickert preferred to be quiet Taylor would contrive that someone else should take the floor, if he decided to hold forth, Sickert could be sure of an attentive audience. As he was not really a great talker these monologues were rare, but always received with the deference which was due to the elder statesman.

But now? He had not bargained for the new turn that Taylor's life had taken during his absence. Sickert had been away from London too long. Perhaps it is always a mistake to return. Bereft of Sickert's company and the set he drew after him, Taylor had had perforce to seek other companions; he was a lonely man, infinitely tolerant of youth and easily seduced by novelty. The Sickerts that had graced his dining room with their good manners had been replaced by the latest experiments and young artists who had recently made a splash at the London Group or the New English were invited not only to formal tea parties at his studio in Fitzroy Square but to the intimate charmed circle of diners in his private house. These up and coming youngsters were not always modest or adaptable; they might dispute, insist, lay down the law or argue fiercely about their latest theories. They even introduced politics into the conversation, a subject that bored Sickert to death. He had always refrained from dissipating his energies in a battle of words; debating, especially angry debating, was a waste of time . . . It was ironic that he, the champion of youth, should find these boys so exhausting. They were not at all like the young people he had known.

An especial trial was Mark Gertler, whose work Taylor much admired. Sickert admired it too and wrote of Gertler's 'Fruit Sorters', shown at the N.E.A.C., that 'the picture is justified by a sort of intensity and raciness . . . it is important also because it is a masterly piece of painting in well supported and consistent illumination and the work of a colourist at the same time rich and sober.'

Gertler was too intelligent not to appreciate the society of Sickert but he was difficult, excitable and moody, with a bristling inferiority complex. The gulf between them was not merely a question of years; many people of Gertler's own generation found him exhausting. Few were aware of the tragedy of his life, they saw him as a privileged boy whose early promise had received ample recognition. These early efforts were certainly brilliant, memories of the most part of his colourful youth in the East End of London. But Gertler was consumptive, and with all the intensity of the consumptive he tormented himself about his broken health and his early poverty. Above all, he was obsessed with fear, the fear that his talent was not powerful enough to stay the course. There were ominous signs that already he was repeating himself, that he had nothing more to say.

It is doubtful if Sickert knew the background of Gertler's life; on the whole, he was infinitely patient. But sometimes the temptation was too great and he could not resist poking fun at him. One evening, over coffee, the conversation turned on birthplaces; we were all speaking at once when Gertler crashed in with—

'Well, I was born in Spitalfields and I don't care who knows it.'

'Deutsch über alles,' retorted Sickert promptly.

Poor Gertler looked puzzled at the ensuing laughter. He did not know that Sickert was born in Munich.

Chapter 13

The Girls' School

In 1927, I was teaching art for a few terms at a large school for girls on the east coast. Soon after my arrival, the Headmistress asked me to arrange a lecture for the older girls, whose ages ranged from sixteen to eighteen. I thought at once of Sickert. I knew how much he enjoyed lecturing; it would be a privilege for the school if he could be persuaded to come and his advice about the general policy of the Art Department would be invaluable. So I suggested that he should be invited to address the girls.

The Head was much gratified; I doubt if she had seen many Sickerts; few people had in those days; for that matter, nor have they in these. But he was already a legend, she had heard a good deal about him at Garsington, the home of her friend Lady Ottoline Morell, she took a lively interest in painting and she had a good modern collection of her own. A fiery little Celt with glittering, almost yellow eyes and dark hair, her appearance was unusual; although short, she moved well and wore clothes that gave an impression of line. Impetuous, ardent, without rancour, brimming with drive and imagination, gracious when not overwhelmed with work, she was the most outstanding Head I have known. Socially, she was unpredictable. She had a masculine quality which did not make for ease with strangers; like Christine, she spoke only when she had something to say. If the conversation failed to stimulate her or if she was just plain bored, she remained silent. But if stirred she could burn, as recommended by Walter Pater, with a hard gem-like flame. I thought that if anyone could move her to eloquence it would be Sickert; I knew he would appreciate her passionately-held views and the lucidity with which she would express them; if repartee was not her forte, she could take the cut-and-thrust of argument surprisingly well for one who was seldom contradicted on her own ground. I hoped that on this occasion their flames would fuse and we should have a display of fireworks that would give us something to remember.

Situated on one of the bleakest spurs on the east coast, the school grew rapidly under her direction; parents favoured it because the climate was bracing and the pupils throve exceedingly, although one suspected that a Spartan régime of early hours, plain food and regular exercise contributed as much to their welfare as the invigorating blasts that buffeted them all the year round from the North Sea. Now, shortly before her retirement, her life's work was crowned with an array of solid red buildings and a large new studio, her latest present from a grateful Council. For the studio, she needed a few contemporary pictures. Would I enquire if Sickert had a suitable oil to spare? In my mind's eye I had already seen a choice Sickert brooding on those blank walls and I was delighted with her request.

The prospect seemed rosy enough. Except for that one word, 'suitable'. It had a knell-like sound, displeasing to the ear. But I went forthwith to Sickert to sound him about the lecture and to beg for an oil. He was immediately interested in the lecture, bubbling over with all he wanted to say to the fledgelings, although he did not take up the matter of the picture. In fact, he was so carried away by the novel idea of talking to schoolgirls that he began his discourse there and then and it was with difficulty that I steered him back to sales. But he agreed carelessly to let us have 'something'.

'It's a huge studio,' I hinted, gazing at the rows of canvases which presented their back to us along the walls and hoping desperately that the 'something' would be suitable. 'It's still quite bare except for a few of the usual reproductions that all schools seem to have, Monet and Gauguin and, of course, Van Gogh. But the Head is very keen to collect originals.'

So far so good. But alas, this plan of mine was a mistake from the word go. Between such opposing forces as Sickert and this enclosed order I can only wonder that their encounter was not more disastrous than it proved.

Difficulty number one. There was no intimation from the Head that she would be expecting Sickert to dine with her on the appointed evening, in which case the honour of his company would devolve on a housemistress. But none of the housemistresses was anxious for the distinction. Having found these ladies always kind and friendly, this grievous lack of hospitality distressed me but the real reason seemed to be that they were all, unaccountably, scared. 'We don't talk painting, what shall we say,' was the burden of their song. In vain one assured them that Sickert would be only too happy to hear them talk about anything that interested them but then difficulty number two arose. Other men should be asked to meet him; but who was sufficiently equipped to compete with this phoenix? Again, one argued that painting was not the only subject for conversation, that Sickert loved meeting fresh people, *any* people, and hearing about their lives and occupations but several likely candidates whom I was sure he would have liked and who would have liked him were turned down as being unworthy of his steel, which left us with no men for the dinner at all.

In despair, I was contemplating a humble meal in my cottage with a few cronies, which hardly seemed to be paying him the respect due to an elder statesman, when the Head suddenly recollected her duties and announced, at the eleventh hour, that Sickert was dining with her.

This was a weight off my mind. The French mistress was to be present at dinner and I rejoiced to think that he would certainly feel at home with Mademoiselle.

When I met him at the station, he was carrying the famous Gladstone bag which I took, rightly, to contain the desired picture. I gazed affectionately at that old friend, which still bore traces of the address he had so carefully painted on its battered surface, 'The Shrubbery, 81 Camden Road'. Another hurdle surmounted! A procession of magnificent Sickerts marched across my mind. Dieppe cathedrals, Old Bedford music-halls, Venetian bridges, Georgian squares in Islington, garrets in Camden Town, dawn in Mornington Crescent . . . perhaps a swaggering portrait of the Colonel's lady or Judy O'Grady . . . of all these riches, which would it be?

'This is fun,' remarked Sickert. He never complained, so there was no reference to his long, cold, complicated journey. We went to my lodgings, and when my landlady appeared with boiled eggs and tea to restore the traveller he was immediately amused with her mountainous proportions and made himself so agreeable that she was loth to leave us. The tea was rather black but what perturbed me most was the consistency of the eggs. They were as hard as bricks. I had asked that they should be boiled as lightly as possible; Sickert maintained that an egg should only be 'shown the fire' and how often, at the Frith, I had swallowed a nearly raw egg, trying to conceal the discomfort I felt! However, on this occasion he was in too complacent a mood to notice any shortcomings. The charming prospect of exhorting the young was uppermost in his mind; he ate two bricks and drank several cups of ink without teasing me about the fare I had provided, talking all the time about what he would say to the girls and the points he would drive home for their benefit. But I could not keep my attention from straying towards the precious bag. When he saw my impatience, he opened it with his usual leisurely precision and produced an ominously small parcel.

'You'll like it, I think. It's a portrait of Thérèse, they ought to have her. *Such* an important painter!'

To my dismay, he revealed a tiny, very slight, very dark oil sketch of Thérèse Lessore.

I do not suppose that he could ever have painted a smaller picture. He had caught her in severe mood; the sittings, perhaps, had tired her and she looked, as Marianne Hunt said of Byron, 'as if she had been given a plain bun instead of a plum one'. In short, it was a very difficult Sickert indeed.

I cannot speak of its merits as a picture, as I was too disappointed to do it justice. Instead of the adviser who had backed the firm to some purpose and laid the foundations of an exciting modern collection, I now saw myself in an ambiguous position, defending, condoling, explaining . . . if any explanation *was* possible. This ill-fated production would be lost in that enormous studio, he could ask comparatively little for it although the school was prepared to pay handsomely for an important Sickert. I saw an embarrassed interview before me with a bewildered Head. And I had so counted on his work being greeted with grateful appreciation, and on his receiving a fat cheque . . .

After tea, we took a turn by the sea; shaking off my worries for the time being, I gave myself up to the charm of his company. He was enchanted to renew his acquaintance with the old town of Southwold, which he had visited once before with Whistler, in the nineties. To his great satisfaction, it had hardly changed since then and he diverted me with stories about the Butterfly, how he insisted on wearing his pumps when walking, or rather limping along the beach, how discomfited he was generally with life out-of-doors. I did not gather that much work had been done by either on this occasion; Whistler destroyed most of what he did do and the place, much as Sickert enjoyed it, was too cosy, too picturesque and prosperous, to stir him to action.

On our return to the town he went off to his hotel to dress for dinner and I to gaze despairingly at the portrait, propped up on the chimneypiece in my sitting room. It gave me increasing food for thought. There was, of course, no hope of securing another trophy from the Frith. Memory tormented me with visions of the imposing rows of canvases around those walls; almost any of them would have been more appreciated than this. We had, so unfortunately for us, caught him at the height of one of his fervent enthusiasms; he did really think at the moment that nothing could be more charming for us than to have a reminder of Thérèse Lessore. If I stated my main objection to the portrait, that it would look like a postage stamp on the studio wall, he would be merely shocked and distressed that after all these years I understood his work so little that I failed to distinguish between quantity and quality and he would remain unconvinced that an enlightened Head, any enlightened person, could hold so Philistine a view as to demand of a work of art that it should be judged by its mere physical size. I cursed myself for forgetting that it was all of a piece with his general perversity about his own work; when asked to provide a picture for public exhibition, he would invarably choose the smallest, slightest, most insignificant sketch he could find, regardless of its future setting, whether it was intended for my lady's chamber or a Victorian town hall.

Although the Head had large ideas about housing and education, her aspirations did not run to food and this attitude was reflected in her dining room; it was hardly bigger than a nun's cell, the sort of cupboard that would suffice for a highminded and preoccupied intellectual who dines alone with something on a tray. When planning the cupboard, she had evidently not allowed for male guests, especially those of the dimensions of Sickert. By the time that he, she, I and Mademoiselle were crushed together round her little table, it was an acrobatic feat for the parlourmaid to present the dishes. Sickert was seated with his back in the fireplace and one leg of his chair almost in the fender; as he seldom bothered about the temperature, this might do. But other embarrassments soon arose. Mademoiselle promptly adopted him; plunging into French, she spoke of Paris. This was naughty; the Head had no French and Mademoiselle knew it. He was now enjoying himself hugely; the little dining-room, the grave Head, the demure and comely country parlourmaid, the ebullient Mademoiselle, his own precarious perch, the whole affair tickled him; it was all so unlikely, a novel and absurd situation. If I had congratulated myself previously that he would feel at home with Mademoiselle, I now had qualms that their mutual response was perhaps excessive. Mademoiselle was not young or especially handsome but in any case, these were not considerations that would affect Sickert; he had the French rather than the English outlook about women, he ignored age and held unexpected views about feminine looks.

When meeting strangers officially as on the present occasion, he could be vague about appearances and all he asked was that they should be good company and above all, intelligent. He was never vague about that. And Mademoiselle was certainly intelligent. Moreover, she was gay and not in the least overawed by him. But as the purest torrents of French streamed back and forth between them he turned a bright puzzled glance every now and then towards the Head, concerned that she was not taking part in the conversation at her own table. He was so unused to an aloof and frowning hostess; this amused him too; it was quite an experience for him and he sought to beguile her with some of his best Parisian stories, only to find her more and more absent. I had told him that she was a personage, and it was plain that he was wondering what on earth I meant. From time to time I managed to catch his eye and try to convey the fact that she did not understand French but he could not make head or tail of all this pantomime and the simple truth did not strike him; he always supposed that everyone spoke French. The meal ended as it had begun, in an unholy triumph for Mademoiselle.

I was thankful when we went to the Head's study for coffee. Now, I thought, she will score; he will be delighted with her Epstein, her Marie Laurençin, her Constable. But no sooner had he begun to adjust his pince-nez to examine her things than we were switched away for the lecture in the Great Hall; we were already late. The hall was some distance away from the Head's house and what would have been a pleasant stroll in the night air was ruined by rain, a hopeless drenching downpour. Sickert followed the Head and me along the dark paths with resignation, murmuring 'tiens!' thoughtfully to himself as he trudged through the mire and hopped over the puddles and was finally deposited, wet pumps and all, upon the rostrum.

He beamed upon the assembled school, awaiting him in their white dresses and white shawls. 'Charming!' he remarked to the Head, 'like a flock of little white doves.'

The lecture began. No sooner had he plunged into his theme than I began to wonder how I could ever have supposed that he would be able to adapt himself to the immature minds around him. I had been entirely misled by his eager talk in the past about teen-agers of both sexes, what should be done for them, what should be avoided, how they should be guided and encouraged on the thorny path to painting, so that I had overlooked the fact that he had no practical knowledge of adolescents. One week as visiting professor at a boys' or girls' school would have been a chastening experience for him. Whatever their natural bent may be, the English young—I do not presume, of course, to speak of other countries—are mostly ignorant about painting, past or present. Perhaps their darkness has been lightened during the last few years but rarely so in the case of boys, and one cannot wonder; there is little place for the history of art in an already overloaded timetable and it is a mistake to suppose that all pupils are interested in painting or would certainly be interested if they had the chance. As Stevenson pointed out, the world is full of a number of things ... And I have found that however enthusiastic heads might be about my subject, when it was a question of art appreciation, their interest slackened. 'I don't want them to hear about painting, I want them to do it,' they generally insisted. Whether it would be advisable for those who cannot be performers but who show signs of developing a love of art, to study the historical side of the business, is beyond the scope of this book; it seems only common sense that the more interests people can cultivate the better but on the other hand I have know art historians whom I feel in my bones, from their general demeanour, have never been fairly thrilled by a picture in their lives. Be all that as it may, for Sickert, painting was the crown and summit of human endeavour; he assumed a like ardour on the part of his audience and, taking for granted that they shared the same sense of values, he let himself go.

Warming thoroughly to his task, he referred to painters of whom they had never heard, to pictures in European galleries that they had never seen; he compared procedures of painting, he analysed, he philosophized, he cracked jokes in his best boulevardier French. When dead silence ensued after he had made what he considered to be a particularly telling sally, he paused, awaiting the laughter which never came. Looking down on their bemused faces, he said plaintively, 'But you do learn French here, don't you? I thought this was a school!'

Before we broke up he was asked to come again next day to see the studio and the work of the pupils. He was looking forward to this and by 10.30 on Sunday morning he was already at my garden gate, bustling me into my coat. Rain had ceased but the weather was still wan, misty and bitterly cold; there was a level light over the empty Sunday-morning fields which I found *triste* and he found enchanting. The Head met us in the drive and we went to the studio. She had taken endless pains with this fine room and it was furnished with every modern appliance. For Sickert, it was too much like a glorified classroom; he would have installed blinds forthwith to temper the strong north light and create more mystery, atmosphere. But he realized that she was pardonably proud of her spacious and comfortable workshop and he spent happy hours pronouncing on all the drawings he was shown. He loved searching for talent and found it sometimes in unexpected places, but he always gave his reasons for his decisions, which interested the Head profoundly. They were getting on very nicely now; I prayed that this gratifying state of things might continue. Before we left, however, he caught sight of a timetable hanging on the wall.

'Tiens!' he exclaimed, his upper lip lengthening. It was the usual school timetable, comprising about nine different subjects weekly.

'What do you suggest?' asked the Head.

'Three subjects are enough,' replied Sickert firmly. 'Latin, English and mathematics. Then the pupils may leave school knowing a *little* about *something* which would give them the confidence which is so necessary for their future studies, instead of *nothing* about anything at all. Nine subjects, indeed!'

The Head sighed; in silence, we followed her back to her study for coffee. Sickert admired her pictures and they discussed mutual friends; as he was going, she collected herself for a final appeal.

'Mr Sickert, what aesthetic influences do you suggest for the girls?'

But Sickert had dismissed the subject of education for that day; it was getting too near lunch time.

'Pretty creatures!' he exclaimed fervently.

And we took our leave.

After his departure for London, the Head asked to see me. I knew only too well what she would say; I attended her with reluctance. She was frowning fiercely at the portrait on her desk; there was no need for me to enlarge on her difficulty, I saw her point only too well and had rehearsed already all the objections she would raise. It was a distressing interview for us both but she seemed greatly relieved that I raised no protest against her decision. At last, she decided to decline the portrait with thanks and to send Sickert the fee that he had asked for it.

'But he won't take the cheque unless you like the picture.'

She looked very unhappy.

'Oh dear. What *is* the answer?'

'I don't think,' I replied gloomily, 'that there always is an answer.'

'Life is *too* difficult sometimes,' the Head assured me.

Sadly, I left her study and met the head girl in the passage. She had been introduced to Sickert the night before and they had exchanged a few words; promptly, she summed up for me the reactions of the school to the visit of the master.

'Of course we didn't understand a word that he was saying,' she announced cheerfully. 'Right above our heads you know. Palio stuffers and neo-stinkers. What *does* he mean? All that French too. My!'

But she added suddenly:

'We all thought he was a dear old chap, you know.'

I smiled at the irreverence; she looked at me thoughtfully with her clear young blue eyes. It seemed that Sickert had struck a blow for culture after all.

Some weeks later, the Head and I went to Mr Marchant at the Goupil Gallery where we chose a larger and more important Sickert, a three-quarter length portrait of a woman (plate 38), which is still in the possession of the school (I understand it was so unpopular with one subsequent art teacher there that it spent some years languishing in a cupboard). For the school, the incident was now closed. Everybody had behaved beautifully, the engagement had been conducted with the utmost gallantry on both sides; the Head had written a remorseful letter to Sickert, presenting her compliments, Sickert had responded, acquitting her of all blame and presenting his. All the cruder aspects of the affair were draped in mutual admiration. It only remained for me to face the ordeal of returning to him the unwanted portrait of Thérèse.

At first, I began to launch out in a long and confused description of the pleasure the Head had experienced when she saw his things at the Goupil. But it was not going down very well. In despair, I put the portrait on the table and stated what had happened in the baldest language, shorn of apology.

'We went to Goupil's and bought another of your pictures instead of Thérèse. The Head is delighted with it.'

Sickert would hardly have been human if he had not seized his opportunity here. After all, I was, actually, the villain of the piece; had it not been for my misplaced scheming, he would never have been involved in this coil.

'Ah well, I am pleased that the good lady is pleased. Probably it is another of these forgeries, and not by me at all.'

But he could seldom remain disagreeable for long. Soon, we put the kettle on and exchanged views about his ill-starred journey.

'I had a letter from Mademoiselle this morning,' he confided as drank his tea. 'Quite long and newsy and a great deal about Paris. I really ought to answer it. But one must paint sometimes,' he added, gazing into the fire.

Chapter 14

Noel Street

In 1934, the younger members of the Royal British Artists decided that Sickert must be invited to become their new President. Wishing to put new life into the society, they managed to override some doubting Thomases among the older members who felt that he was too unpredictable for their purpose, even though they were impressed by his reputation. Claude Flight, the leader of the Sickert faction, thought that in any case they might not be able to secure him but he little knew how gratified Sickert would be with the invitation. The society was associated for him with his beloved Whistler and other friends of his youth; nothing would please him better than to follow in the footsteps of the Butterfly.

He would have been shocked to know how little most of the members cared about Whistler or the past of the society, but it was agreed that the master must be reverently approached to find out if he might accept the presidency and I was asked to put the matter before him.

Feeling almost certain of success, I went hopefully to Islington. Sickert had a charming first floor flat in Noel Street, overlooking the Regent's Canal, not far from Duncan Terrace, his earliest recollection of north London. I wondered if he would hear me ring the bell, but the front door was ajar and I entered a square little hall with a pretty curving staircase of the Regency period. The place seemed empty, then I saw the familiar leonine head, now cropped, with beard in full spate, looking through the banisters with an expression of acute apprehension.

'It's all right, who did you think I was?' I enquired?

'I thought you must be Lady Oxford. I met her at dinner last week and she asked where my studio was and I said nowhere. She said, "But you must paint somewhere," and I said "No I don't," and she said "I shall find you, never fear! *One day you'll open the door and I shall be on the doorstep." '*

Seeing that he was genuinely scared, I forbore to laugh and followed him upstairs, but he was still full of Lady Oxford.

'It's like Cézanne,' I said. 'When his friends pursued him, do you remember, he told them: "I live a long way off, down a street." But they never found him, did they?'

'Ah, but you don't know Lady Oxford. She's a very determined woman.'

'She must be rather fun. After all, she wouldn't be so talked about if she hadn't got something.'

'Got something, indeed! The woman's an exhibitionist, always trying to hit the headlines. *I* might be talked about too, you know, if I took my clothes off in Piccadilly Circus.'

That was a lovely floor in Noel Street. I wonder if the house is still there. An archway led into the inner room and there was a large window overlooking the canal. Sickert had papered the walls with crimson paper flecked with gold, and decorated them with an odd little collection of prints and drawings. The light was beautiful, there were comfortable, shabby chairs and the whole place was a little Paradise; Lady Oxford would have been charmed with it.

Sickert was in great form. I sat opposite him, the better to contemplate the beard, which was enormous and absolutely square, like a spade. He would never have been permitted to grow such a furzebush in Christine's day; there were limits to the amount of beard she could stand and constant arguments as to why he must shave his head so often, where the hair should be. I reminded him of this; he fingered the preposterous growth complacently and when he had quite forgotten Lady Oxford, I began to explain my mission. The R.B.A. need not have feared that he might make difficulties; he was delighted to become their president. In no time he was toying with the idea that he would design a medal for himself with P.R.B.A. on it. A gold ground, he thought, with a blue band . . . yes, blue and a black ribbon . . .

'So I can go back and tell them you've really consented?'

Of course he consented. Was he not following in the footsteps of Whistler? If there had been no other inducement, was it not enough that Jimmy had been president before him? That should suffice for anybody.

For the benefit of those who do not know the end of the story of the R.B.A. I will add that although he was entranced with his new role as president, he never did himself justice in it. He looked the part to perfection, sweeping about the charming old galleries in Suffolk Street in his Venetian cape and talking to the members with his usual graciousness, but old age was upon him; he could no longer spark off the amusing speeches and lectures for which he was once so famed and there was the regrettable occasion when the society turned out in force to welcome him at an inaugural meeting and he forgot the whole thing. A good quiet little secretary would have been a godsend at this stage of his affairs but that alas, he could not afford, even if he could have borne the restraint that her presence would impose; needless to say, however, the incident, vouched for me by an elderly member who was a great admirer of Sickert's, had left an indelibly painful impression on their minds. There were, of course, some members who would have preferred another candidate as president and they were especially vocal. To think that so many people had taken long railway journeys to be present at this important meeting, which should have been a historic occasion! And that they had waited patiently for him to put in an appearance, but he never came or sent a message or anything. But what could you expect from a president as temperamental as Sickert?

They little knew what an effort he was making. He did not want to be outshone by Whistler but he was too set in his ways to adapt himself to the rules of the society. Administration irked him; there were tiresome minor difficulties. The treasurer clung to the fiendish tradition that the president should study the accounts of the society. Faced with ledgers and rows of figures that meant nothing to him, Sickert's precarious resilience was severely taxed before it occurred to someone that he should be relieved of this burden. But serious trouble came when he suggested a no-jury hanging for their exhibitions, so that everyone would get an equal chance to display their work in advantageous places, combined with the shock they received when he sent his own contribution, on which they had set great store. It was the smallest, slightest and darkest picture he could find. In the end, he and the R.B.A. parted company with goodwill on both sides and the society sought a more practical president, who would study their ways, give big parties and remember to attend them.

To return to Noel Street. It was good to see him in such splendid form, fighting fit in fact, laying down the law and airing his likes and dislikes as he had not bothered to do for so long, spicing his sallies with flashes of the old wit, himself again as I had not seen him for a long time. Life was opening up for him instead of closing down as he had expected it to do, and it was moving to see how quickly his spirits responded to the least semblance of public recognition.

Interest in old friends was returning; he spoke of many people that he must have been meeting again recently and the name of one mutual friend cropped up: a portrait painter, who was rather on my mind, as he was having a struggle to pay his way.

'What makes it worse is the heavy rent he has to find for his address,' I added, rushing upon my fate. I had forgotten that I was now on perilous ground.

'And why, pray, must he pay an exorbitant sum for rent? There are plenty of good studios in Camden Town.'

'Yes. But he says it must be S.W.1.'

'I see nothing wrong with N.W.1.'

'No, but do you think people would go out so far?'

This led, of course, to a solemn little lecture on snobbery and its attendant evils. Sickert deplored the fact that we were all a lot of sheep, trying 'to astonish the Browns' (a pet phrase of his) or keep up with the Joneses. And what was the matter with Camden Town? Who had decreed that business must be exclusively transacted around Piccadilly or Knightsbridge? I was encouraging pretentiousness by taking that line. He had hoped I was more intelligent.

In fact, he got quite severe about his unfortunate friend. I was delighted to see how far he had emerged from his apathy. He enjoyed laying down the law so much that I did not try to point out that it was all very well for him to talk; he had a unique position, he could live where and how he liked and if he chose to inhabit a slum, it would be considered a quirk of eccentricity rather than a confession of failure.

Chapter 15

Bath 1941

In the autumn of 1941, I was looking after an exhibition of paintings at the Bath Art Gallery and welcomed the opportunity of calling on the Sickerts. The war had played such havoc with old friendships that I had not seen them recently and I was delighted to find that Bathampton was so near, only just outside the city, and I soon proposed myself for a visit one evening.

Thérèse met me at the door of their charming Georgian house, looking tinier and more frail than ever but otherwise unchanged; no one would have guessed from her contained manner all that she had on her mind. Old friends were kind but often perfunctory; they had their own problems and those who would have surrounded her with help and sympathy in peace time were now trying to keep their own heads above water in the general deluge. She did not know many people in Bath. The townsfolk had called when the Sickerts arrived, although there had been keen debates among them about this—'Surely we ought to call...' 'I don't know about that, I don't believe he cares tuppence whether we call or not...' But Thérèse had not returned the calls because she had no time to spare for making fresh contacts. Her greatest friends in Bath were the Headmaster of Bath School of Art and his wife, the Clifford Ellises, who stood by her through thick and thin until Sickert's death in 1942. Few people realized the strain she was undergoing with a sick husband, wartime restrictions and very little money; fortunately, she had Sylvia Gosse and Sir Alec Martin to help her with pressing money and household problems.

During supper, she told me about their life in Bath. For some time past, Sickert had been failing rapidly. He was suffering from a succession of small strokes, which had culminated in a more serious attack so that he was now upstairs, unable to leave his room. But until recently he had persisted in his old way, disappearing suddenly into Bath to potter among the second-hand book-shops as he had liked to do at Brighton, to search for subjects that he would never paint again. She was not worried about these flittings, as he was well known to every taxi-driver in Bath; matter-of-fact, efficient, benign, these men had adopted him long ago and soon discovered him as he wandered, confused and weary, along the great grey streets; one of them would cruise beside him, swoop him into the hovering cab without more ado and bring him home.

'And they never cheated him of sixpence,' said Thérèse. 'Even when Walter twice produced a fiver, he was given the right change.'

She thought he had been happy at Bath, as he believed that he was still working. Sometimes he pleaded to be taken back to Fitzroy Street but that was part of the old restlessness that nothing could assuage. And until his final collapse he thought that he was still teaching. Every morning, he would start off gaily to the old barn in the gardens to 'take his class'.

'When I went after him, I would find him waiting for the students who never came. I tried to cheer him with promises that they would be there next day, and take his mind off the subject by talking of something else. He seemed contented for the time being but next day he always went back to the barn to look for them again.'

The changes wrought by the war bewildered him. When evacuees arrived from Balham, he was much mystified to find these strangers walking about his house and making themselves at home; his memory had to be constantly refreshed about them. Meeting them on the stairs or in the hall, he might remember the reason for their presence, which he was inclined to consider an intrusion, when he would bow graciously to them and murmur to himself, 'Ah, the Balhams!'

Thérèse said that her chief difficulty was sorting out the differences of opinion between him and the nurses who attended him. Needless to say, he was an impossible patient. Having had complete freedom all his life and not realizing that he was ill, he was outraged to find himself in their hands; as with 'the Balhams', he could not understand why they were making free of his house and disputes were frequent when they were obliged to impose certain restrictions on him. We laughed over this, although we sympathized whole-heartedly with the nurses, faced with their hopeless task. 'If only,' sighed Thérèse, shaking her hair over her eyes in the old familiar gesture, 'they found they could manage him as well as the taxi-drivers!'

After supper we took a turn round the garden, as Thérèse wanted me to see it before nightfall. It was quite a substantial affair and must at one time have been well stocked with plants, when there was somebody to look after them. We saw the old barn where Sickert had hoped to teach again and then came across a large canvas propped against the wall with only a smudge on it, like the pressure of a moist thumb. Thérèse brought the canvas out into a better light and gazed at it with absorption.

After a while, she turned to me and said: 'What do you think he means to do with it?'

It was rather a shock to realize that I was being asked to contemplate a Sickert. To me, it seemed we were discussing a blank canvas and I wondered if she saw aright and I was blind, so reverently did she gaze on the smudge on its broad surface. But I thought her loyalty was wonderful. Never would she admit to others, and I doubt even to herself, that his painting days were over.

When we returned to the house she asked me to take him some supper. It consisted only of his favourite rice pudding, but she warned me that he would forget to eat it unless he were firmly reminded to do so.

'You'll find him better looking than ever,' she remarked, as she pointed the way to his room. 'Which is more than you can say for some of the rest of us,' she added thoughtfully.

Sickert was sitting with his back to the window, dark against the ebbing day. He was so still in his pose of dumb acceptance that he seemed like a figure in one of his own interiors; drifts of light floated over his head and shoulders but the rest was lost in shadow, all depths and blurred contours, losing and finding themselves in the gathering dusk. He was thinner, the concavities of his face more sharply marked, but his hair was thicker than ever, rising from his head in close-piled curls, his eyes blue and clear in their deep orbits. He moved slightly and the shadows fled. I thought what a portrait he would make with his lime green checked coat, the crimson rug wrapped round his knees and the background of trees beyond the window.

I put the tray down beside him as he turned to greet me with the old affectionate warmth. He was not surprised to see me; he always took the comings and goings of his friends as a matter of course, however long the intervals between their visits might be. But although he knew my face, his memory was almost gone. How ironic that he of all people with his superb memory should be living in this bleak no-man's-land! Did it irk him, I wondered, or did he not even remember how rich his life had been? Evidently, he was eager for company; after joking with me a little about his infirmities he lapsed into silence and I felt that he was contented. For a long time, it had all been 'a little much' for him; now, life's effort was over, he could sit back idly and watch the dying light beyond the trees and dream of the pictures he wanted to paint. I tried to interest him in his supper, which was getting cold, but he brushed the tray aside; his attention wandered back to the window and suddenly he started to tell me about the picture he saw there in a torrent of words, moving in its broken vehemence. Then he pointed to the foot of the bed; he wanted a figure in the composition. I seated myself on the bed and his face lit up, he had now got what he needed, the fall of light on the object 'Yes, yes, that's it!' then he fell back in his chair:

'But I can't do it today.'

'Never mind, you'll do it tomorrow.'

'Yes tomorrow,' he agreed eagerly, 'tomorrow.'

When he died, some six months later, Thérèse wrote to me.

'St George's Hill,
Bathampton, Bath,
March 1st, 1942

'... thank you for your kind letter. I know you would have come to help if you could I had one great difficulty which was solved by the very great kindness of Clifford Ellis No words can say how kind he has been He came in every day and sometimes twice, to lift Walter for weeks. When you think of his busy life, it was wonderful. Doing it with such tact and tenderness.

What I shall do now, I just do not know. Find a studio somewhere I suppose—are there any Hendon way? At present I have no desire to do anything.

Love from,
Thérèse.'

Chapter 16

Envoi

Soon after the end of the last war, I found myself one winter's afternoon in Tottenham Court Road; now that I was so near to Fitzroy Street, I could not resist the urge to see the old haunts again. People had warned me not to go—'it's all to pieces, a regular shambles, most depressing'—but the desire grew stronger as the familiar smells of fog and smoke and garlic called up their poignant reminders of the past and when I came into Fitzroy Square it did not seem so altered as I had feared. The tall, dark houses frowned on me in the sullen light, their façades battered but intact, hiding their wounds; there was little outward sign of the hollow shells within, save here and there an ominous gap where a bomb had uprooted the whole dwelling. The front door of Number 8 was on the latch, as it always used to be, but when I entered I found the great winding staircase shot away except for a few steps leading upward from the hall, which ended abruptly in a rough wooden fence. I looked over it with a shudder as I saw the sheer drop to the ground far below and the vast spaces filled with weeds and rubble . . . only a few scarred walls, some patches of willow herb, a heap of stones to touch the nerve of memory. I gazed at the desolation around me, cold, bleak, indifferent in the December dusk and wondered that so much laughter and wit and kindness should be stilled for ever.

'If there are ghosts to raise
What should I call?'

But the answer came—

'There are no ghosts to raise
Out of death lead no ways . . .'

All, all lost! And then I remembered, the pictures were still there, two world wars had failed to destroy them. The ghosts of Fitzroy Street had triumphed after all.

Restored by the thought, I stood alone in the gaping ruin to bid them farewell. Then I closed the great front door behind me and went away down the silent street.

Index